REMATERIALISING CHILDREN'S AGENCY

Everyday practices in a post-socialist estate

Matej Blazek

First published in Great Britain in 2016 by

Policy Press
University of Bristol
1-9 Old Park Hill
Bristol
BS2 8BB
UK
t: +44 (0)117 954 5940
pp-info@bristol.ac.uk
www.policypress.co.uk

North America office:
Policy Press
c/o The University of Chicago Press
1427 East 60th Street
Chicago, IL 60637, USA
t: +1 773 702 7700
f: +1 773 702 9756
sales@press.uchicago.edu
www.press.uchicago.edu

British Library Cataloguing in Publication Data
A catalogue record for this book is available from the British Library

Library of Congress Cataloging-in-Publication Data
A catalog record for this book has been requested

ISBN 978 1 44732 274 0 hardcover

Cover design by Policy Press
Front cover image: Matej Blazek
Printed and bound in Great Britain by CPI Group (UK) Ltd, Croydon, CR0 4YY
Policy Press uses environmentally responsible print partners

Dedicated to the memory of
my grandfathers
(and their role in shaping
my childhood)

Contents

List of tables, figures and maps

Tables

Figures

Maps

About the author

Matej Blazek is Lecturer in Human Geography at Loughborough University, UK. He is a social geographer with a particular interest in the geography of marginalisation, childhood, migration and emotions. He is also active in community youth work as a practitioner and trainer.

Acknowledgements

This book has developed from a doctoral project undertaken at the University of Dundee (2008-2011) and later during my work as a lecturer at Loughborough University (2012–15). The seven-year span means that the number of people who impacted on the project and who supported me is far too great to name them individually but I am certain that they will find their imprints in the book and accept my gratitude. Still, some I want to thank more clearly.

First, I am greatly indebted to my supervisors, who were extremely supportive throughout my time as a PhD student. Fiona Smith showed amazing patience and care for my work and her encouragement and insights were crucial for me to persevere through my fieldwork challenges. Chris Philo's knowledge and encouraging attitude helped me to feel comfortable with my own work at the early stage of the project. Later, Donna Marie Brown was always generous in giving her time and providing me with quick, rigorous and encouraging feedback throughout the process of writing.

Second, I greatly enjoyed the hospitality and cosy atmosphere of Geography at the University of Dundee. For more than three years it has been a great place to do PhD and to develop academically as well as personally. Special thanks to Morgan Windram-Geddes for sharing a passion for the geographies of childhood.

Third, I was lucky to get on with my academic career at Loughborough University. A hub of work on children, youth and families, the Geography Department there made finishing this book possible. Of all colleagues, I am especially thankful to Darren Smith for guiding me through the first few years.

Fourth, I owe too much my closest ones and little would have happened without them.

Fifth, and most importantly, my greatest thanks should go to those who hosted my research and made it possible. The time I spent with children and young people in Kopčany was a life-time experience and I can only hope that this book will do them and their lives a justice. The support I received from the Community Centre exceeded all my expectations and several of the staff I have to thank for so much more than their collegiality. The biggest thanks go to Petra Hricová, who stood behind the project in a way I would not have imagined.

I also wish to extend my thanks to Policy Press, in particular Isobel Bainton and Rebecca Tomlinson for their editorial support and patience. Finally, the project would not have been possible without support from the Economic Social and Research Council (ESRC), the Royal Geographical Society with the Institute of British Geographers (RGS-IBG), the Dudley Stamp Memorial Fund of the Royal Society and the Institute of Geography of the Slovak Academic of Sciences.

Part One

ONE

Introduction

This book asks four questions: What do children do? Where do their actions come from? What *can* they do? And what does this imply for adults? It explores everyday practices of children (aged 5–14) from Kopčany, at the time of the fieldwork a deprived and isolated neighbourhood on the outskirts of the Slovak capital Bratislava, where I spent one year in a dual role of ethnographer and youth worker. By investigating the circumstances in which these practices are embedded and from which they emerge, the book builds an account of the formation of children's agency and of this agency as constituting the place where children live.

The question of children's agency has come under the spotlight in a range of recent debates, including the scholarly interest in children's capacities to act and 'make a difference' (Oswell, 2013, p.6), the policy-driven focus on children's wellbeing (van Nijnatten, 2013), or on children as social agents with distinctive rights in the context of global development (Lieten, 2008). I seek to address some gaps in these debates and contribute to the existing understandings of children's agency in three ways. The main contribution comes from the material on which the book is based. This is first and foremost an ethnographic story of children's practices, a thick empirical account generated in the role of a youth worker in Kopčany. The book employs a strongly empiricist approach to theorising children's agency; the theory is grounded in, and built from, the field experience. I offer a justification for this approach in three chapters of Part Two on the grounds of the links between the social *and* spatial positionality of the children in Kopčany and the marginalisation they experience. But the ethnography is also a reflexive account of my encounters with children and adults (neighbourhood residents, youth workers and others) in the neighbourhood. Adults–children is thus only one axis of difference reflected in this book. Another one is established between my roles as a researcher and a youth worker, and I unpick how different preconceptions of who we make ourselves as adults are important for how we can engage with children. I refer to my stay in Kopčany by various terms in the book – as research, project, practice or fieldwork – underlining the complex and yet heterogeneous nature of the work.

The researcher–*practitioner* couplet also opens up space for problematising two especially important facets of children's agency – ideas of children's participation and of politics. In the first venture, the book exceeds the framework of children's participation (Percy-Smith and Thomas, 2010) by disrupting adult-centred geometries of what participation means. Rather than exploring children's involvement in adult-driven agendas, regardless of how well intended, the book positions children themselves at the heart of processes that shape communities. What if we ask about adults' rather than children's participation? As an answer I offer an expansion of theories of (children's) *agency* into a theory of *action* – a relational account of adults' capacity to acquiesce in the fact that children are able to make a difference in the world and to conceive of a way to act upon it. Additionally, unlike a range of recent authors who theorise children's agency in terms of *political* agency (Kallio, 2008; Kallio and Häkli, 2011; Mitchell and Elwood, 2012), I am cautious of scrutinising children as political actors, given the adult-based definitions of politics, whether as referring to institutional participation, civic actions or ongoing practices in everyday environments. Instead, I seek to reconsider *adults themselves* as political agents, building on an empirically grounded account of children's practices, and making the aforementioned theory of action explicitly a theory of *political* action.

The second contribution of this book comes from its geographical lens. Throughout the book, I employ *place* as a central conceptual tool to understand children's practices beyond their immediateness and confinement in individuals, tracing connections between different children and upscaling the prospects of children's agency from individual children to wider society. In Chapter Five, I take an interest in how everyday public *spaces*, with their material and immaterial qualities, generate conditions that make children's practices possible, and how they are in turn shaped by children's agency. And throughout the book, again, I track the formation of children's agency through the concept of *scale*, from the contiguity of children's bodies and material things in mundane moments of everyday activities to the connections of these moments to structural forces impacting on the infrastructure of the neighbourhood. Writing as a geographer in dialogue with other fields of social sciences and humanities, I make an argument that 'spatiality', the inexorable interrelatedness of society and space (Merriman et al, 2012), is not just a different angle to approach children's agency but also provides both epistemological devices to expand understandings of how children come to do what they do and a political compass to navigate how adults might come to terms with it.

The third main area of contribution of the book lies in its geographical scope. Some 25 years after the collapse of the Soviet bloc, many authors have firmly assigned post-socialism to history, and East and Central Europe (ECE) has nominally become part of the Global North. Yet life in post-socialist Europe (not to mention post-socialist Asia or Africa) differs from its Western counterpart in more than just a stage of institutional development, as researchers attentive to experiences of those who have been marginalised in the transformation processes have showed us (Stenning and Hörschelmann, 2008). Academic literature, however, still remains lacking in empirical investigation about what it is like to be growing up in ECE in the context of the social, economic, political and cultural changes that came with the transition from state socialism to liberal capitalism, particularly with the focus on younger children (Trell et al, 2012). This book brings a detailed empirical account of childhood in one of the more marginalised places in ECE, mapping the mundane everydayness of children's lives and its connections to global changes, responding to the calls to consider the diversity of children's experiences around the globe (for example Jeffrey and Dyson, 2008; Holt, 2011). It problematises the grand narratives of post-socialism, globalisation and neoliberalism but avoids romanticising the local and intimate by tracing the presence of the particular in children's lives to wider conditions and possibilities. It does not reject post-socialism or globalisation as adequate frameworks for understanding children's experiences in ECE but principally seeks to bring such terms down to earth, to ground the idea of historical, geographical and social difference in empirical understandings of everyday experiences of children born well after the collapse of the Soviet bloc.

In sum, this book launches three interrelated intellectual projects, developed through a dual academic-practitioner interface. Chiefly, it looks at children's capacities to act and make a difference in the context of their communities and beyond. It extends debates on children's agency by reversing the views of community and society as defined by adults' agendas. It adopts an empiricist approach to consider children as significant social actors in their own right, re-determining such a significance by attending to what 'matters' (Horton and Kraftl, 2006a) in children's lives and tracking which elements contribute to the constitution of children's practices and their very capacity to act, constructing an empirically grounded account of childhood. Then, within the frame of community, the book juxtaposes the ethical and institutional frameworks of adult–child relations with the intimate intersubjective experiences of such engagement, and it questions the prospects, horizons and limitations of how adults can coexist, connect and collaborate with children. While situated at a particular positionality of researcher-practitioner, this argument gives more than a methodological account of how to do research with children or be a youth worker. It speaks back to the prospects of social life and development across age and generational differences and distances (Hopkins and Pain, 2007). Finally, engaging with critical studies of the post-socialist change of ECE, the book approaches the macro-scale of global processes by addressing mundane embodied practices of individual children at a particular locality. Simultaneously, it stands out as a critical ethnography of post-socialist change and as an account of connectivity between global dynamics and embodied experiences of children in a marginalised area of ECE.

In the rest of Chapter One, I present a core theoretical framework that will guide my argument over the course of the book. This is based on four pillars: a theorisation of childhood within and beyond relations to adults as a process of incompleteness; a conceptualisation of social practices as an ongoing process of diverse relations; an understanding of place as a matrix of social connectivity in which children's agency actualises to make a difference; and finally an idea of counter-topographies of children's agency, a methodological approach to reassemble contexts, moments and effects of children's practices. Finally, I give a synopsis of the rest of the book.

Children's practices and place: towards counter-topographies of children's agency

Childhood

One long-standing view on childhood revolves around an essential and inescapable difference between children and adults. Children have been considered as 'human becomings rather than human beings, who through the process of socialisation [are] to be shaped into fully human adult beings' (Holloway and Valentine, 2000); as 'fundamentally different types of human' (Lee, 2001, p.5); or as 'adults in the making rather than children in the state of being' (Brannen and O'Brien, 1995, p.730). This distinction between 'human beings' and 'human becomings' denotes the difference between adults as 'stable, complete, self-possessed and self-controlling' individuals (Lee, 2001, p.5), and children who are deemed 'changeable and incomplete and [lacking] the self-possession and self-control that would allow [them] the independence of thought and action that merits respect' (2001, p.5).

This question of children's 'in/completeness' is central to this book. My research draws on the critiques of popular thinking about children as incomplete in comparison to adults (and thus incompetent), as fragile (and thus in the need of protection) and as non-socialised (and thus savage, harsh and in the need of surveillance). It extends the claims that childhood is at least partly a social construct (James et al, 1998) and, as such, it is contingent upon the particular societal mechanisms that frame it, so its production as a social consequence cannot be universal. It draws on the traditions that understand childhoods variously as simultaneously and relationally biological, legal, social and cultural constructs, situated in different times, places and cultures (Heywood, 2001; Mayall, 2002), but crucially as formations existing on their own. Although children can be dependent on adults (on adult individuals or on adult society), and such dependence would differ in various contexts, this does not take away from the rationale for studying children's lives as unfolding on their own as there are additional factors in 'being a child'.

Lee's (2001) thoughts about children's 'incompleteness' take the discussion even further. In line with the arguments of much of the late 20th-century work in philosophy and social theory that questions the idea of the fully constituted human subject of the Enlightenment (for example Bauman, 1991), Lee proposes destabilising the notion of the human subject entirely rather than just establishing a new sense of the child's subjectivity. His key claim is that 'even though [the being/ becoming] distinction is still an important aspect of the regulation of childhoods, [it] is becoming "outdated" as a way of understanding childhoods' (2001, p. 121). Lee's primary aim is to break the being/ becoming and completeness/incompleteness binaries. However, rather than establishing the term 'childhood' on its own in a parallel to the idea of fully constituted, complete and independent adult subjectivity, he seeks to understand children's lives by destabilising the latter and asks 'how we are to understand childhood when *both* our human categories are coming under question' (Bauman, 1991, p.6, italics added). This call does not dismiss the existence of 'childhood' and 'adulthood' as distinct categories in culture, policy or law, but it recognises them only as such, not as fundamental essences of being.

I approach childhood and children's agency as incomplete, always in process of constitution. This approach – its theoretical and practical implications and the strategies I employ – is further developed in Chapters Three and Four, but here I wish to present three ideas from which it springs. The first is Lee's understandings of agency through 'extensions and supplements' (2001, p.131) upon which a person depends in order to act. These 'extensions' or 'supplements' include a diverse and heterogeneous range of issues such as emotions, memories, knowledge, physical objects, spaces, people, social institutions, cultural patterns or bodies. Lee sees children neither as independent human subjects nor as mechanical machines (in contrast to fundamentally materialist readings of agency; see Lee, 2013), as their actions depend on the capacities of their bodies and minds, but also on the presence of and relations with other people, objects or environments. Ontologically, children's agency does not differ from that of adults in principle; yet this difference needs to be examined by paying to attention to the character of all the kinds of elements already mentioned. The second idea is essentially a geographical parallel to Lee's sociological conception of relational agency addressing the concept of scale. Current geographical debates on children's agency have presented conflicted views over whether more attention needs to be paid to the mundane contexts of children's lives, such as play, embodiment, emotions or popular culture (for example Harker, 2005), or whether celebrating the banal obscures children's positioning in wider structures of power relations and inequality, effectively depoliticising the question of children's agency (Mitchell and Elwood, 2012). In response, the book follows Ansell's call for 'descaled geographies of childhood' as a careful examination of 'the nature and limits of children's spaces of perception and action' (2009a, p.190) as a key determinant of the agenda for research with children. In other words, my interest begins in moments and sites of children's practices, but analytically, I track them consistently to connections well beyond the immediate range of children's everydayness.

The third idea underpinning my approach to childhood is about epistemology and politics. Jones (2008) is among authors arguing that childhood is constructed as an inferior reflection of the adult order. This justifies the process of what he terms as the 'colonisation' of children's lives, the regulation of children's 'opportunities to control his or her own relationship with time and space' (Jones, 2008, p.196). Jones argues that childhood is constructed in relation to adults through uneven power relations and, because of its otherness to adulthood, the authenticity of children's experiences and agency can be never fully approached by adults. He then turns this epistemological question into a political one and suggests that, as a way 'to resist colonising' childhood (Jones, 2013, p.7), adults need to '"give" children space in literal, metaphorical and political terms' (2013, p.6). Translating this idea to my work means that I also need to approach my own engagements with children and my capacities to capture, understand and (re)present an account of their agency as incomplete.

Practices

This book maps children's everyday practices in Kopčany and the circumstances in which these practices are constituted. The notion of mapping does not refer to simply plotting the spatial range of children's experiences into a cartographical representation. It stands for an investigation of what the children do and which factors matter for their practices, for example, enable, instigate, constrain or disable them. Building on the reading of Lee and Ansell explained in the previous section, I am inspired by Latour's (2005) idea of 'tracing associations' in children's lives, by Pile and Thrift's (1995) notion of 'mapping the subject', and especially by Mathy's metaphor of 'visiting in turn all, or most, of the positions one takes to constitute the field ... [covering] descriptively as much of the terrain as possible, exploring it on foot rather than looking down at it from an airplane' (1993, p.15). Instead of observing only certain types of practices and categorising or comparing them (that is, defining prior to the fieldwork what themes are relevant), my objective was to undertake an open-ended experiential procedure of recording the fieldwork encounters that reveal something about children's practices, a procedure that would be 'open ... and connectable in all of its dimensions' (Deleuze and Guattari, 2004, p.13).

Practices themselves, in this context, can be understood simply as 'the act of doing something' (Setten, 2009, p.1), as the 'ongoing mix of human activities that make up the richness of everyday social life' (Painter, 2000, p.242) or, more profoundly, as 'a series of actions that are governed by practical intelligibility and performed in interconnected, local settings' (Schatzki, 1988, p.244), highlighting their incomplete logic and interrelatedness. This conceptualisation is also sufficient as it embraces broadly the contents of children's everyday actions and helps in keeping the epistemological openness and flexibility in relation to a range of experiences, an implicit requirement of approaching agency as incomplete.

My argument for focusing on practices is based on the conceptual interconnectedness between children's activities and their everyday surroundings. On the one hand, practices are embodied, that is, located and entwined within individual human bodies. On the other hand, how they evolve depends on the presence of a range of other circumstances, including material objects, other people, discursive practices, or institutional functioning. My empirical interest is located at the connections between these two dimensions – children's individual bodies through which their practices are located and a range of issues that matter for how children's practices take place. Throughout the book, I use Lee's (2001) term 'extensions to agency', as it emphasises how children's capacity to act is dependent on a range of circumstances that 'extend' children's simple presence in the world and create the possibility of action.

Not all practices and not all their necessary pre-conditions were always intelligibly mediated by the children in this book. Their actions were often driven by tacit knowledge, customary routine, or unarticulated affective states. While there exist ways that pre-cognitive or even pre-conscious features that matter for the constitution of children's practices can be explored, this does not mean that such inquiry can be always fully transparent and fully comprehensive. To explore the circumstances of children's practices requires adopting an ad hoc set of analytical tools, reflective of the situations and experiences. I discuss some of the general strategies in this section and later in Chapter Four, but each empirical chapter is also accompanied by additional conceptual and methodological synopses that help to illuminate the particular experiences outlined in the chapter narratives.

Themes that are presented as circumstances of children's practices in individual empirical chapters have been selected on the basis of a range of rationales. The choice is primarily field-driven, based on the occurrence, intensity and impact of certain circumstances on the constitution of children's practices (these factors largely underlie how I understand the 'everydayness' of children's lives). However, other criteria were also employed: how well the themes can be transferred from the research experiences in the field to research outputs and how well they can be expressed in written work; how representative the selection is so it covers the richness of children's agendas; but also how relevant the themes are to scholarly debates. The book does not attempt to cover all children's practices and all their extensions. The criteria given earlier also indicate limits of the research that cannot reach beyond the opportunities provided by the ethnographic approach (see Chapter Three) and by (re)presentation (see Chapter Four). Rather than providing an exhaustive summary of children's practices and their circumstances, the book seeks 'an understanding of [their] complexity which is correspondingly modest' and which attempts to 'simultaneously see ... everything' about them (by taking most from my ethnographic presence in the site of children's practices) while 'inevitably missing most [or, at least a lot] of it' (Thrift and Pile, 2000, p.xiv).

Place

Where *practices* provide a concept that helps explore a range of immediate moments in children's lives, the idea of *place* helps integrate those moments as a way of coming to a broader understanding of children's lives. Place has been theorised in distinct and even contradictory ways, but most approaches usually come from the understanding of it as a 'meaningful location' (Cresswell, 2004, p.7) or a 'known and definable area' (McDowell, 1997, p.2), as opposed to an undifferentiated 'realm without meaning' (Cresswell, 2004, p.10). What I find more helpful, however, is thinking about place as a *way of understanding*, that is, an 'aspect of the way we choose to think about' (2004, p.11) world phenomena, particularly those that are intertwined or juxtaposed in various spatial and social networks of flows, relations and processes. Cresswell emphasises how places as objects 'are obscure and quite hard to grasp' (2004, p.11) and, as such, place conceptualised in an epistemological sense, that is, what 'we decide to emphasise and what we decide to designate as unimportant' (2004, p.11), can be as illuminating about social life as the usual ontological definitions of place.

In this way, Kopčany can be approached as a place if a view centred on the children's lives reveals understandings of the location that question or add to the existing imaginations in the public, academy or policy, thus contributing to the book's objective of rethinking the horizons of children's agency beyond the adult realm. In Chapter Two, I introduce Kopčany as an area that is depicted through often simplistic ways, either as a neglected area associated with crime, unemployment, danger or poverty, or as a territory that could be interpreted within broader structural explanations of post-socialist transitions. However, this book is committed to undertake an in-depth investigation of everyday experiences in Kopčany, but additionally with a focus on a social group that is itself often neglected in academic, professional but also everyday public considerations of social life, namely children. The research thus connects with the long-standing tradition of geographers interested in relations between children and place (for example Hart, 1979; Matthews, 1992), and particularly with the work interested in how places can be produced differently by children themselves in relation to their agency (Aitken, 2001b; Kjørholt, 2003).

Understanding places as spatial nodes that bear distinct (though possibly multiple) meanings implies that they are more than just 'simply bounded locations' (Laurie et al, 1999, p.13). Moreover, different places are necessarily *differently produced* but also *producing difference*. In turn then, paraphrasing Laurie et al, it can be said that childhoods, as features in social life, are 'constituted differently in different places, and that they in turn help make those places what they are' (1999, p.12), that is, they 'are part of what shapes those places' (1999, p.12). This proposition leads towards two implications that the idea of place brings for the research. First, it opens up the question of what kind of location Kopčany is, if we decide to think seriously about Kopčany as co-constituted by children's practices rather than imagine it as produced entirely without considering the effects of children's activities. Second, it opens avenues towards understanding how children's practices are shaped in certain ways because of other features that are present in Kopčany and which the children encounter. Kopčany is then thought of as a place with regard to what effects the processes and relations in the locality have on children's practices.

Counter-topographies of children's agency

I introduced the ideas of place – as a concept *integrative* for the contents of lives of particular children – and of practices – as a concept *revealing* them. To make a methodological link between the two – that is, between revealing the particularities and understanding the broader associations – this book adapts a variant of Katz's (2001a, 2001b, 2004b) method of *counter-topography*. Whereas Katz uses it as a study of global processes through a connective analysis of social reproduction in various places, I have reworked the approach to study the constitution of *place* through individual and collective, or at least shared, *experiences of particular children* in Kopčany. After explaining my links to Katz's work, I introduce the analytical method that followed the ethnographical fieldwork.

Katz describes *topography* as a critical method that examines 'places in their broader context and in relation to other areas and geographical scales' (2001a, p.1228). Discussing topographic maps, she writes:

> Just as topographic maps connect sites of equal elevation through contour lines, so too can particular relationships across localities be revealed and examined using topographies. That is, the trace or effects of particular processes on various places can be demonstrated through this methodology to suggest their translocal bearings. (Katz, 2009, p.762)

Katz's interest lies in studies of particular places and in 'the grounds of and between multiply situated social actors in a range of geographical locations who are at once bound and rent by the diverse forces of globalization' (Katz, 2001a, p.1214). The issue of connections between different locations is crucial here, as it enables the identification and exploration of often subterranean or latent effects of global forces and processes, or, as she writes, topographies 'allow us to look not only at particular processes in place, but at the effects of their encounters with sedimented social relations' (Katz, 2001b, p.719). Topographies offer a thick description, but this is situated and links dynamic processes with their local points of contact, with the very particular moments of everydayness. Katz mentions how 'the place-based knowledge produced as topographies sustains and enables the exercise of power at various geographic scales and can transcend the specificities of the locality in which it was gathered' (2001b, p.719).

The topographical method as Katz provides it is inherently critical (and Katz labels her own approach as 'counter-topographies'), as it aims to produce a political alternative to imaginations about areas that are used and reproduced through dominant institutions and their mechanisms. Exploring the global through local connections and thus opening up recognitions of encounters between processes and material responses is for Katz a political means to build alternative and more just spatial and social networks – and there are very practical examples of this strategy (Katz, 2004a; Nelson, 2004; Nagar and Swarr, 2005).

My method for analysing and interpreting the ethnographic data can be described as a counter-topographical analysis on a smaller geographical and social scale. The scope of this research lies not in comparing Kopčany to other places, but in connections between everyday practices of *individual* children and relevant broader circumstances. I am interested in how similarities and differences in everyday circumstances instigate similar or different effects on children's practices, and in an identification of the significant connections between various circumstances that affect individual children's practices differently (analogically to how Katz investigates global processes through their different or similar kinds of affects in various places). This takes advantage of several features indicated by Katz, who herself emphasises that the topographical method can be used 'at *any scale* from the body to the globe' (Katz, 2001a, p.1228, italics added). It helps me understand children's practices in the context of their encounters with the practices of other people as well as with other relations and processes that affect them. As many of these have effects on a broader scale, tracing connections between the experiences of different children helps me to investigate different ways in which the immediate circumstances of children's lives connect together differently, and what the diverse consequences are that this brings to individual children or specific groups of children.

I began the project by writing individual stories about everyday practices of individual children from the neighbourhood. Extracting a list of the most relevant practices I have experienced, I further traced those circumstances that mattered for the constitution of these practices – enabling, triggering or constraining them – mapping the 'networks of extensions' to individual children's agencies. In the third stage of the analysis, I was looking for particular practices and circumstances in individual 'maps' of children's actions as they emerge across several individual files. By identifying similarities among the children, broader themes were selected as central foci for individual chapters on the basis of their frequency, importance or transparency in a number of individual accounts. For the purpose of writing the book, I then tracked the presence of these themes (for example, bodies, things, notions of social identity) in children's individual accounts and searched for differences and similarities both in the ways that they emerged in these stories (for instance, the presence of things versus their absence, or practices of affirming or challenging the labels of one's social identity) and in the eventual practices of the children. I focused on the lines of similarities or differences in connections between children's practices and their circumstances, while I also explored the presence and genesis of these circumstances, particularly in relation to their location in Kopčany.

The topographical method builds a link between the particularities of individual children's practices, and the contexts of their lives in Kopčany that are to some extent shared, although the experiences of life in Kopčany can be enormously different for individual children or groups of children. Katz labelled her own use of the topographical method as 'counter-topography', to emphasise how her analysis of globalisation creates alternative contours of the global flows, processes and relations, and how it can be used for emancipatory politics. I follow this stance and use the same term. In this case, the 'counter' in the name refers both to the production of a grounded account of children's agency and its implications for politics, and for an alternative understandings of Kopčany against the existing imaginations that either too vaguely comprehend Kopčany as a transitional area in a post-socialist territory or provide a stereotypical image of Kopčany as a neglected area without closer engagement with or experiences in the neighbourhood. By emphasising the 'ways of understanding' Kopčany, I use counter-topographies as an epistemological approach that opens up new directions to think about Kopčany as a place; by emphasising 'connections', I build an account of children's capacity to make a difference as constituted beyond their bodies/minds but enacted through individuals.

Book synopsis

The book addresses the question of children's agency over the course of twelve chapters organised into four parts.

Chapter Two introduces the area of Kopčany within the local and regional context of Bratislava, Slovakia and the broader East and Central European region. It locates the neighbourhood within the concept of post-socialism and then identifies key social, economic and demographic data that situate the livelihoods of children from Kopčany, along with a local history of housing and social development. The chapter gives an account of the double marginalisation of children in Kopčany – due to the deprivation of the area and to the position of children in the society – and highlights implications of this for children and their agency.

Chapter Three adopts a reflexive approach to fieldwork and provides an account of how field practices shaped the research questions, settings, process of knowledge generation and impact. The chapter contests a view of methodology as a coherent set of practices and instead develops understandings of the embodied intersubjective dynamics of the fieldwork and their effects on the research. Particular attention is given to intricacies of doing research as a community-based practitioner.

Chapter Four continues the discussion of how the research is framed by exploring the issues of conceptualisation and presentation. I explain the concept of minor theory as a mobile practice of theorising the fieldwork events locally and in accordance with the empirical experiences while building a wider narrative. The chapter sketches the underlying theoretical propositions for the book, reflecting on the problems of openness, complexity, essentiality and im/materiality in field encounters by employing theoretical perspectives of empiricism, relationalism, non-essentialism, and (relational) materialism.

Chapters Five to Eleven form the empirical core of the book. Each of them addresses a particular domain of extensions to children's agency and explores what diverse impacts these have on the constitution of children's practices. **Chapter Five** explores the significance of everyday spaces in Kopčany for children's practices and introduces the links between spatiality and other aspects of children's agency. **Chapter Six** explores children's bodies as both the material location and the symbolical attribute of children's practices. The analysis breaks down the material/immaterial dichotomy and identifies the ways in which children's material bodies 'come to matter', emphasising the notion of immediacy in children's actions. **Chapter Seven** pursues the interest in everyday objects ('things') and their role in the constitution of children's agency. The conclusions of the chapter link the role of things and of children's experience as an intertwined factor in how children's practices are formed. In **Chapter Eight**, I am interested in how children's social life begins to be shaped by their everyday encounters with other people. The importance of children's experience is here explored again, and the chapter leads to the next discussions of children's ongoing social relationships. **Chapter Nine** discusses the role of family life in children's practices (and vice versa) and addresses the links between family patterns and children's agency. **Chapter Ten** provides a similar discussion with a focus on friendship. Links between the institutional roles of family and friendship are identified and discussion of them contributes to conceptualising the formation of children's social relationships more broadly. This theme is concluded in **Chapter Eleven**, which discusses how the notions of children's social identity (related to age, ethnicity and gender) come to matter in their everyday practices and how childhood can be seen as a specific mode of forming an attitude to others as well as to oneself.

Chapter Twelve responds to the themes introduced in Chapter One. I draw a connection between the conceptual and practical strategies presented in Part Two and the empirically driven discussions in Part Three, and I propose what is implied in the title of the book: to 'rematerialise' children's agency. This stands for three issues: to recognise heterogeneous elements that constitute children's capacity to act; to reconnect this capacity with children's everyday environments; and to establish this capacity in how we, as adults, act towards children but also the rest of the society.

Although all empirical chapters can be read on their own, the circumstances of children's practices are often shown to blend together or be crucial components of each other. The linear style of presentation is therefore artificial at least insofar as the impact of all circumstances on children's practices is simultaneous but also interrelated. I tried to adjust the style of writing so references to other discussions or evidence would primarily refer to previous chapters and cross-referencing would not address what yet remains to be read, although this was not always possible.

Some key themes are not addressed within a single chapter but are presented recurrently through a number of chapters (for example issues such as emotions or knowledge). Some other themes are presented only through specific conceptualisations (for instance, gender, age and ethnicity are discussed specifically in terms of their expressions as notions of social identity in Chapter Eleven, or as embodied inscriptions of social practices in Chapter Five, rather than as themes on their own).

The themes are ordered starting with the most explicitly spatial theme – everyday spaces in the neighbourhood. This chapter also serves to situate further discussions graphically. Next chapters explore circumstances from those localised at the most instantaneous spaces (body, things) and temporalities (immediate moments), towards those that are spread and settled through broader social ties. However, I agree that scale constitutes, rather than represents, the truth (Marston et al, 2005), and this statement is valid for both ontological and geographical scales, therefore entanglements of various themes and scales are presented as crucial for understanding the complex constitutions of children's practices.

Part Two

TWO

Locating the field

An extract from the research diary:

> ... although I lived in Petržalka [the largest district of Bratislava, Kopčany lies on its outskirts] for the first twenty years of my life and was proud to be familiar with the area, this was the very first time that I was going to visit Kopčany. For one reason, there seemed to be nothing to do in the neighbourhood – located at the end of the city near the Austrian border and with its image of a neglected and dangerous area that one should avoid, especially at night. For another, only to access it was difficult – one had to cross a motorway and a railway, or, if coming from another direction, a zone of former industrial plants ... After this, from the overpass that bordered Kopčany, the neighbourhood was below me, five eight-storey prefabricated panel buildings separated from the bridge by a strip of neglected greenery and by an abandoned construction site. I walked down the stairs and entered the actual neighbourhood ...

Figure 2.1 The landscape of Kopčany

As I was looking for the Community Centre where my interview with the staff was scheduled, I was reflecting on what I actually knew about the place I had just entered and

about the children who lived there whom I was supposed
to study. And what *I thought* I knew...

'Non-payers',[1] unemployed, people without money,
alcoholics, drug dealers and their customers – people with
the most diverse social problems live together in a couple
of buildings where the authorities concentrated them. A
few ordinary tenants got stuck among them...' (An extract
about Kopčany from the most popular Slovakian broadsheet,
October 2008)

I was familiar with the reputation of danger and mess but
I was also aware that no one who told me about Kopčany
had ever visited the place or had known anyone from the
area. While I grew up just a couple of hundred metres from
Kopčany, in what was, at the first glance, a very similar
neighbourhood ('...although', I was thinking, 'we had
benches ... and no CCTV ... and a *tarmacked* car park
full of cars ... and the adults usually were not sitting on the
concrete wall and having a chat ... and this young woman
would not stop by me and ask if I was looking for the shop
...'), and while I read newspapers and listened to my friends
talking about all the dangers and mess in Kopčany – I
realised that I did not really know what it was like to live,
and particularly to grow up in Kopčany – what problems
these children might have, what dreams, desires or simply
how they spent their time. Actually, despite the feeling of
superficial uniformity that the landscape of the wider district
of Petržalka gave off, I did not know *anything at all* about
these children before I entered Kopčany because there was
no way I *could have known* ...

The introductory vignette is an illustration of a common urban paradox
of spatial proximity intertwined with social distance. In this chapter,
I explain the rationale for focusing solely on Kopčany in exploring
children's agency by outlining the contours of a dual marginalisation
experienced by children in the neighbourhood: due to the history
of underdevelopment of the locality in the uneven post-socialist
transformation; and due to children's unequal power relations with

---

[1]   The term, a direct translation of the Slovak word '*neplatič*', refers to people who
do not pay their rent and does not differentiate between various reasons for this.

adults. I draw on this argument to amplify two of the book's rationales: the analytical importance of place in understanding children's agency and the critical responsiveness to children's agency as a political responsibility of adults.

This is the first of three chapters in Part Two that explicate how this book has been written. Where Chapter Three gives a first-person account of engaging with children's practices and Chapter Four explains how I theorise them, Chapter Two is concerned with the setting of what children do. I approach this in two ways. One is about outlining the character of Kopčany, a tangible site and home of the children this book is about. But before this, I place Kopčany conceptually within the broader narratives of social, political and economic processes that shape the wider region and span well beyond the boundaries of the neighbourhood.

Post-socialism: marginalisation and the global

In 1998, Smith and Pickles argued that in the analyses of changes in Eastern and Central Europe (ECE), 'mainstream theory of transition ha[d] been written in terms of the discourses and practices of liberalisation' (1998, p.2). The attention of both neoliberal (for example Sachs, 1994; Åslund, 2002) and neoconservative (for example Fukuyama, 1992) approaches focused on political and economic macro-structures as determinants of everyday circumstances. The liberalisation of markets and macroeconomic structures (Gros and Steinher, 2004) and the installation of democratic institutions serving pluralistic democracy and civil society (Kaldor and Vejvoda, 2002; Sakwa, 1999) were considered as 'an expression of a universal trend' (Musil, 1993, p.10), and as flat and 'normative' (Outhwaite and Ray, 2005) trajectories supposed to determine the particularities of social life. Focusing on the transformation of political and economic macro-structures was considered as sufficient conceptual material, too, for the assessment of wellbeing in the region (for example Åslund, 2002).

A contrasting perspective was developed in parallel in anthropological literature (for example Verdery, 1996; Burawoy, 1999; Ekiert and Hanson, 2003) and elsewhere (Hörschelmann, 1997; Smith, 1997; Stenning, 2000), with the focus 'shifted from the "transition" ... to "actually-existing post-socialism"' (Stenning and Hörschelmann, 2008, p.314). Bradshaw and Stenning (2004) highlighted uneven development in post-socialist regions as the central theme within this approach. While still considered in the context of broader institutional changes, the focus shifted to 'diverse and even divergent local meanings and motivations' (Creed, 1999, p. 223) and to what Hörschelmann (2004) labels 'everyday life conditions', with a special focus on the 'losers' from economic changes, political exclusions and cultural commodifications. While moderately more interest has been given within this vein of research to women (Hörschelmann and Van Hoven, 2003; Johnson and Robinson, 2007), those with low incomes or at risk of poverty (Smith et al, 2008; Stenning et al, 2010), minority ethnic groups, particularly Roma (Fonseca, 1996; Sibley, 1998), or teenagers (Hörschelmann and Schäfer, 2005; Pilkington et al, 2010), little attention has focused on younger children, despite evidence of different experiences of childhood in Western and Eastern Europe (Tomanović and Petrović, 2010; Blazek, 2011).

This is in a stark contrast to Katz's (2004a, 2006, 2008, 2011) argument about the intense and intensifying risk of children's lives being constituted as disposable and negligible within the processes of neoliberal capitalism, of which the countries of ECE are a striking contemporary example (Stenning et al, 2010). This does not mean that neoliberalism needs to be ultimately a starting point for exploring children's lives in ECE, as there are other important factors shaping children's everyday experiences (Blazek, 2011), and as there are other processes and domains in which differences of post-socialism unfold geographically and historically (Harutyunyan, 2009; Hirt, 2012; Hörschelmann and Burrell, 2013; Ramet, 2014). Yet there is an array of analysis showing that socioeconomic transformations in ECE fashioned previously unknown layers of marginalisation and processes of stratification (Hirt et al, 2013), and, if the evidence from elsewhere (Holloway and Pimlott-Wilson, 2012) is any indication, children are likely to be among those most affected. I pick Kopčany as an example of such a collective experience, as I map the development of the neighbourhood relevant to the lives of children and contribute to the rationale for paying attention to children's lives in the region because of the immense risks of exclusion that the children are exposed to, and which are also distinct from those experienced by adults.

Kopčany: marginalisation and the local

Kopčany is a small peripheral neighbourhood of Bratislava, a detached residential area of Petržalka, the largest housing estate in Central Europe (Figure 2.2). Petržalka, including Kopčany, was completely rebuilt from a previous rural settlement between early 1973 and 1987 as a modern and exemplary estate of state socialist urbanism, becoming both a tangible monument to the political regime and a site of the future residence of more than 100,000 citizens (Figure 2.3).

Figure 2.2 Location of Petržalka within the boundaries of Bratislava. City boundaries are displayed in grey, state boundaries are in bold black

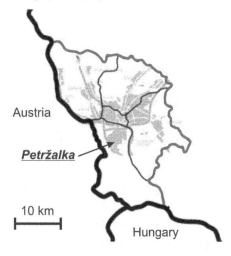

Figure 2.3 Landscapes of Petržalka

Kopčany consists of five 12-storey panel-block buildings with a total of 212 flats, most of them used for residency. Its official population in 2001 was 651, but with 'temporary occupants', it was 1,027 (according to the Census 2001 – more recent demographic data do not provide details at the level of the neighbourhood; the research itself took place in 2008–9). This difference was interesting on its own and unusual in the context of Bratislava. There are two categories of residence in Slovakia. Every citizen must have a permanent residence, which is registered with the police and creates a basis for the taxation system, and so on. In Kopčany, many residents had their permanent residence mostly outside the neighbourhood, and their address in the neighbourhood was their temporary residence, hence the status of 'temporary occupant'. The share of population with permanent residence (56.5%) was unprecedentedly low among other areas in Petržalka, as the share of citizens with permanent residence for the whole district was 95.1%. Kopčany was thus an area with an extraordinarily mobile population in comparison to the surrounding neighbourhoods, largely a result of the socioeconomic circumstances of the residents.

Kopčany has some of the highest levels of deprivation and negative perceptions of quality of life (Andraško 2006) in the whole of Bratislava. The neighbourhood itself is detached from the inner areas of Petržalka by a motorway, railway and industrial estates (Figure 2.4). The only other buildings in the neighbourhood are a large eight-storey commercial hostel for workers from the surrounding industrial plants located in the centre of the neighbourhood, and a small shabby pub on the outskirts of the area. Land surrounding the neighbourhood is mostly private areas, gated from the public.

The initial rationale for the development of Kopčany in the late 1970s came from the proximity of the industrial plants and the aim of providing accommodation for workers and their families, a role that the site had played historically, spanning back to the 19th century. After the formal end of state socialism, the ownership structure diversified and the use of the area changed in the 1990s. Some flats in two of the buildings were made available for private purchase, while other flats in these buildings and all flats in the other two buildings were transformed into council flats managed by the Petržalka District Council, which adopted a policy of resettling there tenants who were not able or willing to pay their rent elsewhere. The fifth building was governed by the Bratislava City Council and was transformed into a fixed-term social lodging house for families with young children and for former residents of foster homes (Figure 2.5). While the other four buildings

Figure 2.4 Location of Kopčany within Petržalka and Bratislava. The Bratislava 'Old Town' is located immediately to the north of Petržalka across the River Danube. The proximity of the state border and of major motorways can be seen, as well as the separation from the rest of Petržalka.

shared some similarities with the social lodging house (for instance they all had a porter's lodge), the lodging house itself operated within a distinctive regime. Accommodation was provided for a fixed-term period of a maximum of three years, and it was guaranteed primarily to families with children and without any other accommodation. All tenants and their visitors had to report to the porter and visits were permitted only until 10pm, with overnight visitors obliged to receive approval. Basic infrastructure, such as water and electricity, was supplied at a flat rate and at reduced tariffs, and the management of the lodging house provided all basic maintenance, while the other four buildings were not subject to these additional regulations.

The area was notable for the high number of children and young people. Even among the permanent population (for which the 2001 Census data were available), excluding residents of the social lodging house, the proportion of those under the age of 16 was higher than in Petržalka, the average age of the citizens was lower than in Petržalka and in Slovakia as a whole, and the proportion of households with dependent children was also higher than in Petržalka and Slovakia as a whole (see Table 2.1). Including the lodging house, where the ratio of families with young children was almost 100%, this proportion would be much higher.

The area, due to its physical detachment from the rest of Petržalka and the city, was characterised by the absence of, and difficult access to, basic social facilities and services, such as shopping (only one small corner shop in Kopčany), public offices, health services or school

Figure 2.5 Landscape of Kopčany. Four of the five 12-storey buildings can be seen on the photo. The social lodging house is on the right and it hides the fifth building. The workers' hostel is hidden behind the building in the middle of the photo. The trees on the horizon of the photograph are in Austria.

services. The nearest elementary schools (schools for children aged 6–15) were situated two bus stops from the neighbourhood and it was difficult for young children to access them on foot due to the motorway and railway. This is in contrast to the rest of Petržalka, where every neighbourhood had an elementary school within walking distance and without the need to cross busy roads or railways. Before 1989, at least one nursery existed in each neighbourhood of the size of Kopčany, while there was none in Kopčany (see Blazek et al, 2015). In addition, the local infrastructure lacked tangible facilities for children's leisure time activities. There were just two small playgrounds: one consisting of a deteriorating sand-pit and a self-made seesaw constructed from a tyre hanging on a chain; another consisting of a small slide (Figure 2.6). No grounds for sports activities existed in the area and there were no benches.

Table 2.1 Selected demographic statistics of Kopčany as compared to Petržalka and Slovakia

	Kopčany	Petržalka	Slovakia
Percentage of persons aged under 16	20.3%	14.2%	20.5%
Average age	31.0	34.7	36.0
Percentage of households with dependent children	45.3%	42.7%	37.8%

Source: Census 2001

Figure 2.6 Playgrounds in Kopčany

Another factor of social exclusion in Kopčany was the planning policies of the local authorities. Kopčany is an example of the policy common in both Slovakian and Czech urban development in the 1990s and 2000s, where tenants not paying their council flat rent were resettled into separate zones of usually low-quality housing and often neglected by the authorities (Temelová et al, 2011). In the case of Kopčany, this spatial and social isolation led to widespread associations of Kopčany with features such as low income and high unemployment, low quality of public spaces, low social cohesion and a high rate of crime and of drug consumption (Andraško, 2007). Kopčany has gone through a change more recently, due to a combination of citizens' involvement, District Council initiatives (focused especially on evicting drug dealers and increasing security through police patrols, but also on enhancement of street lighting and installation of CCTV and security services at the porter's lodges) and the activities of social and community workers.

Nevertheless, during the time of my fieldwork in 2008–9, Kopčany was one of the two areas perceived most negatively in Bratislava (Andraško, 2006). Media reports pictured the neighbourhood in a negative way and associated it with incivility, deprivation, crime and drugs. The opposite sort of media outputs were accounts produced under cautious supervision of the local Community Centre, which usually focused on the activities of the Centre and children's involvement, and emphasised the notion of normality in children's lives in Kopčany. Children were, to the contrary, notably absent in any other media representations of Kopčany. Everyday discourses about Kopčany to a great extent replicated this image of the neighbourhood as only very few citizens had any contact with Kopčany because of its isolation and marginalisation. The negative image was usually based on associations with a few key notions, such as drugs, violence and crime, incivility, poverty, dirt and the relatively large Roma population (in Chapter Eleven, I discuss how public discourses about Roma in Slovakia and the tensions between the non-Roma majority and the Roma minority affected children's practices in Kopčany). At the same time, children in the neighbourhood, especially the older ones, were familiar with this image and claimed to have experienced stigmatisation or even discrimination based on their residence (for instance, when their friends refused to visit them or even ceased contact with them, when they heard negative comments by strangers on public transport, or even remarks from their teachers in school). The image and representations of the neighbourhood thus affected children's everyday experiences significantly, along with the material development of the place.

Conclusions: connecting macro and micro and understanding marginalisation

Not only people but also places can become the 'losers' in transformational processes (Massey, 1984; Smith, 1984). This highlights the risk in choosing any place as representative of the broader range of circumstances that impact children and others in the wider region of ECE. The situation in Kopčany is not typical of all large panel-block housing estates across Slovakia, nor indeed Central Europe, in terms of children's experiences. I outlined a brief genesis of Kopčany, along with a detailed overview of the neighbourhood as a marginalised area with a high proportion of young people. The level of deprivation is high compared to other neighbourhoods of Bratislava, including other areas of panel-block housing such as Petržalka, and other factors such as family structures or spatial and social isolation are also distinctive. It is the contrasting perspective of Kopčany – as one of the most deprived areas in the Bratislava region, itself now one of the ten economically strongest regions of the European Union according to regional gross domestic product (GDP) per inhabitant – that opens up the rationale for this study.

It is not just the social vulnerability of children in general that raises their risk of exclusion. Residence, that is the place where they live and where their activities are concentrated, is also an important factor as, both through the paths of social reproduction in families, and through the lack of opportunities in their geographical area, children are exposed to vulnerabilty. This means that Kopčany should not be understood as representative of childhood in general in ECE. However, to ignore or underestimate children's experiences in Kopčany means potentially to overlook significant processes of marginalisation and socio-spatial inequalities in the region, some of which might reveal also more widespread and far-reaching patterns of social exclusion in ECE. There are two key benefits that the choice of the field site might additionally bring. First, it enables the research to explore a range of marginalising processes that are both *socially* and *spatially* instigated. In other words, patterns of inequalities can be revealed that have their roots in a range of grounded social relations, but also those which affect only some areas and in different ways. Second, taking seriously *children's* everyday experiences in Kopčany adds to an overall image of the place and opens unexplored paths of research that can also illuminate broader processes and relations of marginalisation to include a fuller range of human subjects.

Processes such as neoliberalism and globalisation are nowadays seen less in terms of pervasiveness and totality (Gibson-Graham, 1996) and more as 'a series of local, but interconnected' (Peck, 2008, p.33), multiple, fragmented, and 'migrating set[s] of *practices*' (Willis et al, 2008, p.2, italics added). Broader social processes and structures are connected to local embodied performances in particular times and places (Hörschelmann and Schäfer, 2005) and embodied practices of individuals are constitutive of broader processes and structures (Stenning et al, 2010). To explore the particularities of children's individual lives, as I set out to do in Chapter One, is thus not in contradiction with the arguments about the possible existence of commonalities in children's experiences in Kopčany due to broader factors, such as the marginalisation of the area. Following Philo's claim that children's worlds are 'structured "from without"' but 'experienced "from within"' (1992, p.198), this rationale instead articulates the need for a framework that would adequately forge the 'connections between the micro and the macro' (Philo and Smith, 2003, p.111) in children's lives, and especially 'transitions from the one to the other' (2003, p.111), at which particular moments in children's everyday lives are 'anchored' (Philo, 2004, p.97) within their broader circumstances. As Philo argues, there is:

> the need to study connections *of all sorts*, adopting a diversity of theoretical perspectives, in exposing the spaces of childhood to a critical scrutiny which might herald 'real' changes in the conditions of existence for children who are in poverty, being excluded, suffering abuse or simply enduring neglect. (2000, p.253)

In Chapter Three, I explain how I set about identifying these connections in a dual role of researcher-practitioner. Then, in Chapter Four, I introduce a series of conceptual queries and answers that helped me create an account of those connections, presented through empirical themes in Chapters Five to Eleven.

THREE

Practising the field

Can we find common ground? Talk? Love? Create
something together? (Irigaray, 1993, p.178; in Rose, 1996,
p.61)

In this chapter I wish to expand on the fieldwork story through
enhanced reflexive analysis of *my* practices in Kopčany. Beyond just
reflecting on what I have done, a much more fragile account of what
constituted the fieldwork is presented, that is, practices of mine and
of others, and the 'in-between' and 'additional' that they formed.
Against the coherence that the notion of 'methodology' might imply,
this chapter is an unsettled process of reasoning about 'what happened'
in the course of the research, in order to identify what findings such a
reflection *can* provide, and *how*. I concur with Law's (2004) argument
that '[m]ethod is not ... a more or less successful set of procedures
for reporting on a given reality. Rather it is performative. It helps to
produces realities' (2004, p.143). As I will argue in this chapter, the
'production' of realities by research method does not refer only to the
knowledge about realities that different methods are responsible for, but
also to the intersubjective practices of research that *reshape* different
realities in the course of research.

As I aimed to render an account of the multiplicity of ways in which
children's practices are constituted, my strategy was to engage with
the field, to step down from my original academic background and
to be open to the field '*coming to me*'. By the effort to 'divest [myself]
of the theoretical and philosophical pretentions to attend the urgency
of [my] participants' context' (Aitken, 2001a, p.125), I responded to
the initial drive to explore the formation of the place by focusing on
children's lives, and, in turn, on what matters for them. Then again, as
Von Eckartsberg (1986, p.98) notes, 'we cannot [entirely] escape our
theoretical presuppositions. All we can do is try to make our approaches
as explicit as possible.' In this chapter, I therefore focus on practices
of the field as features that make up the social life of the research
process. The 'relative autonomy' (Hitchings, 2010) of practices refers
to how they often exceed understandings and discourses produced by
social actors and unfold to a great extent through tacit propensities of

particular social settings (Bourdieu, 1990). By focusing on practices of the research, I think about the field only as *fieldwork*, a dynamic and performed composition that destabilises boundaries between the researcher and the researched (Massey, 2003) and challenges the imagination of the passive field and the active researcher (Nast, 1994). However, such a view also helps bridge the different positionalities I will explore – of a researcher and a practitioner – as the emphasis is on the relationships with other people rather than with professional goals.

The chapter consists of three unevenly long sections and a conclusion. First, I introduce the Community Centre which I joined as a researcher and where I took on the practitioner/researcher role for the duration of the fieldwork. I also give details of my involvement with the Centre and with children from Kopčany. After that, I elaborate on the idea of *reflexivity* as a complex and essentially practical tool employed for an advanced approach to the research process which is then provided in subsequent sections. Finally, I provide in-depth reflections on the nature of the practitioner-based research, tracing connections to the theme of adults' coexistence with children in a community space by exploring themes of power and ethics.

The Community Centre

I undertook my fieldwork in association with the Community Centre Kopčany, who accepted my request to host the research in exchange for at least a year-long commitment in the youth work role (although the collaboration went well beyond it, see Blazek and Lemešová, 2011; Blazek and Hraňová, 2012; Blazek et al, 2015). The Centre was founded in early 2004 with the aim of tackling social exclusion among children and young people in Kopčany by providing a range of advisory, counselling, leisure-time and educational programmes otherwise absent in the neighbourhood. Ulita is a third-sector organisation financed from a mix of temporary sources (independent foundations, the local municipality or private corporations) on a project-by-project basis. The Centre is based on principles of mobile youth work, locally labelled as a 'low-threshold programme', which is underpinned by the following:

- Reflexively *reacting* to the needs of children and young people instead of fitting them into pre-existing agendas.
- Tackling the demands and barriers that clients cannot meet, so the Community Centre services are *accessible* to all children and young people for whom usual institutional (leisure-time and counselling) services involve impassable obstacles (due to financial, social, travel or

other reasons). This applies also to the policy of penalisation in the case of misconduct which aims not to exclude children and young people from the activities of the Centre, but rather to involve them in alternative forms of sanction. Other key principles include no fees for using the services and no need to register or to attend regularly.

• Working with children and young people *at the sites where they spend their own time*, that is, in their own neighbourhood, on the street, and to create opportunities for involvement of both individuals and the whole community.

The Centre was located in a small flat on the first floor of the social lodging house and the staff consisted of psychologists, therapists, social pedagogues and social workers, including part-time professionals, volunteers and students. It operated all year, usually in afternoons and evenings between Monday and Thursday, and on an occasional basis also on weekends or holidays. It ran a range of activities, of which I was involved especially in two:

My main source of contact with children was street work (Figure 3.1), based on the direct contact of the Centre staff with children and young people that took place on the street. The nature of the contact with children varied and responded to children's immediate requirements and expectations. Usually, it consisted of play and entertaining activities, but also of individual and group advisory, counselling or crisis interventions. I spent time in street work usually twice a week in sessions that generally took two hours on the street and additional time for preparation for and reflecting on the sessions.

Boys Group and Girls Group (Figure 3.2) meetings were activities organised by the Centre within its indoor premises (hereafter called *the Club*) for children aged between 5 and 13 years. Unlike the street work, this setting involved certain rules partially imposed by the Centre and partially established and negotiated by the children. Time spent at the meetings was usually taken up by creative activities, games, conversations, craft production, or just passive hanging around in a safe space. Involvement of at least two staff members guaranteed both contact with the whole group and opportunities for individual consultations. During my stay in Kopčany, I was involved as the regular staff member in the Boys Group (two hours once a week) and occasionally participated in the Girls Group.

My main source of information about children's lives was direct contact through street work. During one shift on the street, we usually made contact with 15–50 children, depending on the weather and time of the year. The Centre kept regular contact with about 150 children

Figure 3.1 Street work

Figure 3.2 Club activities (the Boys Group)

and young people, most of them aged between 5 and 20, although the number changed rapidly due to sudden moves of children's families to and from the neighbourhood (see Chapter Five). Considering the overall number of young people that can be estimated from the Census data (see Table 2.1), my estimation was that the contact group represented between 50 and 90% of children and young people of the age group that my research addressed, with 70–80% being the most probable range. For my analysis, I processed records of encounters with 67 children (34 boys and 33 girls) aged between 5 and 14 years. The decision to restrict my work only to this age group came particularly from the need to restrict the scope of the research as working with older/younger groups would have required including a much broader set of themes relevant for the research analysis, some of which would be more ethically problematic or sensitive (such as sexuality or illegal behaviour). Moreover, working with older or younger groups of children required different approaches for me as a street worker and often also different sets of skills that would have been too demanding. In other words, this decision was based on the experience of the social context of the field, not *a priori* on developmental models of children's psychology. The nature of contact with the children was not uniform and the level of our engagement or the range of my experiences with them varied highly. In some cases, I was thus quite familiar with children's life histories, in other cases, I did not even know their real names, relying instead on their popular nicknames.

Reflexivity

Consider the following vignette:

> I took part in a hide-and-seek game on a very dark and cold December evening, with almost 15 children participating, aged between 5 and 13. Each turn of the game started with one person (who lost in the previous round) shutting his or her eyes and counting to agreed number, while everyone else had to run away and hide. As soon as Martin (9) turned his head away and raised his hand to cover his eyes, Rebeka (13) grabbed my hand and dragged me towards the dark area of concrete cylinders and trees, about 50 metres from the lodging house where the game took place. As we began to run, Monika (12) grabbed my other hand and ran with us, and I noticed Lina (7) and Peter (5), with a grin on their faces, running behind us. As we left the last lighted areas, the children hesitated, some screamed, and Rebeka let my hand go, saying "You lead now!" Martin almost finished counting, so we quickly took a stance behind one of the concrete cylinders and waited for Martin's steps. (Extract from fieldnotes, November 2008)

This quite mundane situation caused me considerable discomfort, and I reflected on it several times, immediately after my shift in the Community Centre was over as well as during the next few days, and on my own as well as with the Centre workers and the children themselves. Discussing the story, I will outline five important features of reflexivity as the method used throughout this chapter and the rest of the book and the difference it might make in the research practice. By doing this, I want to problematise reflexivity as more than just introspection (Finlay, 2003) and track its importance in all stages of work, from asking questions through encountering others in the course of fieldwork, to generating outcomes (Hertz, 1997).

First, interpersonal reflexivity needs to engage also with intrapersonal qualities, not just to catalogue the social categories of involved persons (Punch, 2012). In my story, I was quite concerned about running hand in hand with two older girls as well as about taking four children into the dark and hiding with them, thinking about the 'appropriateness' of such behaviour from an adult male, even though such an act was not necessary in conflict with the code of practice of the Centre. While gender, age or professional relations between me and the children were important for children's motivations during the event, these came also from more mundane and interpersonal motives, unexplainable by my and their social statuses. The older girls said that they wanted to hide with me as I had hidden so successfully in the last couple of game rounds and they thought they would do well in the game if they hid with me. The youngest children joined us as in this way they could go to a dark place without fear, but they also enjoyed the company of the older girls, who agreed to form such a big party because of my presence and involvement in the game but who would have probably rejected them otherwise. This situation relates to Moser explaining that 'external meta-categories' (2008, p.383) such as gender, ethnicity, nationality or status, even if the researcher is aware of them, 'quickly diminish ... in importance to the people' (2008, p.383) who are 'researched'. Instead, Moser stresses the notion of *personality* as a new approach to positionality, extending the socially based notion of identity that understands individuals as predominantly formed in entanglements of power relations (Sharp et al, 2000). During my research stay, while my social positionality, relative to that of the children or other participants, definitely mattered, a crucial portion of the intersubjective dynamics in the field during the research was grounded in the 'unique individual social and emotional qualities' (Moser, 2008, p.383) of myself and of the children, despite the ultimate social distance between us (Philo, 2003).

Second, reflexivity both helps enhance the generated knowledge and addresses the situated and dynamic ethical relations and practices (Guillemin and Gillam, 2004). Through disclosure and more than introspective critical accounts of the power dynamics in the research, reflexivity can *identify* different vulnerabilities in the research among the participants, but also of the researcher (Clandinin and Connelly, 1994) and others involved. My discomfort when I took the children away holding their hands, amplified by the training in practice with children I had received in the UK, was tackled by my training at the Centre that defined the key principles to follow and some of which I considered during the situation: to let the children initiate any bodily contact (for example, hugs or hands shaking) while monitoring my personal boundaries for discomfort, touch only children's 'hard' body parts (that is, hands, shoulders, or upper parts of back), use my body as a *passive* barrier in confrontations (such as when children aimed to enter the Club by force) or prevent children from taking any risk of harm to themselves. Reflexivity was thus a constant iterative process that *accompanied* the fieldwork rather than *followed* it, and it brought significant benefits to the relational ethics of the research (Etherington, 2007).

Third, reflexivity does not relate only to material practices. In our story with the children, emotions – my concern about the 'appropriateness' of the situation, the older girls' desire to succeed in the game, or younger children's desire to be accompanied by their older peers in a safe way – were crucial for our experience and were an important subject of the reflexive inquiry in that moment – as they 'are [an] inevitable and necessary aspect of doing research' (Bondi, 2005b, p.239) in general. Emotions build a cornerstone of the relational ethics that I discuss in the later part of the chapter. Although illustrations from the field show that reflecting emotions of others can be far from straightforward, understanding emotions through theories of practice can also help advance the epistemological framework of the study as emotions have proved to matter for the constitution of children's practices (as several chapters of the book will clearly show). However, the researcher's emotions are also a part of the research, even helping him/her to protect others (Gaskell 2008) and I provide emotional self-disclosures at various places in the book when it becomes pertinent.

Fourth, reflexivity is already present in everyday, non-professional processes that we encounter. Researchers (when they are away from their research) reflect on the events around them in many ways similarly to the way they do in their professional roles, try to make sense of these events and understand how they are affected, even if in different ways from the research process. Reflexivity should also address other practices of reflexivity (Adkins, 2003) as the same is done by other people around us. In our run to the dark area, I was not the only one who reflected on the situation. The children did too as they evaluated the situation before deciding to join the party and in order to understand their experience, I had to reflect on how they reflected on the situation.

Finally, not all is reflected in the course of everyday lives, reflexivity is inevitably imperfect. As there is much that we encounter but do not or cannot reflect upon (as researchers or not), reflexivity cannot provide an ultimate meaning for the events around us. Instead, it opens new depths of our encounters with the world and its richness, and it intensifies how we enliven it. At the same time, research reflexivity is not just a matter of one passing moment (Doucet, 2008) – it transfers to other daily encounters within and beyond the field and builds – more or less consciously and systematically – a subjective framework for understanding social life. Reflexivity is thus ultimately 'a *chance* rather than a model ... whose serendipity is the paradoxical promise of its achievement' (Stronach et al, 2007, p.196). Reflexivity applied to my field experience can enhance its epistemological standards but still has limits and remains partial.

Researcher and youth worker: the dual positionality

Practitioner

Discussions of the duality in practitioner/research positionalities have been offered mostly by practitioners engaged in research (Fox et al, 2007; Menter et al, 2011) and much less has been put forward by those who were initially researchers and who undertook their fieldwork in the role of practitioners (Bondi, 1999a). The benefits of practitioner research come from both epistemological and political/ethical backgrounds. As Fuller and Petch argue, 'day-to-day experience gives [practitioners] an unequalled degree of insight into, and knowledge of, the real problems which face both client and service providers' (1995, p.9). As such, practitioner research has a potential to explore and illuminate realities of the lives of marginalised social groups that conventional research approaches often fail to attain. However, practitioner research also raises concerns about several issues such as the different priorities of researchers and practitioners (Jones et al, 2000), tensions in gaining consent and managing identities (Dowds, 2008), or multiple institutional placements and responsibilities (Barker and Smith, 2001).

In my daily youth work duties, I was expected to fulfil the Centre's objectives revolving around the improvement of the quality of children's lives. In terms of street work specifically, this meant going out to the neighbourhood at an assigned time and spending time with the children. Usually we (working in a group of two to four youth workers) walked around the neighbourhood, had contact with children on the street and, depending on their reactions, we stayed with them or moved on, possibly splitting and working with children individually. Such reactions were rarely explicit and we even more rarely actually asked the children what they wanted. To consider whether they wanted our company was a matter of interpreting their reactions, as was the kind of contact they required – some wanted to be heard, others to be talked to, and some preferred just silent company. Importantly, our presence was known so children could approach us, but also stay away if they wished.

The nature of the contact depended on the children. They were largely familiar with the service of the Centre so they knew what to ask for and what to expect, often better than I did (see also Chapter Eight). Sometimes they wanted me to take part in their games or to facilitate them, sometimes they asked for some equipment, and often they wanted to talk or to have company. The principle we followed was that, depending on the situation (number of children and their requests), we tried to be available to as many as possible, with preferences given to those children who needed to deal with serious or sensitive issues. In that case, we usually split so one would be with children who sought counselling or advice while others would 'divert' others; or we simply apologised to other children and joined the company of the children with (urgent) problems.

The street was a place where the children made the rules, I had no formal authority and I was not expected to have any (see Blazek and Hricová, 2015, for a closer analysis of the relations between power and space in detached youth work). I was not expected to prevent children's conflicts, for instance, but rather suggest appropriate and acceptable ways of tackling them. At times this even included letting the children fight, and making sure that the fight would be safe and 'fair'. In any case, I was to justify my action from my personal viewpoint, not as an institutional authority. For instance, if I had to intervene to protect someone, I had to articulate why I personally did not find certain actions fair or right so I could not accept them and felt that I had to interfere. The presence of street workers on the street thus signalled certain safety for the children – but this was not supposed to enforce their authority over children's behaviour in the street. Instead, such presence in mutual encounters was based on intersubjective relationships between the children and the workers – negotiated, challenged and constantly reconstituted.

In the rooms of the Club, similar principles were followed, although adjusted depending on the activity. Some activities had an educational purpose and mode (such as school tutorials), but those that involved me most were a sort of extension to the street work. While certain rules were imposed by the Centre (such as no smoking or fighting, and respect of the time when the Club was open), most were negotiated with the children to ensure that they would feel safe and comfortable and, at the same time, would be involved in making the rules. Much of the Club activities allowed passivity, so the children could just spend time inside and did not have to participate. Similar to the street work, key principles were followed and applied – to be accessible and inclusive; reflexive and flexible; and to secure beneficence for the children who received the services.

Interpreting my practitioner role conceptually, the aim of the youth work activities was to *help* the children and as such it was open to a range of practices and approaches, depending on children's situations, needs and expectations, on the skills and capacities of the workers, but also on the relationships between the children and the practitioners. Reflecting on my role in encounters with children, the positionality of a 'helper' in relation to them can be interpreted in three ways as informing also the process of research. First, it is shaped through the *process* of providing the service, which was intentional, motivated, framed and undertaken as an informal 'contract' (Sills, 1997) based on expectations between me and the children. Both the children and I were aware of the essential formal roles in our contact and, consequently, we had certain expectations of each other – such as when children expected confidentiality from me, willingness to help or fair and equal treatment. The course of the research thus unfolded from the range of encounters and practices that happened as a result of the youth work process, structured around my formal duties as a practitioner and children's involvement with the Community Centre. Second, youth work can be also conceptualised as a *relationship* between practitioners and clients. A certain kind of relationship established between the client and the practitioner itself makes a positive difference in the helping process. I was expected, through my role and training as a youth worker, to develop relations with children in which they would feel safe and would recognise my interest and acceptance so that a 'helping' process might occur and this was true of all the other staff. Consequently, the close relationship also enabled my engagement with the field and enhanced the fieldwork. To develop a specific and engaged relationship with children was an expectation based on my role as a practitioner, but also significantly affected my positionality as a researcher, as the range and type of experiences I shared with the children, as well as the epistemological fields I could thus access, depended on the relationships we formed. Third, the research process in a practitioner role was accompanied by the 'use of professional skills' and 'profession-informed practice' (Bondi, 1999b). This view emphasises the often indistinct and blurred nature of my involvement. While I was not a fully qualified social or youth worker or counsellor, several practices of the fieldwork were nevertheless significantly informed by the theory and practice of these disciplines. Youth work activities such as attending to children's emotions, helping them to manage their anger or despair, facilitating their conflicts, or helping them in educational activities all required professional skills provided by the background in disciplines such as social work or counselling that were addressed by a basic training in the Centre, as well as through ongoing monitoring and supervision of my work by the senior workers in the Centre. In summary, youth work with its 'helping' philosophy was intrinsically interpersonal (Bondi, 2005a), explorative (Bondi and Fewell, 2003), value-oriented and engaged (Strawbridge and Woolfe, 2003), multi-perspective and based on interdisciplinary inputs and skills (Thorne and Dryden, 1993), and based on routine intersubjective practices between practitioners (in my case also researcher) and children. Due to its central role in my involvement with the children, it also fundamentally affected the nature of the research

Researcher

The relationship between my practitioner and researcher roles was affected by the initial decision made by me and the Community Centre to enter the fieldwork with children as a youth worker, not a researcher. The decision of the Centre managers was to introduce me as a new member of the Centre staff and to leave me to communicate my research interests to the children. I was introduced as coming from an academic environment and doing a research project in Petržalka, one element of which was my stay in Kopčany, but what the children were told to expect from me was defined according to the youth worker role, familiar to the children. For the purpose of my research stay, this decision meant that the practitioner aspect of my involvement with the children was superior and could not be jeopardised by any interference from the researcher perspective. I became a youth worker and committed myself to participate also in other activities of the Centre, such as engaging in clinical supervision, clerical tasks, organisational duties and planning. As such, I followed the practical, ethical and safety codes of the Centre, and sought to develop a practical approach of 'unobtrusive' ethnography. This unobtrusiveness did not mean that I did not affect the field dynamics (Fine, 1993), but this impact came from my actions as a helper and the affiliated personal dispositions. The key *research* method was participant observation, with the focus on *participation* in children's lives in a clearly definable (yet dynamic) role. I did not interview children for the purpose of the project, tried not to turn our conversations to themes I might have found important and rather made efforts to let them choose the themes of our conservations and activities.

An important question to factor in when reflecting on the research methodology is how to come to terms with the uneven power dynamics embedded in the relationships between children and adults.

A prevalent trend in research with children of the last decade has been to stress participatory, child-friendly or child-centric methods of research (Freeman and Mathison, 2009). The issue of empowerment, as suggested in Chapters One and Two, was essential also for the philosophy of this project, yet I did not devise a research methodology that would be participatory or in any other way attempt to involve children in the design, management or collaborative execution of the data collection or analysis, partly because this would have imposed my research identity over my youth work positionality. Yet, I want to argue that even as a non-participatory approach, the research was empowering through its practitioner (and participant rather than participatory) dimension.

A pivotal argument of participatory action researchers is that participatory approaches have a potential to destabilise the power relations between researchers and participants through increasing the participants' involvement, and thus they empower them. However, as Gallagher, among others, argues:

> On this view, power is seen as a commodity possessed by dominant groups (adults) and not by their subordinates (children). This conceptualization tends to obscure the complex multivalency of power as it is exercised within the spaces where research is carried out. At best, this means that geographers may be unprepared for the ways in which children may exploit, appropriate, redirect, contest or refuse participatory techniques. At worst, it means that researchers may unwittingly reproduce the regulation of children by insisting upon certain forms of participation, in the belief that this constitutes 'empowerment'. (2008, p.137)

Soon after joining the field, I recognised different patterns of inequality and asymmetrical power relations among the children themselves, based on various issues such as social status (related to affluence, gender, ethnicity, age or family reputation in the neighbourhood), belonging (or the lack of) to peer-groups or personality, many of which will be explored in the course of this book. In children's collective activities (such as games or creative activities), their relationships often affected their involvement enormously – several children refused to visit the Club, to take part in group activities, or just talk to the workers if some other particular children were present. Patterns of exclusion existed among different children's groups and some children were rejected, or even harassed, by their peers. I did not have equally frequent or deep contact with all children as their relationship with me or even with the Centre in general was very diverse. Thus, to involve children in participatory research raised concerns whether possibly empowering only *some* children – that is, those with whom I worked most frequently, who would be willing to take part in participatory research activities and would not mind cooperating with their peers – would not simply reproduce and even reinforce the power relations among the children (something I reflect in more detail in Blazek and Hraňová, 2012). My concern was about privileging only some (based on our closeness, frequency and comfort of the contact) while 'hushing' the voices of other children to whom my access was more difficult. The vision of undertaking participatory research without being able to cope with even the very mundane power asymmetry among the children themselves thus raised doubts about the empowering impact of such an approach in this context (Kesby et al, 2007).

The philosophy of the Centre was to design its activities so they would be potentially accessible to all children from Kopčany and, if this failed, the activities were usually expected to be reshaped. This philosophy also applied to my engagement in the neighbourhood, where I was expected to reach out to as high a number of children as possible, rather than being rooted in pre-structured activities that would possibly isolate me from some children. As Riessman argues, as researchers, we 'cannot *give* voice [as] we don't have access to another's experience' (1993, p.8, italics added). The philosophy of the Centre had as its priority encountering and exploring children's experiences in all their breadth, yet without any claim to exhaustive comprehension of children's lives.

Rather than trying to involve children in my research – that had its structural limits in terms of the activities I could provide – my approach to power dynamics between me and the children, or among the children themselves, had to find a different mode, not least to fit within the practitioner perspective of the Centre. Gallagher (2008) provides an alternative approach to the power dynamics of the fieldwork with children, saying that:

> power could be reconceptualised as a form of action carried out through multivalent strategies and tactics, rather than a commodity or a capacity. This complicates the view of adults as powerful and children as powerless, and questions the idea that researchers can 'give' power to children through participatory techniques … This suggests that, for social researchers working with an emancipatory ethics, *the*

question is not how to avoid using power, but how power can be used to resist domination. (2008, p.147, italics added)

Drawing on this perspective, my politics of the practitioner research approach and its philosophy of attending to power dynamics in the fieldwork can be outlined in three points.

First, I based my practitioner research on destabilising the boundaries between 'doing research' and 'providing services'. While conventional research approaches are supposed to cause impact by generating relevant findings and conclusions, and participatory action research is well positioned to make real-world changes as a consequence of the participants' involvement in the research practices, a practitioner's work is supposed to have impact by engaging directly with the clients. In the Centre, the aim was to reach children at risk of exclusion who received little or no institutional support from elsewhere (such as at home or in school), and to improve the quality of their lives by direct contact, not just by advocacy or through policy. The process of encountering children in the field was crucial for my practitioner work, and being incorporated into my research project (or indeed my research project being incorporated into it), its role was equally significant also for my perspective as a researcher.

Second, this perspective requires a reconsideration of the notions of participation and action. Entering the field conceived by the children primarily as a practitioner, my research process was intrinsically embedded within everyday interactions in the neighbourhood (see Percy-Smith and Thomas, 2010), and so was the participation of children in relation to our interactions in the context of youth work. My aim of the children's participation was not based on their involvement in the research design; instead, it stood for children's participation in the community services provided by the Centre – aimed at improving their quality of life – and thus also in the exchange of experiences between the children and the community workers of whom I was one.

Third, such a notion of participation is *directly* and *deliberately* linked to the notion of action, of the real-world changes that the course of the research (rather than just its outputs) brings and to those who take part. It was thus through the research performances and practices, themselves intrinsically relational and intersubjective, and not just through their outputs, at which changes towards empowerment were aimed (see Holt, 2004). The outputs *were* relevant – the findings of the research were used to inform the agenda of the Centre, including negotiations with policy makers (see Blazek et al, 2015). However, the impact of the research came from my involvement in the contact work of the Centre, aimed at the empowerment of the children through a range of areas such as self-development, counselling, social advising, emotional support or education, and through its inclusive policy of access. As an adult youth worker, I had powerful mechanisms at my disposal that the children lacked; although, within the environment that 'belonged' to the children, this relationship was often reversed. In any case, my aim as a practitioner was not to eliminate the capacity for power that lay within my reach (social, cultural or symbolic capital, experiences), but to use them for the benefit of the children through the work of the Centre. That would include supporting them through activities focused on their individual and social development and on the related process of empowerment. The links between undertaking a systematic research inquiry and providing services for children were crucial in this context.

Practitioner/researcher: complementarity, blending, separation and ethics

Participation in ethnographic research is in some way always situated. As the notion of participation presumes that the ethnographer will be active (as opposed to simple observation), he or she needs to adopt certain roles, and along with his/her practices, these will constitute often unexpected positionalities and identities in the field in relation to other actors of the field. In my case, the roles I adopted in the field through my practitioner-based involvement, and which also affected my positionality as a researcher, were shaped at least in three ways. First, through the *process* of helping, in which various routine and (to some extent) formalised expectations from the children were significant. Second, this was based on a certain kind of *relationship* with the children, for my part centred round notions such as accessibility, confidentiality, empathy, positive regard or congruence. Features that fashioned children's attitudes depended on particular relationships but included, for instance, trust (or the lack of it), sympathy (or the lack of it), protection (from other children) or curious inquiry. Third, the positionality of my involvement as an ethnographer was based on ongoing *practical use* of skills that would help achieve the helping process and that I acquired through training, monitoring and mentoring by the Centre staff. This included for instance basic youth work/counselling skills such as active listening, recognising others' mechanisms of communication, empathy, acceptance of and positive regard for the children, or adequate communication of my own understanding of children's feelings to them.

There is a question of the duality between being a researcher and a practitioner. Arguably, it was based on three different types of engagement, gradually merging into each other. First, the roles of researcher and practitioner were *complementary* – my research findings and the analytical conclusions were used to inform the practitioner work, while doing the helping work enabled me to access the children and to explore their everyday practices. Second, the roles were to some extent and at some moments *blending* into each other – exploring children's lives, reflecting on our intersubjective experiences and interpreting these events, were features of both my researcher and practitioner work. Although they seemed to be 'research' practices, they were necessary also for the practitioner practices. Similarly, the politics of the research – to empower, or just in general to 'help' the children – was encompassed within the practitioner work. Finally, the two roles remained to some extent also more or less *separated*. Although negotiations between the two positions existed and shaped my engagement in the field, the rationales behind each perspective ultimately differed (the research itself was not policy oriented and it was not written primarily with the aim of informing professional practice with children in Kopčany). Even more importantly, the two positions worked within different ethical frameworks.

Below is an extract from my fieldnotes from the second month of the fieldwork:

> It is even more complicated with the children. Honestly, I do not know any examples from the literature where participants just do not listen to the researchers who introduce themselves … At my first shift, I was introduced one by one to about 60 children that we met on the street and with whom the Centre is in contact. A colleague told them my name, the fact I would be joining the Centre and then a few details about me – that I am from Scotland, studying there, and doing research about the area of which a part is my stay in Kopčany. But really, most of the children ceased to pay any attention after hearing my name and the fact that I will stay with them for a longer period. They asked more about me – where I live, how old I am, what weapons I have, what car I ride and whether I am a boyfriend of the colleague from the Centre … Three days later, even the kids that I thought might remember this introduction had forgotten everything about Scotland … and my studies … and research. When I attempted to

remind them why I am there, they just interrupted me during the first statement (after the word 'Scotland' [*as I came from the University of Dundee*] or 'University' or 'Research') and took the dialogue away with completely different questions ... I thought it might be easier to introduce my presence and the research during the indoor activities, but it has been even worse so far. The meetings are just too chaotic, with all the kids being concentrated in a small space and they do not really seem to care at all about it ...

I am not quite sure what I could do about this ... (Extracts from fieldnotes included in an email that I sent to my academic supervisors at the beginning of the fieldwork, October 2008)

Concerned with the relevance of informed consent in research with children (following especially Alderson and Morrow, 2004), I was startled by the situation, not prepared for it, and could not even find examples in the academic literature about participants who just did not *listen* to the researcher's disclosure. Yet the feedback I received both within the Community Centre and at my university was the question (from youth workers) why *this* was really so relevant for me and (from academics) why I thought that the children *should* be interested in my research, as something completely remote and abstract for them, no matter how simply I tried to explain my position and background. I was aware that for the children, my 'research [was] hardly at the top of their priorities' (McDowell, 2001, p.7), but this still did not answer the ethical questions.

There is a lot of discussion in qualitative research about two ethical frameworks; the institutional, or 'bureaucratized' (Martin, 2007), notion of ethics defined by ethical review commissions and guidelines; and the relational or 'participative' notion of ethics constructed iteratively in the process of the research and reflexive to what is relevant also to other participants (Pain, 2008). In my case, the institutional ethical framework came from multiple sources. On the one hand, there was the university ethics committee that monitored and approved my research design. On the other hand, my research was subject to local legislation. As such, I was for instance not obliged to provide a Criminal Records Bureau disclosure or its equivalent as the legislation in Slovakia did not require this and the only legal framework that applied to my project was the United Nations Convention on the Rights of the Child (UNCRC; see Bell, 2008). Neither was the disclosure required on the part of the Community Centre – the Slovak legislation did not require it as long as my practice was within certain bounds (for instance, I could not provide certain social care services). I was expected to follow the ethical code of the Centre, which included instructions on how to deal with a wide range of situations, some of which have appeared as causes for concern and perplexity for other researchers (compare the vignette from the 'hide-and-seek game' with Horton, 2008). For instance, I had instructions on how to behave in the case of conflicts or improper behaviour of the children, when children wished to give me a gift, or in the case of physical contact. This also meant that I had to negotiate with the different regulatory regimes of institutions (Martin, 2007), some of which were in contradiction. For instance, as Valentine et al (2001) argue, children technically cannot give informed consent as they do not have necessary legal responsibility for this. Only parents can do so and the children can only give 'approval or assent'. However, approaching the parents of children in Kopčany and negotiating informed consent from them was generally treated with a lot of caution. I was told that approaching some parents with such a request might bring difficulties for the Centre if I were to do this as a Centre worker. The Centre had a relationship only with some parents and to gain access to all of them would be impossible, while in some other cases this contact was very rare or tense, and some parents were expected to react with suspicion to involvement with formal institutions and formal documents, so how they perceived me could have damaged their relationship with the Centre. Not least, in some cases the children did not wish their parents to be involved in their activities in the Centre.

Some of these decisions can be classified as a relational notion of ethics, that is, reflecting on what mattered to other field actors. This approach emphasises that the ethics depend on circumstances (Morrow and Richards, 1996), and that 'it is difficult for researchers to anticipate what ethics dilemmas will arise during the course of the research, so that seeing ethics as situational and responsive is important' (Morrow, 2008, p.56). More importantly, it highlights the institutional but also cultural differences that have been echoed especially in the literature on development and which pose the question of whether researchers (or practitioners, for that matter) should be entitled to follow different codes of conduct in their home country and abroad (Banks and Scheyvens, 2014).

My approach was indeed to see ethics as incomplete and especially *performed* rather than comprehensive (Lee, 2001; Horton, 2008), to refrain from efforts to design an ethically neutral practice and intervention, to see it as a performativity relation constituted through field practices that stem from all that happens in the field, including what is unexpected, undesired and unrecognised (Thomson, 2007). In the context of the overall aims of the book, I find an important point in Askins's (2007) argument that the process of *negotiating* the ethical relations in the field and beyond can tell us sometimes more than the relationships themselves. The *participation* element of ethics is summarised by Elwood:

> Participatory ethics is rooted in assumptions that ethical problems and dilemmas are situational, specific to the relationships and interactions of a particular research context. From this perspective, preemptive proscription of fixed ethical codes, values, and practices is impossible, and the expectation that such codes may be universally applied is unrealistic. (2007, p.331)

Elwood suggests that 'participatory ethics tries to balance sharp differences between ethical concerns raised within an institutional ethics framework ... and the concerns voiced by research participants in a participatory setting' (2007, p.331). The trouble with situated and relational ethics lies partly in the mundane nature of the features that form it and that can be largely elusive from a trained researcher's eye, however. In late November 2008, I was asked by a Centre staff member whether I had been telling the children about my temporary departure from Kopčany, scheduled for the middle of January. I admitted that I had not talked about the issue with children and I thought I would leave it for the final two weeks of my stay. The colleague explained how the notion of departure of one of the workers was often very strongly felt by the children and should be communicated in a proper manner and in advance, so the children would have time to accept it and say goodbye, if they wished (see Iversen, 2009). She also emphasised how my departure was scheduled for just one week after the Christmas holiday, when only a limited number of shifts (and none in the Club) were planned and many children were away, and as children spent less time on the street in winter, it was possible that I would not meet several at all during this approximately six-week period, although we might have been in frequent contact before. The topic of explaining my departure was met with much more enthusiasm by the children than my explaining of the research. Some children protested (some said they were quite happy), some 'forbade' me to go, and I had to make a promise to two boys that I would bring them a present in April should I really leave. At the end of summer 2009, when I was finally leaving the field, saying goodbye was even more challenging and a couple of children ceased talking to me.

The theme of our mutual relationship and engagement contained in the example of taking leave of children is just one of the issues that mattered for the children in a way that I completely underestimated at first. It actually questions whether it is *ethical* at all to assume that what interests us as adults (researchers, practitioners, parents …) is of the same importance to the participants. Institutional ethics are characterised by *a priori* presumptions about what is good for the participants and are based on the notion of powerful adults and powerless children in need of protection, which I questioned earlier. But then, as Kesby et al argue, what about seeing children as 'competent and independent agents of social change and as vulnerable social becomings in need of protection' (2006, p.185) at the same time?

My primary duty at the Centre was to undertake youth worker duties. While it is an imperative ethical principle in social research to avoid harming participants, directly or indirectly (Dowling, 2000), helping professions aspire explicitly for *beneficence* instead, 'striving to enhance client well-being' (McLeod, 1999, p.80). More importantly, this is also what the *clients expect* from the helping professionals. This meant that my primary concern with the wellbeing of the children was developed from the reflexive approach to the priorities that actually mattered to them. Even though I had no informed consent from the children, and some of them did not even realise my researcher identity, I aimed to make sure that children's beneficence would be enhanced through my practitioner involvement. One of the roles of informed consent is to ensure the voluntary and informed participation of the participants in the research. Children gave (although more informal and not written) informed consent for their participation in youth work activities as they were constantly reminded that they did not have to take part in activities they did not like, or in the Centre's programme at all. Parr (1998) highlights that informed consent is never complete, as researchers cannot imagine what will happen over the entire course of the research. The reiterative and situated nature of children's consent in the Centre activities was in that way more suitable to communicate potential consequences of their involvement than a traditional written prior consent. For instance, any case of a private or intimate conversation with children included discussions about confidentiality that the children could expect from the Centre workers, or that our contact and their choice of what they would tell me was entirely voluntary and they could terminate it at any point.

Conclusions

This chapter explored the relationality and intersubjective dynamics of the research process, including a presentation of the field site, practicalities of the research process, its philosophy and politics, multiple positionality of the fieldwork and the dynamics of the ethical relations. In particular, I focused on the significance of the practitioner approach to research, not just for my access to the field but also for the contours of everyday experiences of adults with children.

I have outlined two key positionalities I adopted in the field, being a youth worker and a researcher. I argued that these positionalities were partly complementary, partly blending with each other, but in some aspects quite contradictory. My key claim in relation to the book's scope is that acknowledging the difference between adults and children is imperative, but so is approaching it gradually in daily interactions. Illustrated through the topics of power/participation and ethics, I offered both a *re*construction of how my positionalities were (pre-)defined by my goals and institutional affiliations, but also a *de*construction of how they were negotiated and transformed in unfolding relationships with children.

This account of practice already offers a framework for addressing one of the questions raised in Chapter One, about how adults can approach children's agency. I revisit this question throughout the book and substantiate my account with more empirical material and conceptual tools to understand this relation, before concluding with an account of 'adult politics' in Chapter Twelve. Before that, Chapter Four offers some conceptual tools.

FOUR

Thinking the field

> I will explore the politics of producing theory that is ... interstitial with empirical research and social location; of scholarship that self-reflexively interpolates the theories and practices of everyday historical subjects – including, but not restricted to scholars; and of work that reworks marginality by decomposing the major. (Katz, 1996, p.487)

> In the first place, a theory is always local, related to a limited domain, though it can be applied in another domain that is more or less distant ... Praxis is a network of relays from one theoretical point to another, and theory relays one praxis to another. (Deleuze, 2004, p.206)

As Chapter Three did not provide a systematic methodological framework but rather explored reflectively the sphere of fieldwork practices, so this chapter does not present a systematic theoretical framework that would comprehensively underpin the research. Rather, it discusses *a way of engagement* with theory that has an ambition to unfold from the practical experiences of the fieldwork as well as to respond to its rationales, understanding theory as a 'relay' of praxis rather than its foundation.

In the spirit of the overall research ambitions, to remain open to the field and to engage with extensive variety and multiplicity in the children's lives, the theoretical foundations of the research therefore built upon encounters with the fieldwork rather than a particular theoretical model which pre-existed the research experience. My research is not a-theoretical – there has been a consistent effort to elucidate intellectually the significant moments of children's lives and how I experienced them. However, rather than 'imposing' the theory on the fieldwork dynamics or situating the findings within major conceptual frameworks, the research 'draws' (Reinharz, 1992, p.72) on a range of theoretical sources and explores them dialogically without any single theoretical framework being *a priori* a dominant one.

This approach echoes Katz's (1996) strategy of 'minor theory'. Minor theory is constituted at local sites and through local knowledges and contexts, related to and negotiated through each other, rather than derived out of any specific 'constant serving as a standard measure' (Deleuze and Guattari, 2004, p.116). The notion of minor does not refer to numbers; instead, it emphasises creative departures from models, 'a process ... that would lead into unknown paths if [we] opted to follow it through' (Deleuze, 1995, p.173). In research with a pre-structured theoretical basis, the content of the theoretical framework might inform or even predetermine the research questions, procedures and analysis. In contrast, in the minor approach, 'it is expression that precedes contents, whether to prefigure the rigid forms into which contents will flow or to make them take flight along lines of escape or transformation' (Deleuze and Guattari, 1986, p.85). One effect of this is the choice of thematic chapters included in this book based on the fieldwork analysis, as explained in Chapter One.

The theoretical propositions of the research are thus developed along with its field practice (Hanson 1997) and through fluid and shifted configurations of the spaces of the fieldwork (Nast, 1994), used locally to illuminate particular moments rather than the project as a whole. The minor theory approach inevitably expects an overall theoretical eclecticism that would respond to the richness of the empirical findings. Throughout the book, I offer interpretations based on my direct experience in the field (including both children's words and deeds) which was rich in quantity and depth of engagement with children, as well as on hearsay and stories (and interpretations) told to me by others (children or youth work colleagues) and on of a wide range of readings across social sciences and humanities. Yet, the ultimate insight into extensions of children's agency is anything but complete. Additionally, interpretations were not only a matter of post-fieldwork activities. My practices in the field were also guided by interpretations, generated *in situ* (Blazek, 2013). Many meanings emerging during the interactions with children later evolved or were confronted with different interpretations (Bondi, 2013), and the book thus presents the narratives of children's practices as lines of thinking that span from embodied interactions in Kopčany to the time of writing (and revising) the book. The idea of minor theory underpins all sections of the chapters and unfolds a connection between them – as a medium of theoretical implications of the rationale for the research and as a way of engagement with particular problems of presenting the research in the book.

The following theoretical propositions are responses to my initial rationale for the research as well as to some of the initial experiences with the fieldwork, and they offer some preliminary indications as to how the experiences from Kopčany can be thought together in the forthcoming chapters of the book. In this chapter, I discuss four problems of the fieldwork – the openness to the field, the fieldwork complexity, the problem of conceptual essentialism, and the relations between materiality and immateriality in the scope of the research – and articulate responses that helped me interpret and present research findings in the empirical chapters.

Openness to the field and empiricism

In Chapter Three, I articulated my approach to the fieldwork in Kopčany as an open inquiry into a complex of issues that mattered in the constitution of children's practices and into the ways whereby they might trace Kopčany out as a place. However, the targeted suspension of pre-existing knowledge, in other words an *empiricist* epistemological commitment, should reach beyond a simplified positivist interpretation that 'the scientific status of knowledge [has] to be guaranteed by the direct experience of an immediate reality' (Gregory, 1978, p. 26) as something validated, value-free, replicable and gradually progressive. My perspective on empiricism is instead linked to a phenomenological aim to 'satisfy the *principle of freedom from presuppositions*' (Husserl, 2001, p.177). More specifically – and diverting from the orthodox phenomenological position – I draw on Derrida's (1973) variant of (post)phenomenology which argues that 'the content of consciousness ... is never fully and immediately present to the one whose consciousness it is, but instead is permeated by indicative relations, deferrals, and delay' (Cerbone, 2006, p.175). As such, the strategy of writing the book is not simply to reproduce the content of my experiences but equally to seek the emergence of these experiences. My approach to empiricism methodologically does not 'begin *from* an idea ... and then use that idea to explain life ... [but] chart[s] the emergence of the idea from particular bodies and connections' (Colebrook, 2002, p.81–2) as they open up to my experiences as well as to each other. As the research has not been produced in isolation, it follows experiences, and not just my own experiences, but also my encounters with the experiences of others in the neighbourhood, requiring openness to the field, to a 'purely heterological thought at its source' (Derrida, 1978, p.151), or to what Bryant (2008) labels as the '"phenomenology" of encounter'. This commitment to empiricism also opens space for commitment to the experiences of *others*, to mutual dialogue and juxtaposing, and not least for constant doubts about fits and clashes among them.

The story I presented in Chapter Three, about the hide-and-seek game with children, illustrates some of these issues. While I had cognitive access to my own practices and emotions, I presented them beyond how I initially interpreted them within my initial expectations about the context of our run to the dark area in Kopčany, particularly regarding the inappropriateness of running away with young children while holding the hands of the older girls. Instead, for the account of the story, I considered what the children told me about their feelings and intentions at the time, their previous histories (from the long-term, such as when the younger children were afraid to go into the dark, to the very local, when they wished to take advantage from my recent 'success' in the game), the code of the Centre and opinions and suggestions (about the situation but also about the children) of the senior staff, or reactions of other people (including ones that might emerge in the future). It was the encounter with all these issues – representing as a broad range as I could manage to capture, although it still remains incomplete – that formed the account of children's practices that is presented in the book. However, this story also suggests another problem of an empiricist approach, namely that of complexity.

Complexity of the field and relationalism

The second problem relates to the range of themes that emerged in the course of the project and the connections among them. Those themes did not emerge in isolation – very remarkable though diverse connections among issues such as bodies, things, family relations or everyday spaces exist in children's lives, and they underlie the formations and operations of each other, but at the same time result 'in a distinct entity' (Barker, 2002, p.50) in which children's practices emerge. To approach the variety and significance of connections among different issues in children's lives, I adopted a *relational* way of thinking about Kopčany. I understand relations as immanent and affective processes that perform simultaneously, that is, as 'embedded practices' (Massey, 2005, p.10). Using Deleuze's terminology (2001), the way children's practices are thought of in the research is not based on "is" – that is, on their intrinsic features. Instead, the "and" thinking is employed – where subjects and objects emerging in the research are thought through their connections to other subjects and objects. As an example, in later chapters, I will emphasise the role of football in the everyday practices of children from Kopčany, particularly younger boys. However, beyond the simple description of children often playing football, this practice can be interpreted as a series of connections in children's lives – the fact that football was one of few outdoor activities that could be undertaken in Kopčany, that it carried a strong emotional context through the friendships that were performed through collective practices of football games and the organisation thereof, that playing football illuminated the role of material objects (ball) in children's everyday practices and their social relations, or that football games also revealed something about exclusionary relations among children from the neighbourhood, such as how younger children or many girls were excluded from this activity. Quite often, this means that to understand children's practices as presented through specific illustrations in empirical chapters requires tracing their connections to other stories and associations and the style of the book attempts to allow this by highlighting cross-references between individual chapters. At the same time, 'it is not enough to simply assert that phenomena are "relationally constituted" ... rather it becomes necessary to think through the specificity and performative efficacy of different relations and different relational configurations' (Anderson and Harrison, 2010, p.16). That means that rather than just flatly mapping associations of children's practices, the book also explores the genesis and effects of the relations that form and instigate children's practices.

Vocabulary and non-essentialism

The third problem of conceptualising my research encounters is a problem of vocabulary. Even with the most basic concepts in the research, diverse meanings in different contexts often had to be employed. When using the very key term 'childhood', there are moments where it helps me to articulate biological implications for bodily activities of the children; in other cases, it helps to explain that children seek for various things around the neighbourhood due to the lack of means they have in their families, that is, it illustrates their social position; and in other cases, the notion of childhood emerges in children's plans and dreams about the future as a medium for the idea of growing up and maturing (see Chapters Six, Seven and Eleven). Hence, 'childhood' is enacted in biological, cultural *or* social modes, sometimes clearly simultaneously, and it bears very diverse expressions even within these particular modes (see the discussion in Chapter One for links to literature on this problem).

This theoretical problem is then the issue of *non-essentialism*, a possible constitution of objects beyond any notion of substance and through exploring their difference and dynamic interactions with other objects. A non-essentialist perspective is in this case an extension to empiricism

– besides suspending presuppositions about the field, generalisations from the experiences are also limited. This responds to what Latour (2005) describes as a confusion of 'explanation' and 'what should be explained', arguing, using the example of sociology, that '["mainstream" sociologists] begin with society or other social aggregates whereas one should end with them' (2005, p.8). Latour criticises the process of essentialist inquiry that first defines a concept 'as possessing specific properties' (2005, p.3) and distinguishes it from other concepts this way (childhood from adulthood, for instance), and that goes on '[o]nce this domain had been defined, no matter how vaguely ... to be used to shed some light on specifically ... [concept-intrinsic] phenomena' (2005, p.3). An example of such a fallacy could be explanations of discourses on dependency, vulnerability or incivility of children (Jenks 1996; Holloway and Valentine 2000) because of the 'nature' of childhood itself. Latour argues that concepts of as abstract a degree as 'society' (or 'childhood') should not really be used for explanation of mundane, everyday moments – '[n]o social explanation is necessary' (2005, p.99). Instead, they should be explained on their own, through their particular elements and their interactions, associations and relations, not confusing thus the 'cause and effect' (Latour, 2005, p.13). This perspective informs also my practical vocabulary procedures where use of particular terms is related to events from the fieldwork, even if the ultimate use of terms is different from how children or other actors in Kopčany use them.

Mattering and relational materialism

One more question needs to be addressed, linking to all three areas discussed so far. If the research aims to reflect on 'anything' that matters for the constitution of children's practices, what is the *range* of these 'anythings' that is significant for children's practices? Following the rationale about openness to field experiences, I presume that to approach the variety and extensive dimensions of children's practices, the research cannot:

> limit *a priori* what kind of beings make up the social. Rather everything takes-part and in taking-part, takes-place: everything happens, everything acts. (Anderson and Harrison, 2010, p.14)

I explained in Chapter One how the choice of particular themes for the empirical chapters followed a range of criteria, including their occurrence, intensity or impact on children's practices, and I explained Lee's (2001) and Ansell's (2009a) arguments that emphasise empirical identification of the range of children's activities and experiences over their ontological preconfiguration. However, this still leaves open the question of the variety of ways in which particular issues matter for the constitution of children's practices. For instance, children's knowledge about their bodies is important, but so is the corporeal capacity for everyday practices that children gain (see Chapter Six). The *sense* of family is important in children's daily actions in the neighbourhood, but so are daily *operations* within and across families (see Chapter Nine). Children encounter the *tangibility* of particular sites in Kopčany, but the *imaginations* of these sites and *associations* with issues such as danger or retreat are as important (see Chapters Five and Eight).

However, this short list also opens up the question of the relationships between the materiality in children's practices and the ways in which material objects or bodies are thought, perceived, represented or communicated. As there are connections, for instance between children's corporeal capacities and their knowledge about their bodies, differentiating between the two categories is not my aim. Rather, I am interested in the interplay where experiences need to be explored through the ways in which material objects become entwined with feelings, knowledges or representations to form relational assemblages in which children's practice emerge (Rautio, 2013; Änggård, 2015). This produces discussions about children's passion for climbing trees that embrace investigations of material entities (children's bodies) and their capacities (strength, flexibility or stamina), of the ways they are intertwined with other material objects (trees or ropes) through processes with immaterial conditions (such as knowledge about the technique of climbing, support during the climbing, or relationship with the workers because of whom the rope is borrowed). Reflecting on the importance of investigating the genesis of relations between children's practices and their circumstances, material entities are therefore explored particularly in relation to how they 'come to matter' for children's practices, while knowledge, emotions, communications or representations take part also by 'triggering' children's material practices.

In his study of alternative education, Kraftl offers what he terms 'a "weak" version of Actor-Network Theory' (2013, p.147) for an exploration of the agency of both human and non-human elements in schooling environments, but with an ultimate focus on how the 'mess' and contingency of the material world are eventually subsumed (yet not completely) in the social ordering. With similar connotations, I use

Anderson and Harrison's (2010) term 'relational materialism' instead as a signifier of the conceptual process that:

> departs from understandings of the social as ordered *a priori* (be it symbolically, ontologically or otherwise) in a manner that would, for example, set the conditions for how objects appear, or as an ostensive structure that stands behind and determines practical action. In the taking-place of practices, things and events, there is no room for hidden forces, no room for universal transcendental or first principles. And so even representations become understood as representations; as *things and events they enact worlds*, rather than being simple go-betweens tasked with re-presenting some pre-existing order or force. (2010, p.14, italics added)

Anderson and Harrison call their idea a philosophy of immanency, meaning that only what is present in (immanent), and impacts on, processes (children's practices) should be regarded for explaining these processes. For this book, it means that a*nything* can be potentially included in the analysis of children's practices, but nothing will be unless it *enacts* them, unless there can be an association identified between the existence and presence of this 'anything' and particular children's practices. Discourses, imaginations or representations might be triggers of children's actions and this is the moment when they become important also for this research – in the same way as a range of other entities, from public spaces, through bodies to institutions do. Drawn together, issues of openness, complexity, conceptual vocabulary and im/materiality in field encounters as linked to the theoretical perspectives of empiricism, relationalism, non-essentialism, and (relational) materialism help inform what the limits and expectations of the research might be.

Conclusion

Chapter Four extends the reflexive analysis of the fieldwork dynamics given in Chapter Three by elaborating on the ways in which the fieldwork experiences are transformed analytically into the book while the research outcomes aim to remain faithful to the research objectives and rationale. I outlined Katz's idea of *minor theory* as an epistemological strategy that forms the conceptual tools through connections with particular research locations, experiences and practices, as opposed to grand theories that define the theoretical approach of the research prior the fieldwork process. Subsequently, I elaborated on some basic expectations on the research and on some fundamental reflections on fieldwork, situating the research in relation to the approaches of *empiricism*, *relationalism*, *non-essentialism* and *relational materialism*.

This chapter emphasised that even in an empiricist approach to research, theoretical connections are necessary as a naively empiricist approach would not be so much a-theoretical as theoretically hypocritical, working on a basis of implicit conceptual assumptions. By drawing on the idea of minor theory, I build a theoretical basis that follows the empirical experience rather than the other way around, and although it stems from individual moments of the research, the theoretical and conceptual implications can be connected together in a way that mirrors the connections identified in the empirical work.

The next seven chapters provide discussions of different types of circumstances that are significant for the constitution of children's practices. The first empirical inquiry in Chapter Five explores how children's practices are placed in the area where my contact with children primarily took place – in public spaces in Kopčany – thus also localising other empirical discussions of the book.

Part Three

Part Three

FIVE

Public spaces of Kopčany

We left the lodging house and a few children were already awaiting us near the entrance to the building. A girl halted one of the colleagues and screamed at her for something while the other colleague took me down the stairs and introduced me to other children. I ended up with a group of young boys who were playing near a puddle at the verge of a humpy parking place, probably a result of a clogged sewer.

Figure 5.1 Puddles in front of the lodging house

We brought skipping ropes for the children and we played with them while I started my first conversations in the neighbourhood, although the game attracted the boys more than my words. After a while, one of the colleagues came and suggested that we would have a walk while our other colleague would stay with the boys. We walked anticlockwise around the workers' hostel but no children were around. The colleague told me that most of the children we had just met were from the lodging house and that it was a place where especially younger children could be often seen gathering. She also said that it was a usual practice to walk around the hostel if the Centre workers wished to talk to someone (as we just did), as most of children would be concentrated in just a few areas and for most of the path [Figure 5.2] no one would approach us. Indeed, we passed another building but only a young girl waved from the window. It was not until the next building that we met some other children. As the colleague told me, walking around the area of the hostel had also the advantage of getting a look at the whole neighbourhood and seeing who is outside. It took only a few minutes, but if children were on the street and unless they wished to be unseen, we would meet them as the path provided a view of almost all areas of the neighbourhood. (Extract from fieldnotes on my first street work shift, September 2008)

Figure 5.2 Paths around Kopčany (a view from the rear of the lodging house – the path to the left circles the lodging house; the path to the right is a part of the pavement that encircles the workers' hostel)

Some of my very first impressions from the contact with children in Kopčany indicated that a range of micro-geographies existed that had an impact on children's practices. To meet the young boys in front of the lodging house was not accidental. They were close to home as most of them lived in the building. This was important, especially for the younger ones, as their parents could see them from their windows. Others came to the front side of the lodging house as their friends assembled here, several expected the Centre workers to come, and the site also provided opportunities for play as the pavement broadened here. The area around the next building we passed was on the contrary empty and no children were on the street. The pavement was very narrow here, surrounded by a fence, walls of the building, and an unkept lawn full of litter with little space for children to meet in a larger group (see Figure 5.3). It was also the site most remote from the 'entrance' to the neighbourhood, as the main bus stops were at the area at the opposite end, and this corner was only barely visible even from the nearest building and practically invisible from other areas. Still, as I later noticed, small groups of children who wished to be alone, away from the company of their peers, or when they wished to talk in peace, often gathered here.

This chapter explores how different configurations of everyday public spaces (spaces that are formally, if not necessarily practically, accessible to anyone, including the children) in Kopčany are important for children's practices. This scope is set as a response to my fieldwork experiences, most of which came from my contact with children and their practices *in* the neighbourhood rather than elsewhere. It is not the purpose of

Figure 5.3 The corner of the remote building (on the left) where the pavement is at its narrowest

this chapter to suggest that spaces of the neighbourhood are necessarily more relevant for children's practices than other spatial configurations. Therefore, I also situate the significance of public spaces in Kopčany within children's experiences of other forms of spatial relationships, at least the ones that I was aware of.

The scope of my interest and the links between the chapter and the focus on counter-topography (Chapter One) are based on three ideas about space and its role in social practices. First, I adopt a loose *definition* of space following Philo, who defines various spaces as particular 'types of settings for interaction' (2000, p.245) (as opposed to 'specific sites of meaning' [2000, p.245], that is, places). This is a path that allows, in accordance with the minor theory approach, the exploration of space conceptually as it emerges from localised experiences from the fieldwork. Using the freedom that this definition provides, spaces will be thought of as both tangible and intangible types of setting, or rather as complex amalgamations of the two, formed at the interface of material and immaterial processes that envelop children's actions. Second, the chapter focuses on a *spatial scale* that responds to the range of children's practices in the neighbourhood and elsewhere, linking back to Ansell's idea of descaled geography from Chapter One. Although, in practice, this leads the analysis to considering spaces such as 'pavements', 'playgrounds' or 'green areas', this is not a result of segmenting the physical environment into discrete tangible plots. Instead, these notions of spaces come from segmenting – but also reconnecting – *children's interactions* and their *settings*. Finally, I explore spatialities of children's practices in their 'perpetual dynamism' (Horton and Kraftl, 2006b, p.86), that is, as always in a constant process of production and disruption (see also Massey, 2005), as practised and performed *doings* rather than pre-existing *beings* (Rose, 1999), or as *spacings* rather than spaces (Horton and Kraftl, 2006b) that are 'always open to negotiation and thus always in a process of becoming', unfinished and subject to change (Malbon, 1999, p.94; also Massey, 2005). Focusing on the spaces of children's practices as constituted, and as (co)constituted *by children's practices*, they can be explored through similarities and differences in individual cases of children, drawing a counter-topography of children's agency from the everyday spatiality of children's practices.

The chapter should be read along with three maps located at the end of this chapter that display and discuss children's practices at the edge of the neighbourhood (Map 2), within the neighbourhood (Map 3) and outside the neighbourhood (Map 1). While the central visual contents of the maps are representations of the absolute spaces of the neighbourhood, the textual annotations and the accompanying photographs in the chapter provide a *relational* segmentation of children's practices so the described spaces are delineated as results (but also conditions) of children's interactions.

The chapter is organised into three sections. First, I explore the circumstances in which children spend their time elsewhere than on the streets of Kopčany and what the significance is of such a locating of children's practices for the spatialities of their activities *in* the neighbourhood. Exploring the character and extent of children's mobility, their spatial experiences and knowledges, and the role of home helps in understanding how important the public spaces of Kopčany are for the constitution of children's everyday practices and what a difference this might make among individual children and groups of children. The next section of the chapter then provides an analysis of the outdoor public spaces in Kopčany and of the role they have in the formation of children's practices. This section is central not only to the chapter but also to the whole book as it illustrates the main portion of my experiences with children's practices during my fieldwork and it also situates the empirical contexts of further chapters. As a conclusion, I reflect on the dynamics of children's spatial practices and the differentiations these make within the neighbourhood, outlining also links to circumstances discussed in the rest of the book.

Children's practices outside the public spaces of Kopčany and the significance of the neighbourhood in children's activities

Children's mobilities and spatial experiences beyond Kopčany

Children's spatial movement outside of Kopčany was generally rather limited. Especially for the younger children, the journey to or from school, and the time spent around the school grounds was the main experience of time spent outside the neighbourhood. Most children attended one of two schools situated two bus stops away from Kopčany, that is, in a relatively close range. This distance was usually travelled by bus as walking required crossing busy roads, so children's territories during the journey were also limited. Two axes of differentiation were then crucial for the range of children's spatial experiences beyond the neighbourhood and journeys to and from school.

The first was age. Older children, usually over 12, tended to spend more time away from Kopčany, although usually in areas that were not too far from the neighbourhood and located within Petržalka.

These children quite frequently visited hypermarkets, two of which were located within walking distance from the neighbourhood, and especially a shopping mall situated just about 10 minutes by bus from Kopčany. In the summer months, a swimming pool and especially a small lake (without entrance fee) within the housing estates of Petržalka, both located within a 10-minute journey by bus, were frequently visited by children, including the younger ones, although usually in the company of their older relatives or friends. Some older children, although with some as young as 12 or 13 years old among them, also frequently attended discotheques and music bars in Petržalka, or even in the centre of Bratislava, on Fridays or Saturdays, or they at least attempted to enter bars even if they were often refused the entrance. Yet older children (usually around 13–14 years old) spent more time in other neighbourhoods where their friends, mostly from the school, lived. Occasionally, children also attended sport or cultural events, or a group of boys (aged 9–13) for instance used to play football at a pitch located three bus stops from the neighbourhood.

The factor of mobility, and especially independent mobility (that is, without parents) in general increasing with age of children could be seen among all groups of children, and it corresponds with some other relevant studies (for example, Prezza et al, 2001; Fyhri and Hjorthol, 2009). Older children had more freedom from their parents to move beyond the boundaries of the neighbourhood, they had more knowledge about other areas of the city, and they usually also had more friends from Kopčany who were allowed or willing to take a journey outside of the neighbourhood with them. This was quite important as children took most of these journeys in groups of friends from the neighbourhood. Only occasionally did they travel alone, and this was mostly the case for the oldest children (13–14 years old), often with the purpose of meeting their friends from outside the neighbourhood. On a few occasions when I met children from Kopčany outside the neighbourhood, it mostly happened very close to the neighbourhood (near local stores or near children's schools), and they were usually in groups of at least three or four friends from Kopčany.

The collective character of journeys outside Kopčany (Pyyry, 2015) was significant for the mobility of those younger children who had older siblings who often took them outside Kopčany and whose mobility was higher than that of their peers. In general, the youngest children had only very limited experience and awareness of geographies beyond the neighbourhood. When the children who took part in a summer pre-school educational programme of the Centre (mostly 5–7 years old) went on a trip to museums and the zoological garden in the city centre, some of them did not recognise the Danube River that borders Petržalka (about 10 minutes by bus from Kopčany), and some even called it "a sea". On the other hand, those children who had older siblings were more often allowed to accompany them outside Kopčany and they usually also began to undertake their independent journeys earlier than those young children who had not moved outside the neighbourhood with their older relatives. The range and depth of children's social contacts was thus the second important factor for their independent mobility.

Another area of children's social relationships that had an impact on their mobility (though not necessarily independent mobility) was the role of family. Most parents did not take their children outside the neighbourhood during the weekdays, including taking them to and from the school, where children travelled either on their own or with their siblings, except for a few of the youngest children who were taken by their parents. Many parents did not make any trips with children even on the weekends. Only a few families had a car, so even their family trips took place mostly in areas within a range comfortably accessible by public transport. On many occasions, children went to help their parents with shopping, or joined them for shopping for more valuable items (such as clothes) for them. Other children's trips with their adult family members included trips to swimming pools or public events for children, especially in the summer. Parents' socioeconomic situation was an important factor in this, as many parents worked on weekends or late evenings too, some had two or more jobs, and especially single parents with more children had less time to spend with them in general, and even less to take them outside the neighbourhood (see McLanahan and Percheski, 2008).

A related factor in children's movements outside the neighbourhood was their visits to their (extended) families. Children who had their families in Bratislava (mostly grandparents and/or cousins) made such visits more often, and some even stayed with their extended families for a night or more, especially during school holidays. However, for families with relatives from outside the area this was far more complicated because of travel circumstances and the fact that most families had no car. Family affluence was an important factor in children's mobilities in other ways too, as only very few children I knew attended organised leisure time activities and those who sustained this for a longer period were usually from families with relatively higher incomes.

These limited patterns of children's mobility meant that children's activities were significantly concentrated in the neighbourhood from an early age, and only a few children spent considerable amounts of time outside Kopčany. Those that did were primarily children whose families could afford to pay for their attendance at organised activities elsewhere (dance clubs, sport clubs), those who had close relatives living near Kopčany, or those who had older siblings who took them outside the neighbourhood (so their parents would consent to this). The last factor also meant that children's spaces outside Kopčany were not strictly isolated from their activities in the neighbourhood. Children met other children from Kopčany in the schools and often travelled to and from the school together, they did their homework together in the Community Centre, they visited swimming pools or shopping malls together, planned their activities, and shared or discussed their experiences. Even in those cases where some children attended an organised activity, such as when a group of boys played football for a local team, they often did this with one or more friends from the neighbourhood. Although spaces outside Kopčany were important for children's activities, the children's associations to other people, or their affiliations to respective institutions often made these other spaces co-present in and through the neighbourhood and activities that took place there. Children's social spaces of the neighbourhood thus intersected with those outside Kopčany, even if the physical spatialities were separated.

Children's spatial knowledge was quite limited and reflected the lack of experiences outside Kopčany. I mentioned how the youngest children had little awareness of places beyond the neighbourhood, but the older ones also had rather imprecise ideas about these wider geographies. When a group of 11- and 12-year-old boys took part in a weekend trip with the Centre and a partner organisation, I asked them about their experiences and finally about the location where they were. Instead of telling me the specific place or at least a broader geographical area they visited, the boys described the forest and the hut where they stayed and their feelings about the generic settings of the trip. Children's knowledge of geography from school was adequate, but they struggled to associate this knowledge to images of the real world outside Kopčany. When I talked to Pavol (13) about my past visit to the Tatras, mountains in northern Slovakia, he surprised me with a fairly good knowledge of its local geographies – he knew the names of several rivers, hills or towns around the mountains. However, he could not really imagine what the Tatras looked like as he had never been there and was not familiar even with photographs and or images of the area. So when I talked about the particularities of my visits, about walking journeys, changes of weather, plants, sightseeing, or huts in the Tatras, Pavol apparently struggled to imagine these and

I had to give a more detailed description, making references to the geographical names he was familiar with and my specific experiences.

While this situation might be itself unsurprising, the impact of children's knowledge of 'other geographies' helped them to establish a relationship to the neighbourhood. Compare the two following attitudes of Nina (10) and Simon (13): Nina expressed her desire to move away from Kopčany and to relocate to her grandmother's house in a village near Bratislava. When we talked about her view of Kopčany, she was critical of the people who lived there, its environment, flat design, her opportunities, or the school she attended nearby. Simon, on the other hand, spoke very positively about the neighbourhood, emphasised how people got on well together, how he could enjoy activities he liked there, and how he took pleasure also in the design of his room. The two contrasting views had their roots in the spatial experiences of the children. Nina, on the one hand, had enjoyed her time in her grandmother's big rural house with her numerous family members present. In Kopčany, she lived in a small flat with her parents and six siblings, her family had few social contacts and quite a bad reputation, Nina struggled in school, had very few opportunities for play in the neighbourhood and not many friends. The rural experience with plenty of spaces to use and play in, a big family that interacted together and provided support, and also the sense of safety against distracting experiences from the neighbourhood (for instance, she mentioned meeting a molester in the area) had a strong impact on how her view on Kopčany was formed. Simon, on the other hand, had previously lived with his family in several places in Bratislava, mostly in what he described as inadequate conditions, in small and unsuitable flats. He had not made friends in these areas as they were often sparsely populated with very few children and even less outside space for play, such as football which Simon was very passionate about. Again, Simon's view on Kopčany was formed through and in comparison to his experiences of other spaces. While Simon's and Nina's expectations about the ideal place to live were similar in several aspects, including for instance their desire to have friends and adequate space for their favourite activities, their previous spatial and the related social experiences shaped their actual attitude to Kopčany in a very different way.

Summarising, children's limited mobility had an impact also on their geographical experiences and in turn also on their geographical knowledge. Children's spatial experiences were limited and mainly focused on Kopčany and the surrounding area. Even when children gained geographical knowledge from other sources (such as in school), it was of little immediate relevance and children lacked actual experience of spaces beyond Kopčany, so the range of their spatial imaginations was rather limited. On the other hand, among the children who had spent a significant amount of time outside Kopčany (such as living elsewhere in the past, or spending holidays with their families), these kinds of spatial experiences also affected their attitude to Kopčany, both positively and negatively, and these children's views on the neighbourhood were often constructed differently and based on their reflections on other spaces as comparisons with Kopčany, particularly in terms of the opportunities they found in Kopčany and those that they would like to find.

Van Blerk argues that it is through their mobility and negotiations of a broad range of spatial and temporal perspectives that children form 'the fluid nature of' their identities (2005, p.5). Although my study explores rather different contexts than those (of the street children) in van Blerk's study (see also Beazley, 2003; Gough and Franch, 2005), the significance of mobility and the spatial range (or the lack thereof) of children's activities can be seen too, even if in a contrary way. Rather than setting children's practices within a mobile context of encounters with different sites and places across the city (or a broader) area, children from Kopčany formed their subjectivities primarily within the scope of experiences located in the neighbourhood, or closely related to it. Emphasising the centrality of the neighbourhood in children's activities (Christensen and O'Brien, 2003; Rasmussen and Smidt, 2003; Spicer, 2008), I will now discuss the kind of space in Kopčany that I had only a limited access to – home – in order to demonstrate the relevance of public spaces of Kopčany for children's lives.

Children's homes

> I arrived in Kopčany at 9.30am and met Peter (7) strolling around the neighbourhood. During the next few hours, I noticed Peter a few times and he even knocked at the Community Centre door a couple of times, asking for water to drink or to wash his hands, or for a ball. Eventually he told me that he had nobody at home and the parents left him no keys. Around noon, Peter's mother returned and he went for lunch, but I saw him shortly afterwards walking around the neighbourhood again, waving me goodbye when I was leaving after sunset at 9pm. (Extract from fieldnotes, May 2009)

Peter was just one of several children who spent literally most of their time on the street, and one of the many who spent a majority of their *leisure* time there, at least in some periods (such as when the weather was nice, see later in this chapter). I did not have access to children's homes, apart from standing at the doorsteps of a few and making one visit inside, and I cannot provide an in-depth extensive discussion of children's practices at home. Rather, I am interested in demonstrating the reasons why many children spent a considerable time outside their homes so their practices were concentrated on the street.

There is a rich body of literature on children and their relationships to, experiences of, or practices in, their homes, that suggest that homes are for children not just sites of play, comfort and safety, but also of contestations and negotiations of power, or even of suffering and abuse (Sibley and Lowe, 1992; Aitken, 2000a; Christensen et al, 2000; Skelton and Valentine, 2004; Hancock and Gillen, 2007). Therefore, home can play not just a positive role for children's practices, but also a negative one, where the absences that children feel at home make other spaces more important.

In the neighbourhood, 45.3% of households, excluding those from the lodging house, were families with two or more children (Census, 2001). Most of them lived in one- or two-bedroom flats, so children usually shared bedrooms with other siblings. In our daily discussions, several children mentioned the lack of "their own space" as one of the most frustrating aspects of their living in Kopčany. Spending time on the street was then often an easier way to find privacy than being at home. Also, several children were not allowed to invite their friends home (or not all of them), or they did not wish to when other members of their family were at home as they would lack privacy. This was especially relevant for children who had a higher number of siblings (that is, they were from families with three and more children) and these especially spent most of their time on the street.

Besides the size of the flat and of the family, children also spent a lot of time on the street because of other opportunities the street provided. Several of the children's favourite activities that included movement, such as football or other sport activities, and that also included meeting their friends, could take place only on the street and not at home. As opposed to home, the street was also the place where children could meet Community Centre staff, which was itself linked to having access to toys or other equipment that the staff provided only for the period that children spent outdoors. Most children did not possess many things and sharing their property with friends was quite a usual practice in Kopčany, one that mostly took place on the street and not in children's homes. Especially among the younger ones, children also spent a lot of time exploring the neighbourhood and looking for thrown away items that might have some use for them. Due to the neglect of the neighbourhood, there was much litter on the ground, but even more in bushes, under stairs, or in the nearby areas surrounding Kopčany (see Map 2), and younger children spent a lot of time there, searching and exploring, often finding relatively valuable and interesting objects. I will also argue (in Chapter Ten) that friendship was an important factor in children's practices, and I already suggested that children's homes were not the main sites of children's meetings. Tomanović and Petrović (2010) show that for children from Soviet-type housing-block estates like Petržalka, public areas in their neighbourhoods are more important for their contacts with their friends than their homes or other institutionalised spaces, in comparison with, for instance, their UK peers (Valentine and McKendrick, 1997; Elsley, 2004; Rasmussen, 2004). In low-income neighbourhoods in particular, this is often a consequence of parents' familiarity with their local neighbourhood as a result of low mobility and developed social networks. In Kopčany, children usually met their friends on the street rather than visited each other's places, but some children actually *had to* spend time away from home because of their parents – for instance, older children were asked to take their younger siblings or other relatives outside and had responsibility for them, and some children simply had no keys for their home and I witnessed a few occasions when they were waiting on the street until their parents came home from work.

The relationships between factors such as children's possessions or peer relationships, and the spatial configurations of the neighbourhood were most definitely mutual and, in order to understand how they mattered for children spending time on the street, this chapter needs to be read along with the chapters that follow, as spatialities also had impacts on how friendship or material objects mattered for children's practices, for example. However, my argument is that, for many children from Kopčany, the street and other public spaces in the neighbourhood were in some ways more significant than their homes. Where several authors argue that there is a tendency for home rather than neighbourhood to become the primary space of children from Western countries, for reasons as different as material provision and popularity, or indoor activities or the sense of fear on the street (Pain, 2006; Talbot, 2013), for children from Kopčany, several of these were to be found on the street rather than at home (material objects for play or the relative familiarity with the neighbourhood and the relative lack of fear of strangers). Some aspects for which home is often considered to be the main resource for children's opportunities, such as being the site which provides privacy, comfort, material belonging, or people's most important interpersonal contacts, thus for many children took place on the street, and the significance of public areas was possibly higher than in the case of other nearby neighbourhoods (with smaller families, higher standards of living, or more affluent families).

Children's practices in the public spaces of Kopčany

Locations and rhythms of children's practices

The public spaces of Kopčany were important for the everyday practices of many children as they did not spend much time elsewhere apart from time spent in school, and the street also served as a site of several practices that might be usually expected taking place at home. However, as Map 2 shows, the area of the neighbourhood itself, and particularly the spaces that children could use, was rather limited. The broader area of Kopčany, located on the southwestern outskirts of Bratislava, is separated from the rest of the city by a motorway and a railway at the northern and eastern boundaries. The areas immediately to the west, south and east from the central part of the neighbourhood are gated commercial and industrial zones to which children had no access and these were connected by relatively busy roads. The only areas close to the inner part of the neighbourhood were green zones to the north and northwest of the neighbourhood (Map 2, areas 1, 2 and 5) and a small green area on the southern outskirts of the neighbourhood (Map 2, area 3), but neither of these was suitable for younger children's activities. They were all remnants of past construction activities without any particular plans for future development, neglected and full of litter but also more substantial and often dangerous waste (glass, car-batteries, old furniture). Apart from area 3 on Map 2, they all were out of sight from the neighbourhood and parents did not like their children to spend time here, but many children were also afraid to be there, especially in the evening. Area 3 could be relatively safe for children's activities, and I was told that children used to play football there, but when I came the weeds there were taller than the younger children, so children could not use this space.

Map 3 depicts children's use of spaces in Kopčany in more detail. Even much of the inner zone of Kopčany was gated as a part of the commercial hostel zone (area 5). Although children occasionally climbed the fence and entered the zone, only the younger children did so and not often, and they used to be driven off by the managers. Also, the only objects of interest for children there were large containers and roofs of low buildings adjacent to the central building. Of the other spaces, the green area at the top of the map (area 1) was an unkempt lawn full of litter, including dangerous objects such as glass splinters. There were no benches in the area and the two small playgrounds (one in area 6), another consisting of a single climbing frame and a slide, located between the local pub (area 9) and the building at the southeast of the neighbourhood (area 8), were highly neglected (Figure 5.4). As a result, children, but also adults from the neighbourhood, usually used the wider parts of pavements to gather (Figure 5.5), and when they spent more time outside, they sat on stepss (Figure 5.6), low concrete blocks (such as pillars of former benches, or of the fence, see Figure 5.7) or other ad hoc solid objects. Alcoves of the panel-block buildings were also used for a shelter against bad weather occasionally, especially by young people(see Figure 5.8).

Children's practices in various spaces depended on the seasons and everyday rhythms (Hitchings, 2010). In Kopčany in the winter, when the sun sets as early as about 3:30pm in December and the temperature can be as low as -15°C, the number of children on the street was considerably lower than in the summer, and the frequency and length of their interaction also decreased. While the average number of contacts with children I made during summer was up to 40 in a two-hour shift and the maximum was over 60, in the winter the average number was around 20, with some shifts when I met only about 10 children. In the winter, children also spent more time just talking to each other, or playing simple games that did not require much light, such as skipping the rope, while in the summer they were more mobile, leaving the neighbourhood for swimming pools, or more often visiting areas such as shopping malls. In the winter, an average period that children spent on the street at one time was also rather shorter, often averaging only a couple of minutes, while during the summer months some children left their homes in the morning and came back after dark. The winter months were also marked by frequent illnesses such as flu or colds, particularly as children often dressed inadequately, but many nevertheless spent time outside, even when they were ill. In the summer, school holidays took place during July and August, so children had more time (see illustrations of the landscape in Kopčany in winter and summer in Figures 5.9 and 5.10).

Figure 5.4 A neglected sandpit at a playground

Figure 5.5 Children gathered at the front of the lodging house where the main pavement meets the one that encircles the lodging house

Figure 5.6 Children gathered at the stairways to the lodging house

Figure 5.7 A neglected playground. The grey pillars of the former benches can be seen

Figure 5.8 Alcoves of the panel-block buildings

Figure 5.9 Front side of the lodging house in the winter

Figure 5.10 Kopčany in summer (note the burnt grass, which often happened in the summer, with temperatures over 30°C and very little rain throughout long periods)

A daily routine also mattered for children, depending on the particular time of the year. Children's school day usually started at 8am, and lasted until 1 or 2pm. Due to the nearby location of the children's schools, most of the children could be seen in the streets of the neighbourhood from the early afternoon and they often stayed out until late evening. Some children stayed out late as their parents worked in the evenings and could not control them, or their following of the rules was rather loose. On the other hand, for some children strict rules existed and they usually had to be at home around sunset in summer, or around 7pm in the winter. I had only limited experiences with the children during weekends, but then they usually woke up later and started their activities around 10 or 11am, with a break for lunch (the most important and most substantial meal of the day in Slovakia), and then engaged in other activities depending on time of the year.

Spatialities of children's practices on the street and contestations of the public space

I identified three significant and distinct ways in which the children claimed the street space in Kopčany. First, children spent time in areas that provided them with the best tangible or even immaterial conditions for their activities. By the latter, I mean, for example, a sufficient sense of safety, or the fact that children could observe life in the neighbourhood, such as seeing from their viewpoint the friends they were looking for (such as the crossroads near the building in the northeastern part of the neighbourhood). By the former I mean the suitability of particular spaces for activities such as sitting, playing ball games, or being protected from the sun, wind or rain. These were the 'main' spaces of children's activities in the street and the children could be most easily found there. They often had several uses for the children's practices.

At the front of the lodging house building (Map 3, point 3) there was a staircase where children could sit, they also waited for the Centre workers there, or for their parents and friends when they went to a small shop on the ground floor. Due to the presence of so many people, as well as of the porter in the lodging house, it was perhaps the safest place in the neighbourhood, especially for younger children. At the rear side, there was a wall where children played football or dodge-ball. Here they were sheltered from the wind (that usually came from west and could be very severe, especially in the autumn and winter) and they later painted the wall and the pavement so they had a pitch for their games. Children also used the small stairs under the shadow of the industrial building opposite the lodging house and a rarely used part of the car park in front of this, either for meetings or for (ball) games, but also for searching for thrown away items on the ground (Map 3, point 2). The playground in the other part of the neighbourhood (Map 3, point 6) or the abandoned concrete cylinders on the outskirts of the neighbourhood, were also among the sites where children most often spent time (Map 3, point 1). Younger ones, and especially those from the buildings in the eastern part of the neighbourhood, did so in the playground, as this could be seen relatively well from all three buildings and the asphalt ground revealed any dangerous objects (unlike the grass areas elsewhere in the neighbourhood). Older children often retreated to the cylinders where they could not be seen and had more privacy. In most of these spaces, children also encountered adults and shared the spaces with them. Those were spaces where they could expect to meet other people, adults or children, and where they would be visible and at the same time able to observe activities in the neighbourhood.

But there were also certain mobilities in children's activities in the neighbourhood evolving from the micro-geographies of children's affiliation to the neighbourhood spaces. In particular, the central area of the workers' hostel (Map 3, area 5) was a barrier that separated the opposite parts of the neighbourhood so they could not be seen from the other side. If children wished to find someone (friends, parents, adults, Centre workers), they could often expect them to be in some particular places of the neighbourhood, but could not see them if the hostel stood in the way. Therefore, the pavement that circled the workers lodging house (Map 3, the white line) formed a kind of local boulevard, a line where children (but also adults, and the Centre workers) used to stroll in circles. The role of the pavement was not just to hang around the neighbourhood. It was also used as the main line of connection between people's houses (for both adults and children) and special sites in Kopčany such as bus stops, the small shop in the lodging house, or the local pub (Map 3, point 9). Other important lanes for the children's activities that can be seen on Map 3 included those that connected the significant points of children's activities or gatherings as already described, or paths leading to the bus stops.

Finally, there were sites that were located beyond the most central and usual scope of children's activities, but children often experimented with them and often managed to change their shape, or find a way to use them for their everyday actions. Only a minority of spaces in Kopčany were specifically designed for children – the neglected playgrounds, for instance – and even these were derelict and unsuitable for play. However, children also explored and reclaimed spaces that were otherwise usually considered to be useless and avoided, such as the abandoned building sites at the edge of the neighbourhood, or overgrown green areas within and outside the neighbourhood as shown on Map 2 and outlined at the beginning of this section. Children found a different use for these spaces, and at the same time they could use them for activities that they could not do in other parts of the neighbourhood. For instance, I have seen young boys building a shelter from mud and sticks in one of the building sites (Map 2, area 2), or a young boy constructing a swing on an abandoned tree in the overgrown green area outside the southwestern border of the neighbourhood (Map 2, area 3), where it was so well hidden that he was not afraid that other children would damage it. In other cases, children painted and decorated areas where they spent a lot of time, on some occasions with help from the Community Centre (see Figure 5.11 and Map 3, area 1).

For this kind of activity, children had often exceptionally good knowledge of the spaces in Kopčany, usually exceeding that of the adults. For instance, I took part in the cleaning of a nearby underpass (Map 2, area 1), where young people wanted to create a community space for a film screening. The waste container was placed quite far from the underpass and we had no truck or barrow to transport the waste. I met three young boys, aged between 6 and 10, and asked them whether they knew about any shopping cart or buggy that had been thrown away that we might use. The boys gave me a reply immediately, informing me about a cart that someone had brought to the neighbourhood and left in the sand pit. While walking there, they also informed me that the cart had been damaged, and had no wheels so it would be probably of no use for me. They also told me that no other similar object that I could use was at that time in the neighbourhood.

Figure 5.11 Children decorating the concrete tunnels

Knowing spaces that the adults did not know, and exploring spaces that were left unattended, children also reshaped some areas so they could use them differently. I have mentioned how they – either in collaboration with the Centre or on their own – reshaped or decorated several spaces of the neighbourhood for the purpose of their daily activities, or at least used them in different ways. They played dodge-ball on an unused part of the car park, or football using the walls of buildings as goals. An old carpet-hanger that was turned into a swing by hanging an old tyre on a couple of chains (this happened a long time ago and was reportedly done by the local council) was in turn changed into a football net (see Map 3, area 6). Concrete tunnels were shaped into places where children could sit protected from rain and wind, and old abandoned building sites were used as zones where children could smoke or drink without being disturbed. Valentine (1997) and Nayak (2003a) argue that children often have a better knowledge of public spaces than adults due to the time that they spend on the street, but also due to the different and often spontaneous forms of activities that they do. As Lees argues, for children, 'the public space ... has a use value, in contrast to the exchange value it holds for business people, planners and developers' (1998, p.250; see also Chapter Six). Such a feature of children's activities – re-appropriating and reshaping public spaces that were not used by the adults – was also characteristic for children in Kopčany. This use value was further sedimented and transformed by children through an order that was partially based on their own conventions and only partially responding to the usual use of and ideas about this space by adults. Children's use of some of the spaces that they discovered and explored thus became more than spontaneous or 'opportunistic' (Philo, 1992) and displayed signs of established routine and habits. For children in Kopčany, a lack of space designed specifically for them motivated them to engage with spaces that were designed and left for nobody, and to experiment with the ways in which these spaces could be utilised. Children managed to transfer the former 'non-institutional' character of these public spaces (Matthews et al, 2000; Tucker, 2003; Veitch et al, 2007), and to foster an alternative, liminal culture of use of these spaces driven by orders that were formed and adhered to by the children themselves (Winchester and Costello, 1995; Beazley, 2000; Pain and Francis, 2004).

The role of spaces in some of the children's particular activities is further illustrated in later chapters, but it still needs to be placed within a context of adult appropriation of the space. In Kopčany, very few outdoor spaces were designed even for the adult residents, let alone the children. The area had no benches, and no accessible greenery, and adults' use of and affiliation with the spaces was almost as opportunistic as the children's. The workers from the lodging house spent a lot of time on their balconies that overlooked the neighbourhood; several adults, particularly men, tended to spend their time in the local pub; parents (especially mothers), who spent time outside with their young kids and babies, often tried to make the most out of the uncomfortable design of the neighbourhood so they claimed stairs, kerbs or pillars of the fences, or just took their own chairs outside. They used the buildings as shelters from the sun or wind in a very similar way to the children, so the eastern edge of the buildings was the more common site of gathering – it was protected from the prevailing western wind and in the evening from the sun. Spatial resources in Kopčany were thus a subject of constant negotiation and contestation, not only among the children themselves, but also between them and adults, or various groups of adults. Children were at times sent away by disturbed adults when they made too much noise or were damaging lamps or walls, but they also fought each other for the few suitable spaces for play.

Even though children's use of spaces was characterised by an order manifested and reinscribed in children's habits over various areas in Kopčany, it still remained highly organic, opportunistic and less stratified (Jones, 2000) than the range of ways in which most adults used the public spaces. Adults, in general, engaged in a smaller number and a more settled pattern of practices on the streets of Kopčany, such as visiting the pub, the shop, walking with babies in a buggy, or sitting together on stairs. The range of children's activities, as well as the range of spaces they appropriated, were much greater, diverse and innovative, and also subject to more frequent changes if a particular site was suddenly transformed.

Thomson argues that the 'segmentation of space', the segmentation of the interface of human activities and their settings, serves as 'a source of power' (2005, p.64) as the unevenness of social relations is amplified and transposed through their spatial configurations. In Kopčany, contestation over the spaces in greatest demand, such as stairs or crossroads of pavements, was a part of children's attempts to increase their capacities for everyday practices, including mundane activities such as just sitting with their friends, or playing ball games without the risk of being hurt by splinters of glass. However, even if the children had, as Matthews et al (2000, p.64) put it, '"won out" [some spaces] from the fabric of adult society, [these were still] in constant threat of being reclaimed' by other people, including both adults and other children. Jones (2000) declares how adult spaces usually have a certain 'purity' that children subvert and disrupt. In Kopčany, such purity was more indistinct, as most public spaces were being constantly reconfigured and reclaimed, not just by children but also by adults, who had only very few 'reserved' or 'privileged' sites, such as the pub (which is itself not so much public as perhaps 'shared'), and even those were visited by only few of them. As the public spaces in Kopčany did not provide distinct opportunities for spending time on the street besides just walking home through the area, and because of the limited spatial extent of the area and the high demand for spaces by both children and adults, a constant process of interaction in spaces and over spaces penetrated all social groups of all ages. The rich body of literature on children's exclusion from public spaces (see in Hörschelmann and van Blerk, 2011) because of the risk they bring to social (or spatial) order (and the risk they are at) can be extended in the case of Kopčany to include a multiplicity of habitual social and spatial orderings of particular groups (of adults or children) that contest each other in their claims over particular spaces in the neighbourhood. This finding arguably relates to the idea of ongoing negotiation and contestation as the essence of the public space (Fyfe, 1998; Malone, 2002), but rather than understanding the social (or spatial) orderings of Kopčany as being significantly a result of an active formal and institutional design or management of public spaces, they need also to be recognised as consequences of embodied practices of individual actors (including children in a significant role) and of their contestations over specific sites for contrasting reasons.

Conclusions

One of the key arguments of this chapter was that the limits of children's independent mobility, to a great extent being a reflection of their socioeconomic as well as spatial marginalisation, underpin the centrality of the neighbourhood in children's socio-spatial experiences. Further chapters of the book will draw on this premise and develop also the reverse argument, that this centrality further reinforces children's marginalisation in terms of their social and material experiences. Outlines of such a reverse connection could be seen already in this chapter, though, particularly in the discussion of children's spatial knowledge as linked to the limits of their spatial experiences, since they lacked practically any beyond the immediate surroundings of Kopčany.

Following Ansell's (2009a) call for descaling geographies of children's lives, I focused on the public area of Kopčany not as a pre-defined spatiality but as a projection of the spatial range of children's everyday activities. This revealed the public spaces of Kopčany as central for understanding children's everyday practices – on the one hand as a result of the limited independent mobility of the children, and on the other hand, as for many children the street and other open areas in the neighbourhood also filled the roles that home is usually expected to provide, such as being the source of material possessions, place of routine emotional engagements, or space of privacy.

Topographic contours of how and why the public spaces in Kopčany had diverse importance for children's activities highlighted the difference in children's age, affluence and whether they had siblings or close relatives from Kopčany or living nearby, as important factors that determined the extent of children's independent mobility. Factors such as the family size, flat size but also family affluence and relationships were relevant for how important children's homes were as sites of their practices, and what in turn the implicit significance of the public spaces for children was. There is a relatively high variance in how all these factors contribute relationally to the significance of public spaces in the neighbourhood (as complex settings for children's activities [Philo, 2000]) for individual children, and other chapters will illuminate some of these differences in more detail. Crucially, though, Chapter Five emphasised that space, as an extension to children's agency, is manifested in the neighbourhood in a simultaneous and dynamic multiplicity (see Massey, 2005) rather than as a resource that provides all children with identical and homogeneous traits. Public spaces were shown not only as extensions to children's agency, but also as actively shaped by children's practices and their complex agencies. Public spaces in Kopčany were sites negotiated and challenged by various social groups, both children and adults, and the ongoing contestations of the spaces were related not only to the affiliation with, and appropriation of, the most attractive spaces (such as sites with provisional seats or those that are sheltered from the sun, rain and wind), but also to activities that tangibly transformed particular spaces in order to fit the needs and capacities of the residents, again, both adults and children. Despite limited means, children were active actors in changing their everyday spaces, and many of them actively appropriated and reshaped their everyday environment in order to balance the shortages that the design and management of the public spaces provided them with because of the lack of suitable facilities or services located in the neighbourhood.

The topographical analysis identified key circumstances of children's lives according to the effects they have on the significance and modes of engaging with public spaces in Kopčany for children's agency. The analysis contained also an inherently critical thread, one contributing more directly to a 'counter-topographical' account of the neighbourhood. A critical account of the neighbourhood surfaced in the chapter by focusing on the emergence of children's practices in the context of children's transformative activities, various and complex patterns of marginalisation within the neighbourhood or families, and both affirmative and antagonistic social ties with other residents across diverse age groups. In order to unfold some of these themes in more depth, I follow the discussion in Chapter Six by focusing on children's practices as situated through their bodies, and I will discuss how the body acts as a complex circumstance in the constitution of children's practices.

Map 1: Sites of children's practices outside the neighbourhood

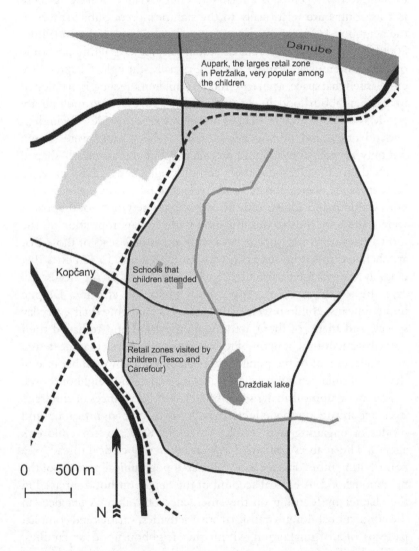

The map shows the residential area of Petržalka and the location of Kopčany.Main highways (full line) and railways (dotted line) are shown.

Map 2: Kopčany and its surroundings

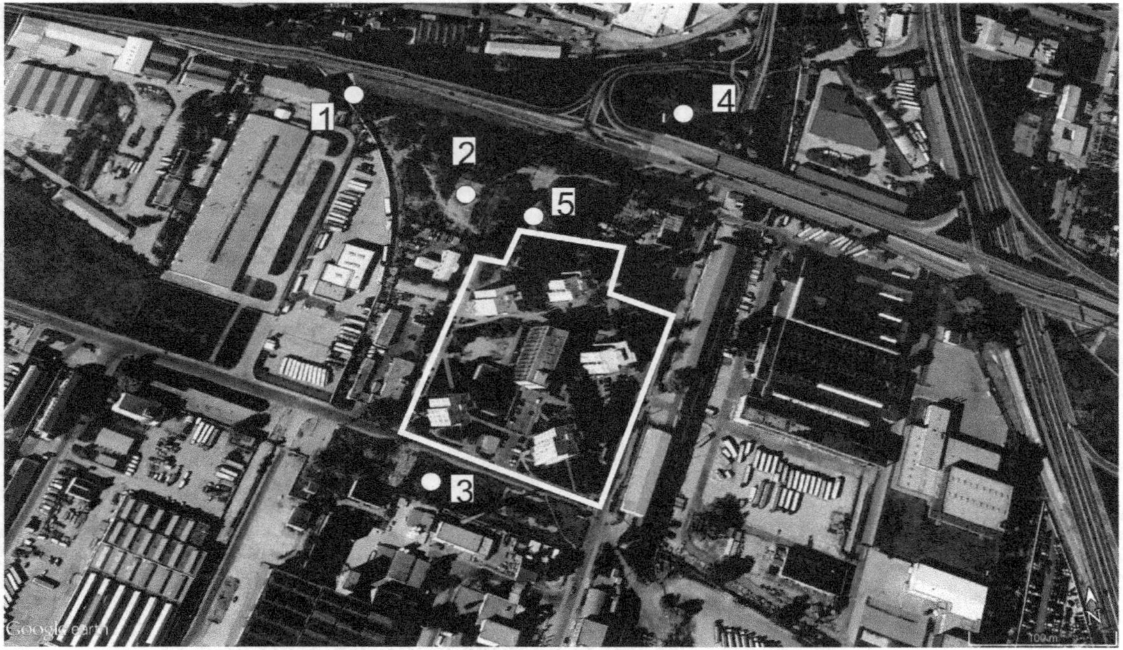

Legend

1. An underpass beneath the motorway at the northwest end of the neighbourhood. Rarely visited by children, it marked the end of Kopčany.

2. An abandoned construction site. Of interest to children as it could not be seen from the neighbourhood and was rarely visited by adults.

3. A grass area which was rarely mowed and although it was a good hiding place, it was not suitable for everyday activities.

4. The 'meadow', a green site circled by an exit from the motorway. The slope was used in the winter for sliding and sleighing, the Community Centre ran various activities here in the summer.

5. Another abandoned building site. Separated from the neighbourhood by concrete cylinders and rarely visited by children.

The white line marks the part of the neighbourhood where children spent most of their time.

Map 3: The inner neighbourhood of Kopčany

The white line marks the fence around the hostel and the main path around the neighbourhood.

Legend

1: Concrete cylinders near the lodging house separated the neighbourhood from an old construction site (Map 2, area 5). The cylinders were a common meeting point for children and for street work encounters. A grass area stretched to the east, which was the largest open space in the neighbourhood.

2: A sparsely used car park, frequently used by children and also adults. Its end was sheltered from the sun in the afternoon by the nearby administrative building.

3: The lodging house where the Community Centre was located. Areas around the building were frequently used by children. The front (west) side was a common meeting point and place where street work shifts started. The rear side provided a shelter from the wind and there was no window on the ground floor, so children also used it for ball games.

4: Two buildings with mixed flat ownership were situated in the northeast part of the area and were in a better state than others. Occasional place for meetings as trees offered a shelter from the sun, but a CCTV was installed here.

5: The workers hostel, an area completely fenced and (in theory) inaccessible. The pavement around the fence constituted a 'boulevard', a path that connected all areas of the neighbourhood. The basic track for the street work.

6: The main playground in the area consisted of a neglected sandpit and a swing made of chains and a tyre.

7: A council flat building at the very end of the neighbourhood (as the entrance to the neighbourhood was from the northeast). A place for children to have some privacy.

8: Another council flat building and a common place for adults to gather.

9: A small local pub, detached from most children's activities.

SIX

The body and embodiment

Physical contacts with children were a routine element of my fieldwork. Hugs, taps, handshakes, strokes, I received even a kiss or two ... Also bumps, kicks and spitting once. I was instructed by the Centre staff that there were no strict formal rules about touching children – such as that one *could not* hold them or hug them. However, there were some principles I was supposed to follow – to be very careful about initiating bodily contact with children and rather let them decide and perform when and *if at all* they wanted any bodily interaction; to consider what impact this could have on children, especially if performed frequently/regularly – for example whether it could instigate too intensive attachment by the child or s/he would receive too much attention if compared to other children; and, not least, to monitor my own boundaries beyond which I would feel uncomfortable – that is, to do what I feel at ease to do.

I became a highly appreciated member of the staff as I usually did not mind lifting the children or carrying them around the neighbourhood, either on my back, shoulders or in arms. I had to monitor and limit such behaviour as the kids were often overenthusiastic, fought each other for a chance to be carried (so I had to organise a queue) and with some, this became too much the core in our relationship (and yes, my back often ached). After a couple of weeks, however, I began to reflect also broader dimensions of physical interactions with children, those that went beyond the actual interactions between two (sometimes three or more) of us.

I was carrying Rebeka (13) on my back around the lodging house and we chatted about some recent events when suddenly a man roared from above:

'REBEKA!!! WHO'S THAT PERVERT?'
'HE'S NOT A PERVERT, HE'S FROM THE CENTRE!!!' – Rebeka yelled back.

'You are not a pervert, are you?' – she asked.
'No. I'm not.'
'Great. Let's go.'
(Extract from field notes, October 2008)

The incident with Rebeka illustrates how bodies take an important role in children's everyday practices (as well as those of other people). In this short story, our bodies were not just passive matters but also the interfaces of our contact and at the same time the signifiers of our social positions, articulated through the intervention of Rebeka's father. After discussing everyday spaces of Kopčany as a crucial contextual setting for children's practices, this chapter focuses on the body as the most intimate location of practices. This rationale does not refer only to the crude materiality and the physical location of individual practices but also to the specificity of embodied capacities such as tacit knowledge or dispositions, reflecting on wider theories of practice (Schatzki, 2001). More specifically, this interest reflects the calls in social sciences to take children's bodies 'seriously' (Colls and Hörschelmann, 2009a, 2009b; Prout, 2011) and to localise children's practices and daily experiences within subtle relations between cognition, emotions and materiality that embodiment forms and enables (Rautio, 2013). However, locating practices in embodiment does not necessarily 'exclude or reject discussion of *representations* of body' (Parr, 1998, p.22, italics added), and the chapter also explores what meanings and representations signified by diverse bodies were important for how children's practices were formed.

I examine three modes through which embodiment mattered in how children's practices were constituted. First, I explore those practices that are seemingly not governed by cognitive contents, highlighting the diverse potential of the body against that of consciousness (Dewsbury and Naylor, 2002). In the stories I discuss, children's actions preceded their mediations of the events and I draw on works of Vygotsky, Benjamin and Katz in order to illustrate the 'immediate connection[s] between thought and action' (Katz, 2004a, p.100) as they manifest among various children – a topic that will become central to the book's conclusions. Second, I connect to this discussion and explore how children perceive and recognise the body, discussing in turn how they perceive their own bodies and how they learn to use them in practices, how they perceive bodies of other people, and how their bodies are noticed by other children. This thread of the analysis goes along with the notion of bodies 'as inscribed with social and cultural meanings' (Mowl et al, 2000, p.189) and is situated in social discourses while at the same time intertwined with individual perception and adaptation of bodies for practice. Having said that, this chapter does not actually pay explicit attention to how key axes of social differences – gender, ethnicity and age/development – are discursively constituted and circulated in children's lives as this inquiry takes place in Chapter Eleven, once I have discussed children's social relations. Finally, I am interested in the idea of proximity, that is, in the moments where the body either affirms or contests and even dissolves its boundaries and engages in contacts with other bodies. Ideas of the body as a boundary/ frontier and as a site of connection and disconnection are crucial here for understanding how children's practices take place within social and spatial circumstances in Kopčany and how they in turn contribute to the formation of space in the neighbourhood.

The chapter is firmly placed within the analytical framework outlined in Parts One and Two. It contributes to the topographical analysis by exploring the diversity and similarities of the ways in which the body affects individual children's practices. There is also a connection to the broader theoretical framework (and the perspectives of relational materialism, relationalism and non-essentialist empiricism respectively) by exploring the links between the materiality of children's bodies and the cognitive elements of their actions, identifying other factors that matter for this association, and tracing other circumstances and their connection that can account for how children act on a day-to-day basis.

Body, experience and action

In the first month of my stay in Kopčany, I saw a conflict between two 7-year-old boys, Samuel and Norbert. During a game, Norbert accidently hit his friend in the eye. When Samuel began to cry, Norbert said "sorry" and sought to embrace and caress Samuel, who furiously refused to let Norbert touch him. Norbert stood steadily, looking at Samuel and seemingly not sure about what to do. He was unable to find any other words except the "sorry" that Samuel had already rejected. With his attention centred on Samuel and apparently wishing persistently to settle the conflict, Norbert eventually said "you can hit me too, come on" and made a reluctant step towards Samuel. As his friend returned him an uncertain look, Norbert made another step and indicated a punch to his eye to confirm his intentions clearly. After a short hesitation, Samuel indeed approached Norbert and hit him in the face. Norbert smiled and now stepped towards Samuel and hugged him. Samuel, although still in tears, did not resist and after a few minutes, they went on with their game.

The story of Norbert and Samuel hints at the significance of embodiment in children's actions in relation to mediation and knowledge for understanding the children's practices. A range of psychological theories of lifespan development imply that children's skills shift progressively from intuitive thinking to the formal operational stage, with abilities to think abstractly and draw logical conclusions from available information as a factor of their psychosocial development, and that the development of the verbal register is an intrinsic part of this process (Piaget, 1995). Norbert, instead of devising a 'rational' decision to deal with his discomfort because of Samuel's crying, provided his body as a device for 'reconciliation' of their conflict and against the struggles to translate his feelings into meaningful words that would satisfy Samuel. Norbert's actions followed his emotions, and when we talked afterwards, he admitted that he had not taken account of the risk of getting injured or being seen by adults who would have probably escalated the whole conflict had they stood up for Norbert and punished Samuel.

When children struggled to express themselves verbally, like Norbert did in his conflict with Samuel, they tended to turn to their bodies to illustrate or tackle their perceptions and apprehensions of everyday situations. A 10-year-old boy, Silvester, was known to the Centre workers as often telling tales or showing off. When I met him for the first time, he began talking about his experiences, such as how he had attended courses on various martial arts for a period of time that was unrealistic due to his age, and while he struggled to name some of the activities he did there, he illustrated his words vigorously, performing martial arts moves, such as hits, kicks or swings. Several children similarly feigned punches or kicks when they passed other children just to attract their attention, although they did not actually want to attack them. For instance, Lukas (10) and his sister Alica (8) rarely allowed anyone to get close to them, often resisted any attempt to contact them in our fieldwork and, when asked, demonstrated how uninterested they were in anyone, including the Centre staff, approaching them. However, if they really wished to speak to me, simulating an attack was often a way that the children initiated a dialogue, often followed with: "Hey, don't you worry, I wouldn't hit you. You're a good boy … So what, how are you?" Although I found that they would not hit me and was not really afraid of being hit, both Lukas and Alica just indicated a threat and subsequently assured me of my safety. This way, they could initiate the contact between us without verbally admitting their interest in it – as the talk seemingly immediately followed our non-verbal embodied interaction.

Katz argues that the immediacy between bodily actions and emotional or cognitive experiences is 'one of the key attributes of children's consciousness' (2004a, p.100). This interpretation draws particularly on Vygotsky's (1978) theory of play. In this framework, there is no middle step, such as imagination or mediation, between children's recognition of particular contexts and their actions through which children replicate their previous experiences with this context. In Norbert's acts, there was no middle step between his feelings of discomfort for Samuel's crying and his impulsive desire to reconcile with his friend, and how he attempted to hug him. Norbert did not try to talk to Samuel at first or inquire about his feelings and he acted straightforwardly to making peace with him. Hugging his friend was what he perceived as a position of a positive mutual engagement. After Samuel refused Norbert's embrace, the latter's next step was to offer to let his friend hit him – that is, the very same act that made Samuel cry, but reversed in the direction which Norbert expected also to reverse Samuel's feelings.

Vygotsky's argument is that the way that children act does not come from their psychological developmental stage but rather from their experiences of particular contexts. Importantly, children's recognition of contexts that can later inform their acts is not only conscious and rational, but also affective. Imaginations and abstract meditations become the middle step between experience and action only later, when children have more experience with particular contexts, as well as with their own responsive behaviour. Benjamin's (1978) concept of mimesis gives some additional insight here – children's behaviour initially just replicates their past experiences as they recognise them in the present contexts rather than constructing more abstract and complex behavioural responses. Children such as Silvester or Lukas with Alica recognised the contexts that were relevant for our meetings (the theme of martial arts or the fact that I would react to children if I felt attacked) and expressed their experiences with both issues through their bodies – by showing the martial arts moves to express this theme and by simulating an attack in order draw my attraction. There was arguably more imagination and conscious meditation between children's recognitions and aims and their ultimate actions than in the case of Norbert, but the children still mostly replicated what they already had an experience with – the bodily movement in martial arts in order to describe to me what the training is like, and the invasion of my bodily space by drawing my attention rather than approaching me verbally.

The issue of immediate bodily actions unmediated by abstract imaginations or meditations was important also for older children. Although many of them were more capable of rationalised talk and accounting for their practices, they were still encountering new contexts for which they lacked previous experiences where such a rationalisation could mediate between their experience and action. Children approaching puberty, who experienced intense bodily changes, can be mentioned as an example. I could thus notice boys with deepening voices and able to roar down others as they screamed, seemingly without any purpose; or showing themselves and threatening others by simulated attacks as their bodies put on more muscles. Similarly, older children who experienced intensive bodily changes often modified their clothes and adopted styles that pointed up bodily features of physical maturing. While younger children often styled themselves using jewellery, haircuts or various colours and motifs on their clothes, older children worked more ingeniously towards stylising their actual bodies and to manifest their body shapes. Older girls, unlike their younger peers, thus wore close-fitting clothes that emphasised their legs or upper bodies, while older boys preferred loose outfits that, on the contrary, hid their body shapes – changes in embodied expressions were thus differentiated not only depending on age but also sex/gender of the children.

The role of the body and bodily perceptions and affective experiences was important also in the contexts where there were seemingly no external impulses that would impact children's practices. As Bissell emphasises, 'the inert body is always already experiencing a myriad of affectual complexes and sensations' (2008, p.1709). While children's lives in Kopčany were indeed full of bodily activities – movements, bumps, tactile explorations and contacts with the world – even when they were bored and seemingly passive, they experienced the world. The uncomfortable feeling of boredom that has a bodily dimension often initiated actions such as teasing other children or adults, or damaging objects in the neighbourhood (street lamps in the neighbourhood, vulnerable to strong shaking, were often kicked by the children as they could be turned off in this way). Anderson describes boredom as a 'suspension of the affect through an incapacity in habit' (2004, p.739), a reference that shows explicit links between the immediate context of circumstances, embodiment, feelings and practice (or the lack thereof). Even when some children mocked other children verbally, they often did so without words, just passing and bumping them until they had their attention. When children were asked about their motivation for such acts without any apparent reason, they tended to answer that they were bored and that was the whole reason. One of the Centre's goals was to provide leisure activities particularly in order to tackle the boredom (and see Skelton, 2000; Morrow, 2005, 2007 on the significance of boredom in the realm of social policy).

My key argument in this section was that the relation between children's practices and their recognitions of the immediate contexts in which the practices took place depended on children's previous experiences with these contexts. In this way, I delineated the contours of difference in which bodies mattered as extensions to children's agencies. If these contexts were rather new, children often drew on their past (conscious or unreflected) experiences and replicated a behaviour that corresponded with these experiences. Abstraction, rationalisation or recognition of more complex associations that would lead to more intensive employment of language as a medium of children's action was not necessarily related to children's age, although older children obviously gained more experiences in mediating the processes between experience and action. Still, children's bodily changes also brought new experiences for older children and initiated behaviour that was seemingly unmediated but responding directly to these new experiences – such as when older boys often shouted after their voice deepened or when older girls emphasised their body shapes extensively after approaching puberty – before children learned to react to the new bodily experience differently. All the practices mentioned in this section highlighted the role of children's bodies as mediums of their actions in not entirely familiar contexts. While bodies can be said to be ever present circumstances of children's practices, they also made individual 'extensions to agency' in these situations, taking a role that was different from and complementary to language or rationalisation.

Meanings of the body and meanings through the body

Descriptions of older children acting through their bodies as they experienced bodily changes in early puberty also lead to the question of how children's knowledge about their bodies was formed. If bodies are among 'the forms of life we routinely consider unremarkable and thus taken for granted' (Chaney, 2002, p.10), particularly older boys and girls who entered puberty represented a counter-argument as they suddenly recognised their bodies and the dynamic changes they experienced very intensely. This was when the themes of sexuality or intimate bodily hygiene (such as skin-care) were raised by boys and girls aged about 11–13 in regular meetings with the Centre staff and became central topics of our discussion with the children. Even in these discussions, the (sexed and already-sexualised; see Gwanzura-Ottemöller and Kesby, 2005) body often emerged in very direct and possibly 'naughty' questions rather than through sophisticated 'adult' discourses. Quite near the beginning of my work on the street, a colleague of mine, absorbed in a discussion with a group of 13-year-old girls, forgot that she had to leave earlier because of an appointment. I interrupted their discussion and reminded her of this after which she left the girls in hurry and I remained with them. I apologised and asked whether I could join them and take the place of my colleague. They agreed, so I asked if they would mind telling me what the topic was and they told me that they were talking about sex. Then I was asked straightaway: "Have you ever fucked someone?" After I asked why they had asked, the girls explained that they wished to know "what it is like" and the debate turned towards sexual health. I had heard several jokes where poor and even alarming knowledge of the body was presented by children (such as with punch lines about carrier bags and adhesive tape being used as a sufficient contraception) and that showed how the body was a relevant theme for children of this age, but how their knowledge about it in general was quite limited, and the knowledge of their own bodies, in particular, often intuitive and explorative, with very little or no sex education in the school (cf. Shapiro, 2001). The shared process of gaining knowledge about the body is important and I return to this question later.

Young children's interest in their own bodies was perhaps less apparent. Still, they occasionally showed off when their baby teeth popped out, or they compared their height together. Younger children talked about elementary bodily feelings such as pain, temperature or tiredness. However, they began to link these expressions explicitly with some of their practices, such as when their interest in being carried in my arms or on my shoulders was linked with tiredness, such as by saying: "Hey, Matej, carry me, at least just a little bit, my legs really ache, I am too tired." Engaging in physical activity, even younger children learned to reflect on their bodily states. For example, younger girls who liked to jump over the elastic rope often contemplated the height of their rope in terms of their bodily abilities and the size of their bodies. For younger children, discussions about "What is it like to be an adult?" with the Centre staff often focused on the bodily experience and children reflected also on their own bodies to an extent, most commonly through contrasts between adults and children in size and strength, but also in features such as body hair.

Engaging with their own bodies, children also learned about bodies in general and began creating meanings about the body related to ideas of bodily normality. An example is the ways that children were mocked for certain bodily features while not for others. For instance, children were very rarely teased for their corpulent bodies, but often were mocked for wearing glasses. Norbert (7), although he had very bad sight, refused to wear glasses even when he attended tutorial classes in the Centre. He explained that, apart from the fear of teasing, he had also experienced attacks when his glasses had hurt him in the face. Similarly Hugo (10), a boy with very bad sight, used to wear glasses, but was particularly sensitive about any jeers and disrespectful comments. Often he reacted sharply, and name-called and attacked others who mentioned his sight. A different kind of example, showing how discourses about the body were related to broader social relationships among the children, is a story of Nina, a 10-year old girl, who had a history of lice which was known in the neighbourhood. One day, several children gathered in the area around the building, so my colleague and I could not give enough attention to all of them. I was carrying various children in turns on my back, but they were still discontented and argued with each other for our attention. As a way to disqualify Nina, another girl whispered to me that Nina had lice and I should not carry her – although she did not have them at that time and this bodily feature was raised because of the significance that having lice was supposed to have for my willingness to carry Nina.

Additionally, children with distinct bodily features were not just passively inscribed with cultural meanings by others as they often negotiated the reception articulated by others. Michal (12) was well respected among his friends. Among the jokes he shared with others, ironic notions of his belly were often mentioned. Instead of being teased, he emphasised his own body, making jokes with other children. Emo (9) was friendly and generally liked among his friends, however, his stuttering attracted several remarks from others. Instead of defending himself or challenging others who teased him, he joined in with the others in laughing about his speech. Both boys thus recognised the cultural meanings that their bodies were given; however, rather than passively receiving remarks from others, they took part in forming these meanings and enacting them in new ways, having fun with their friends and actively pursuing the meanings.

The previous experiences illustrated how understanding one's body and the bodies of others provided children with new capacities to act. However, a considerable part of children's everyday learning about the world was accomplished *through* their bodies and also *aimed at* their bodies (see Ansell, 2009b) rather than just reflecting on their bodies. Much of their education was verbal or visual and focused on memorising. However, much also actively involved their bodies and much targeted bodies as the objects of change. An example would be Peter, a 5-year-old boy who had very few social and practical individual skills in areas such as hygiene, safety, communication or self-presentation. At the beginning of my fieldwork, I met him swashing in a puddle with his shoes on the wrong feet and untied, walking outside the house without his shoes at all during the winter, or playing with the liquid from a car battery. Peter was not allowed to attend regular activities of the Centre in the Club initially, as he was too young, so the only contact we had was during the street work. After a couple of months, he was permitted to participate in the school tutorials and in the meetings of boys aged between 8 and 13 in the Club (after extending the age restrictions). Visiting the Club included certain rituals – every child had to wash their hands after entering the premises; after meetings, children who attended had to help with cleaning up the Club. At the same time, several activities, particularly educational ones for younger children, evolved through bodily actions rather than cognitive activities (see Figure 6.1). Visiting the Club thus became a 'rite of passage' (Teather, 1999) for Peter, an embodied transition towards being what was talked of as a 'big boys' group member and he was very proud of it.

Figure 6.1 Bodily performances in the Club (from the Summer School Preparatory Programme in 2009)

Peter's older sisters also attended various Club activities regularly and he was very keen to be allowed to do the same. As boys and girls had some activities run separately, he even visited the Club without his older sisters, being just on his own without being cared for by them – as was usually the case on the street. At the same time, we emphasised this fact in communication with him anytime he committed a 'mischief' – such as when he had an anger outburst, or when he stole a jump rope from me along with his older sister. After reminding him of his 'new status', he snatched the rope from his sister right away and gave it back to me with apologies, proudly presenting himself as a 'grown' boy. The impact that the Centre workers endeavoured to make on Peter was thus enforced through the verbal reiteration of the fact that he had transitioned towards being an 'older boy' – but even more through repetitive bodily acts. Peter got used to washing his hands and even used to knock on the door of the Centre outside of the opening hours to ask whether he could wash his hands after playing outside. He began to demonstrate his style more in his haircut or clothes, for example showing off when his father cut his hair or when he had a new t-shirt, and was very pleased when an appreciative remark was given to him for this. Peter also became one of the most diligent children in helping with cleaning the Club. In the beginning, it caused more trouble than profit, as Peter tended to wet the whole Club when mopping the floor and consequently trampled the wet floor with his dirty shoes so it needed to be dried and washed again after he left. Nevertheless, Peter managed to achieve a certain amount of skills while he also retained the willingness to do them and an awareness of their significance. Similarly, while being rather uncertain in interactions with other people, after attending a preparatory summer-programme organised by the Centre for pre-school children, he surprised a colleague of mine by shaking her hand with a little bow and asking "So, how are you today?"

Peter learned through the 'ritual' practices at least as much as he learned from the explicit instructions and guidelines that accompanied them. As children learned through their own bodies, they also learned from bodies of others and from the practices that stem from particular uses of the body. This was especially noticeable when children approached adult bodies, that is, the bodies they were not familiar with but were curious about, especially in relation to their own bodies. I have several tattoos on my arms and legs. When I entered the field, I used to wear long sleeves and trousers so none of them was visible as I thought that the tattoos would attract too much attention. In the first four months, I thus revealed only a small tattoo on my forearm that the few children who saw it remarked on as 'nice' and 'cute'.

Initiating the theme of tattoos progressively, I exposed my other tattoos only after seven months in the field as the summer came. I found that several children were actually very interested in tattoos and some thought about getting tattooed, although they had not discussed this theme with other social workers or even their parents before. This gave us a chance to have a very open and in-depth discussion about responsibility and decisions on tattoos, hygiene and safety. This was very important, especially as, because of their lack of financial means, some children even got pierced or tattooed by their friends with a needle, and in general, health risks did not seem always to have been adequately considered. Revealing myself as having bodily experiences with something they often could not really discuss with their parents or other adults – because they were afraid or because they did not expect their parents to have relevant knowledge – triggered the consulting relationship between us. Moreover, such discussion often evolved subsequently into deeper discussions on self-consideration, when the children explained different reasons why they wished to have a tattoo – to improve their look, to have a personal mark, or to resemble their friends.

Likewise, similar discussions were led also in relation to clothes and self-styling of both my own and especially my female colleagues when children inquired about taste and fashion, and the experiences we had with how others reacted or about personal comfort with particular outfits. Similarly, but with a stronger focus on issues such as hygiene and health, discussions about adult bodily features such as muscles, hair, or secondary sex characteristics such as breasts or body hair were held. The children mostly inquired about bodily care, expectations about the normality of the body, or the period in which bodily changes in pubescence happen – all themes that the children were interested in but lacked a source of knowledge about, and for which they used our adult bodies as an illustrating source of learning along with the conversations.

Children gained knowledge about the body and through the body that changed their capacities to act in different contexts. However, certain bodily practices drew simultaneously different meanings in various discursive and regulatory contexts. Sport is an example of bodily acts through which children in Kopčany constituted different and new discourses of the body which fit themselves better than the established institutional ones. In Slovakia, sport and physical education had a long-standing role in the national educational curriculum, with key aims being health advancement among the children (a corresponding context can be found in Jirojanakul et al, 2003 and Tremblay et al, 2005). The District Council in Petržalka focused on sport as a key means to prevent drug misuse and risky behaviour among children and young people from the area, prioritising building new sport playgrounds, organising sport events, and providing financial support to sport clubs that worked with youth. Children of all ages from Kopčany also mentioned sport and bodily exercise as an important aspect of their lives. The youngest children regularly asked for sport equipment such as ropes or balls during our street work shifts. Many older girls, especially in the summer, spent their time roller skating, swimming, cycling or even playing football. When we interviewed children about their everyday needs, many older boys between the ages of 8 and 14, mentioned football as one of the most important activities and hobbies in their lives, stating that building a football ground was the most desired improvement of the neighbourhood they could imagine (see Figure 6.2). Even for the oldest boys, over 15 years of age, sports such as football or hockey mattered much. Many of them used to play football in local organisations and sport clubs and, while frequently complaining about the lack of opportunities and boredom in their daily regime, they often managed to organise and play football together.

My principal claim is that, although health was a frequent theme in our conversations with children of all ages, they rarely associated it with sport, an important element of their daily activities (see

Figure 6.2 Football game during one of the community play days organised by the Community Centre and including external volunteers (in grey t-shirts), several boys from the neighbourhood, one girl and a couple of dogs

Windram-Geddes, 2013). Instead, the key role of sport was in children's 'emotional geographies of pleasure and enjoyment' (Hemming, 2007, p.353). Children – especially boys between 9 and 14 years – emphasised the emotional role of sport in their ongoing self-realisation through physical activities (see Piko and Keresztes, 2006) and related this to their desire to build a new football playground in the neighbourhood. When I tried to get more ideas from Viliam (10), he replied that "Football is all my life, there is nothing else." Sport also formed an emotional landscape and social networks among children from Kopčany, several of which I discuss in detail in Chapters Nine and Ten. For example, Simon, a 13-year-old boy who had moved into the neighbourhood just two years before I started my fieldwork, explained to me how playing football made his integration among the children from Kopčany easier. He even said that while playing football and participating in the Community Centre activities seemed to be the easiest ways of integrating for new children who moved to the neighbourhood, sport activities required fewer social skills, such as being open and talkative, and some children might find it easier to engage with others through sport.

In the account of Simon and his friends, the matter of sport was not recognised through the meanings promoted by the state and educational institutions, that is, health improvement and prevention of anti-social behaviour and drug consumption. Although the children reflected on these meanings, for Simon and his friends sport meant primarily enjoyment, personal satisfaction and self-development, and also a collective space of emotional merging between various children, which helped constitute social ties among them. This example thus relates to previous discussions about children consciously experiencing their own bodies, assigning meanings to various bodies and learning through their own bodies and from the bodies of others, often without concordance with formal discourses and institutional mechanisms over children's bodies.

This connection also expands the discussion of Vygotsky's theory of psychosocial development from the previous section. Piagetian theories of cognitive development suggest that children grow up to fit the society and develop socially appropriate modes of behaviour. In contrast to this, Vygotsky's (1978) view is that children actively appropriate the modes of behaviour they witness, but also transform and rework them in ways that are different from the established societal patterns. Benjamin's (1978) notion of mimesis mentioned in the previous section does not refer to straightforward replication in this context. As Katz emphasises, children's mimetic performances include 'moment[s] of invention' (2004a, p.98), transformative practices that retain a resemblance to previous orders they seemed to copy, but these evolve in different and often unexpected ways. Children's practices are not only forms of 'imperfect performance' within the existing discursive fields (Austin, 1962), but they rather instigate new and diverse meanings and views, disrupting and exceeding these fields, forming different individual and collective subjectivities in the process (see Butler, 1993, 1997). Such a mimesis is ultimately linked with alterity, with one's realisation of the signposts that one aims to avoid (Taussig, 1993). As I suggested in the previous section, children do not just replicate their past experiences, they also perform against what they find as unsuitable in the past experiences of the present contexts. Katz (2004a) highlights how this is a faculty that is developed with social experiences that children adopt, and it is related to the process when children begin to realise that the ways of behaviour that they are familiar with (often tacitly) are just 'made up', that is, transformable and open for reconstruction. Children's interest in tattoos can serve as an example here, as children who talked about possibly getting tattooed in most cases transgressed the rules and expectations of their parents, while their motivations for having a tattoo were different from (and more prolific than) often very simplistic views on tattoos of their parents.

While the distinct role of football illustrated in the last example shows how children re-appropriate their experience with sport beyond the institutional discourses about health, the earlier illustrations in this section take this argument further and show that the range of experiences that children learn to re-transform and re-perform is broad and not limited to institutional or regulatory expectations. Children learning about tattoos and exploring their personal motivation transformed their experiences with tattoos from home (where they are often met with rejection from their parents) or their peer groups (where they might be perceived as an attractive bodily feature). Children who engaged in discourses about the normality of the body played with ways that these discourses affected one's social position. They also transformed or re-established these discourses in everyday practices, emphasising some discourses while ignoring others (such as the example about corpulent bodies vs. bad sight and the significance of wearing glasses). Herrera et al (2009) argue that children negotiate how their own bodies fit or not within ideal expectations and norms about bodies, and if there is a dissonance between the perceived and idealised (normative) image, children use practices of the body to actively challenge this tension. However, not all these practices are fully discursive and, as children's experiences with everyday contexts are often tacit, unreflected, embodied, or habitual, so their critical and transformative practical appropriation of the meanings of body and of the ways the body is employed in everyday practice often exceed discourses and representations.

In the last section of this chapter, I draw on the previous discussion of the body as a location and means of the children's practices, and I explore what the spatialities of embodied practices are in relation to the concept of proximity.

Bodies and proximity

When I met Alena, an 8-year old girl with a complex and difficult history for the first time, she impressed me as very perceptive of particular details of our interaction, but also as being reserved and not expressing her feelings openly. Although she did not spend much time on the street in the first few months of my fieldwork, we developed quite a lot of contact during my street work shifts. There was not much to discuss – Alena at most explained how she was misbehaving in school (having fallen asleep during the class, interrupting her teachers …) and rather repetitively presented herself as constantly rebelling and rarely acknowledging authorities. She usually refused to talk about her own desires, plans or feelings about home or about other people.

Besides talk, a kind of non-verbal interaction that I had rarely experienced with other children in the neighbourhood until then often happened between us. Alena kept me company on the street quite often, and even though she did not talk much, I began noticing her bodily positioning. While other children usually chose to stand opposite to me when we talked to each other, or at least they stood in a closed angle so we could have eye-contact, Alena usually stood next to me so we shared our visual perspective. We only occasionally looked at each other throughout our conversations or if we both simultaneously noticed something that was going on around us and looking at each other was a way to express this. Mostly, we were looking in the same direction and, even if we were in a bigger group of children, Alena kept her position close next to me and shared my visual perspective. I read Alena's position as an expression of trust at the same level as the solely verbal openness of those children who initiated debates about their lives themselves. The intimacy that such conversations created was replaced by the spatial (though non-contact) intimacy of sharing a point of view and the perspective towards the world that Alena herself initiated. I also had experiences where some children joined us and teased me by jumping on my back or trying to steal a ball I held while I was in conversation with other children. Then, Alena acted as what

I considered to be my guard, she 'watched my back', resuming her former position after the situation was dealt with.

Alena's actions (or their lack) were an example of how bodies were used to establish one's position in a way which was intersubjective and still highly personal. My experiences with her in the situations such as the one described earlier were intensive and yet I could not compare or confront my and her perceptions of our interactions as she did not talk about this. Alena was present at our encounters and at interactions that I initiated: in our conversation about the stories she wished to talk about; in my interactions with other children when she was around and situated her presence within my interactive role as an outreach worker in the field; but also in my passive presence with her in the events we jointly experienced. We did not talk about the meanings we found for the situation or about our emotions – to give such a personal account was something that Alena refused and she usually silenced me if I tried to express mine. Only the pure physical presence and particular bodily acts, such as changes in our positions and nearness, thus defined the dynamics of our relationship. A lot of what mattered actually happened without a single word. While I could explore my perceptions of the contact with Alena, reading and interpreting her attitude to our relation through her acts unaccompanied by verbal exchanges was possible only because of the context of other unsaid moments – such as that she was willing to join me almost all the time we met and her behaviour was usually companionate rather than diffident or hostile.

Often, such an interpretation of bodily acts was possible only in the long-term context of experiences:

> I have met Alena for the first time since December. She noticed me from a distance and walked towards me with a kind of stifled and mischievous smile and hugged me, saying:
> 'Hi Matej, ol' bro'…'
> After a second or two, she pushed me fiercely away and said:
> 'So … want a kick or what?'
> (Extract from fieldnotes, June 2009)

This happened when it had been six months since I last saw Alena, and I was told later that she had become more open and talkative meanwhile. Still, our first meeting after this time was similar to our previous interactions in some ways. Although her initiation of the contact was through a seemingly warm and ardent gesture, Alena still refused to express any emotion or engagement that would be explicit and easily readable. Anyway, by stepping towards me and giving me a hug she expressed recognition and even a certain commitment, although she very explicitly disavowed this by her further actions.

The way that Alena approached me through bodily approximation was similar to how many other children used their bodies to approach bodies of other people when they fancied making a contact (see Lukas and Alica, discussed earlier). These moments included a broad range of practices such as gentle touches or jumps into hugs, but also kicks, pushes or stealing things from pockets in order to attract attention. As Alena's case shows, even the supposed nature of these particular contacts did not necessarily reflect the engagement that children felt towards the other person or the intentions they had with a situation that should follow. Alena's invasion of my personal space was paradoxical and contradictory – she initiated a hug and pushed me firmly away within a few seconds while I remained relatively passive and did not give any impulse for such a change in her behaviour. Her actions signalled her intentions to attract my attention and to begin some kind of interaction – a dialogue, or maybe just a passive spending of time as we had done in the past – it was not clear from the first contact. Using the particular dynamics of proximity through invading personal bodily spaces of other persons, children thus created individual codes of meanings that would explain what particular actions, such as a hug, kick or stroke meant for the recipient. Accordingly, I learned that when I received an unexpected kick from Lukas, he would have probably wish to talk to me, possibly even about some serious issues, but he did not say this by words or any other means that would be considered as appropriate manners. Also, I knew that quite a few children were happy to hug me warmly when we met only to have a chance to examine the content of my pockets. The meaning of particular corporeal acts that invaded one's private bodily space thus emerged only through long-time experience rather than straightforward and easily readable explanations.

The children did not just invade the bodily spaces of other people. They also tended to separate themselves physically from others. Several children avoided the nearness of other children very frequently, while others stayed away only from some persons – particular individuals or certain groups, such as older children, children of the other sex, or ethnic background. In some situations, this effort could be interpreted as an attempt to enhance personal security – if children were in conflict with each other for instance. But this happened also in the case when children had some troubles with the Centre staff. For example, Peter was among many children who tended to stay away from the staff if they had done some mischief, or had not returned borrowed things. On such occasions, children, as if incidentally, moved away from me or my colleagues, or even hid for a while until we left the site. Even the oldest clients of the Centre, well over 20 years, tended to avoid the presence of the Centre staff if they, for instance, owed some money to the Centre.

Bodily practices such as these reinforce the argument that the connections between thoughts and actions can be of different kinds and degrees. While in the previous part of the chapter, I illustrated some examples where the association was very immediate, in situations like that, children's actions were more pre-meditated and their distancing from other people was a part of their tactics, that is, children's ways of finding spaces to avoid unpleasant encounters. The level of reasonability in such actions was diverse – sometimes children pretended they did not see other people while it was clear that they did, at other times distancing was a part of very carefully prepared tactics to avoid trouble or unpleasant encounters.

The practice of distancing was a very important tactic in children's everyday actions, a deliberate but still spontaneous action evolved as a reaction to circumstances not dictated by the children themselves (see de Certeau, 1984). A principle of the Centre was to respect children's preferences about their position with other people, so if they wished not to be in immediate proximity to other persons, we tried to support them in this and to help them to create some space of their own. It was, for instance, very difficult to provide such a substantial personal space in the small rooms of the Club. If children wished to maintain distance from other children, they could either take over sites in the room that made physical access more difficult (such as sitting in a corner) or they had to leave the Club. A consideration of children's tendency to avoid physical proximity with a youth worker was a very frequent theme of staff discussions, and it was an issue reflected in strategies for the actual practice during the contact work with children. Reports of the workers from the field often included statements such as 'We saw XY but they had no interest in talking to us and moved behind the building as we approached ...' or 'I approached the group of girls but they were not in a mood for talking and in a few minutes, one by one, went away and later met together near the trees, so I did not approach them again ...'. Even the physical absence of other bodies in the proximate distance of one's body thus could have a positive meaning about the intersubjective relationship between one another. As illustrated through the few examples discussed earlier, the children distanced themselves from (certain) other people with certain intentions or emotions about these persons. The example of Peter, who avoided the Centre staff when he felt guilty for something, illustrates how juxtapositions of bodies and the active negotiation of this juxtaposition by the children themselves were practical mechanisms through which children used their bodies to negotiate and perform their relationships to others.

Examples of both strategies of negotiating the spatial proximity, that is, invasion and distancing, show that children are not just active initiators of bodily encounters, but also *active recipients* who experience changing settings of the proximity and negotiate or even contest other people's efforts to invade their personal or bodily spaces. Such negotiation is always subjective *and* intersubjective at once – it involves negotiation of encountering others within the intensities of one's bodily spaces and, rejecting or affirming them, it leads to practices through which children deal with these tensions, a topic I unpick in Chapter Eight. These findings further imply three crucial notes.

First, bodies served as mechanisms of connection and disconnection between the children and other people, and they formed an intersubjective frame in which children's individual practices emerged. Psychoanalytic geographies suggest (see particularly Nast and Pile, 1998) that 'the social' is formed not only through cultural ties or separations, but also through physical contact, or the lack of it, between bodies. Yet this is not only a matter of the cultural appropriation and significations of the body and bodily features, but also the tacit positioning of bodies against each other in dynamically shaping everyday spaces (Thomas, 2009). I deliberately abstained from debating bodily features signifying gender or ethnicity, partly because of leaving this topic for Chapter Eleven, but partly to show how the very material presence of children's bodies in relation to other bodies acts as a significant extension to their agency, such as when Alena stood next to me facing the same direction (and used this as a way to establish an ongoing interaction), or when both younger and older children stayed away from the Centre workers when owing money (and thus avoided the pressure of actions that would lead to repaying the debt).

Second, through the process of social connection and disconnection, children's bodies act as the boundaries of their subjectivity (see Sibley, 1995a; Longhurst, 2001), that is, as fluid and permeable limits or diaphragms that open up space for intersubjective encounters, or, on the contrary, prevent them by expulsion or distancing. The boundaries of the body often acted as a surface through which children's practices connected or disconnected – along with a varying degree of conscious contemplations and discursive practices. Examples such as Alena embracing me and pushing me away in turn illustrate the perpetual dynamism of the affective drive to be engaged interlinked with the articulated attitude of protecting her personal boundaries and sovereignty. The boundaries of Alena's body, and how she used it to establish and disrupt spatial proximity and social intimacy, was a key instrument in her social interaction and consequent establishment of her own agency in relation to others.

Finally, the dynamics of children's intersubjectivity were intrinsically spatial and connected to the spatial settings of children's practices in Kopčany. Chapter Five showed that children were subject to frequent encounters in a very limited space of the neighbourhood. The intersubjective contact was often linked to the struggles over the public space in Kopčany – how children sought to find some for themselves or for their friends, or when they expelled others (or were expelled themselves) from particular spaces in the neighbourhood. This is an issue that expands the discussion in Chapter Five, which focused rather on the nature of particular spatial settings and their interests to children or other people in Kopčany. The discussion about proximity suggests that other factors mattered in children's spatial practices in the neighbourhood, particularly their social relationships as they were reflected in children's bodily movements and practices of distancing or engaging with other bodies.

Conclusions

By locating children's practices in their bodies, this chapter emphasises how the immediacy between experience (often in the form of unreflected thought or emotion) and action transcends both abstract imagination and rational meditation, and how the body is the key medium for children's practices in various (socio-spatial) contexts. I worked through Vygotsky's theory of psychosocial development, which argues that children's practices draw from children's recognitions of past experiences in similar contexts to those that they encounter, and that their practices also spontaneously aim to resemble those practices that children remember from past experiences, often tacitly or even unconsciously. This is not a re-inscription of the age-based dichotomy between older and younger children. When experiencing quite unknown contexts, even older children tended to draw from the experience most closely resembling their present encounter and used their bodies as the key medium of their practices. While with increasing experience of the same/similar contexts children also increased their ability to reflect deliberately on these, and to employ words for their actions more than their bodies, an experiential focus thus does not presume that it is automatically the older children who would gain more experience. Instead, complex individual life-trajectories need to be taken into account in order to identify the topographical contours of children's actions.

I also discussed children's experience of their own body and of other people's bodies as a kind of experiential learning with a huge impact on children's everyday actions. This factor was relevant in relation to showing how children did not just replicate discourses and meanings of the body (its normality, potential or cultural signification) they encountered elsewhere – and I noticed that portions of children's formal learning tended to concentrate on the body – but they also formed alternative responses. I drew on writings of Benjamin, Taussig, Katz and Vygotsky, who argue that children's practices do not just resemble their past experiences and recognitions, but they also tend to be produced in alterity to what children find an unsatisfactory experience (often just tacitly). The body was then shown as both a medium and a target of such practices.

Finally, I focused on the spatiality of children's embodied practices in the context of spatialities in the neighbourhood and in relation to the idea of proximity. The body was shown here as a spatial domain of individual practices that delimits the fluid boundary of one's subjectivity, but also as a site of connections and disconnections with other bodies and other human subjects through which social and cultural relationships are performed and subsequently re-established or negotiated. This factor was then discussed in relation to the spatialities of the neighbourhood and the discussions in Chapter Five, emphasising that the spatialities of children's practices presented in that chapter are not affected only by the nature of particular spatial settings in Kopčany, but also by children's spatial embodied practices by which they distance or engage with other people (and their bodies).

In terms of the broader scope of the book as a whole, the chapter signified that in order to understand children's practices, the focus needs to be broadened from children's social positionalities to the role of embodied, pre-cognitive and/or unmediated circumstances of children's actions. From the topographical perspective of exploring differences in children's practices and their formation, the discussion emphasises the need to reflect on the constitution of children's practices in the context of their past experiences and the ways in which children recollect and conceive them. The main implication is the need also to consider carefully children's pasts, both methodologically (thus expanding the scope of ethnography using available paths in the fieldwork) and theoretically (including the temporality of children's experiences, perceptions and conceptions in meditating on how children come to act in specific contexts). But, most importantly, and in relation to the *counter*-topographical element of the research, this chapter implies that children's *individual* histories (through their past experiences) are crucial for understanding children's present practices, and there is a high risk of generalisation by overemphasising similarities in children's current situations along the conceptions of developmental lines.

In Chapter Seven, I draw on these notions of locating the children's practices in the body and space, and I discuss the immediate and more subtle material extensions for children's practices, namely 'things', understood as everyday material objects used by children in their actions.

SEVEN

Things

Today, I was at the 'Boys Group' with a new colleague who suggested that boys could water-paint their faces. It went really well, boys, mostly 10-year-olds and younger, managed to help themselves, so we were just facilitating and making sure there would be no harm. I made some tea that boys mostly spilled while trying to pour it into their cups.

The boys had fun and the place was really wet, when Marcel (6), with yellow lion-features painted on his face by Roman (10) and followed by Samuel (6) and Norbert (7), roared at me and with a jump he made a half-hug half-bite on my leg, that is, my black trousers. As the paint was still wet, I saw a yellow imprint on my thigh and I had to go and wash it immediately. Within a few seconds, along with the fact that we had only 15 minutes left for the activities and the Club had to be cleaned, the mood changed. The boys calmed down, apologised for dirtying my trousers, and hastily helped to clean and dry the Club. At least some did. Samuel was afraid of coming home painted, so he washed his face furiously and after a few minutes he left the Club without helping the others. (Extract from fieldnotes, June 2009)

One of the key themes in Chapter Six was the importance of children's practices being located in their bodies. The story with young boys in the Club suggests that the body is not the only material resource for practices. Here, objects such as face-paint and bowls of water acted as fundamental material extensions to what children did.

Considering that 'our lives are characterised by innumerable encounters with objects' (Woodward, 2007, p.vi) and the constant presence of a vast array of material objects in children's lives, this chapter explores what kind of extensions to children's agency emerge through children's encounters with small mundane objects and how children's practices are affected by the presence of 'things', but also what the processes and practices through which 'things' come to matter in children's lives are with respect to differences or similarities among individual children and groups of children. I use the term *things* in order to illustrate the scope of the chapter that focuses on relatively small material objects that children could 'use' in their everyday actions as opposed to larger material entities that 'surround' them (which could be better labelled as 'environments', built or natural, or 'spaces' – and these are rather the subject of Chapter Five).

Despite the enormous role that things play in children's everyday activities, only relatively little attention has been given by social scientists to the complex and dynamic interfaces between children and things (for example, Kline, 1993; Derevenski, 2000; Barnes and Kehily, 2003). While a conceptual framework of approaching the 'hybrid' (Whatmore, 2002) socio-material spatialities of childhood was articulated some time ago (Horton and Kraftl, 2006b; Woodyer, 2008), there is still a lacuna of empirical work on the still conceptually developing topic concerning children's enchantment with things (Burrell, 2011; Woodyer and Cook, 2011), or the intra-agency of things in the constitution of human subjectivity (Prout, 2011; Kraftl, 2013; Rautio, 2013).

In the story from the Club, face-paint and water were material extensions to children's practices located at a very immediate interface with children's bodies. This chapter draws on arguments that human agency and the presence of material things are inseparable (Latour and Venn, 2002), but also that the former emerges 'through site-specific practices' (Kraftl, 2006, p.488) at the *point of contact* between people and things rather than in people's individual capacities or in the presence of material things alone (Latour, 2005). This moment also incorporates a range of other elements, such as the body, spaces, timings, thoughts, emotions, but also broader and often grounded social relations, such as when Samuel had to clean his face before he went home.

These material dynamics thus also have their sensuous, imaginative and discursive dimensions, besides the physical closeness of bodies and things. In our story, this ranged from Marcel acting as a lion when his face was painted in yellow, through the sense of guilt the boys had when they got paint on my trousers, to the effort they made in order to clean the room after the activity. The scope of this chapter is likewise hybrid – it does not examine things in isolation, either as passive matters or as bearers of meanings. I take inspiration from those perspectives in sociology (Latour, 1987, 2005), philosophy (Haraway, 1991) and geography (Whatmore, 2002) which consider things as 'material-semiotic actors' that have the capacity to impact social actions through hybrid interfaces with embodied human actors and their discursive worlds, as well as with other non-human entities. To suggest that 'things have agency' (Latour, 2005) does not mean that they can act intentionally, but rather that things can potentially affect, trigger or even be conditions for some human actions, whether the things 'act' as practical tools, sources of knowledge or foundations of meanings. The material presence and discursive or imaginative contexts of things accompany each other and they often act on each other, as the case of the boys and the face-paint illustrates.

Such a conceptualisation enables me to think about the complexity of encounters between things, people and other entities, the complexity that underpins children's everyday practices and that also highlights the diversity of impacts that individual things can have on the practices of particular children, often in very immediate contexts:

> I was helping Monika (12) with her mathematics homework and we used chalk to draw figures onto the street pavements. Several older children found this interesting – especially as doing one's homework was an activity that usually took place in private spaces, but also as drawing on pavements with chalk was associated with fun, leisure and mostly with activities of younger children – while the younger ones understood this precisely as the latter, as a fun activity of drawing on the pavement [see Figure 7.1 for a similar activity in the summer]. Therefore, when Maros (5) realised that he was not allowed to 'play' with us, and that what we were doing was not really fun (at least not for him), he stomped on our figures and blurred them, something he often did when he got bored of drawing with chalk. His understanding of how we used chalk – and how we possibly *could* use it – was clearly different from mine and Monika's. Other people expressed yet different associations. Silvia, a young mother from the neighbourhood who was outside with her little daughter, joined us with an interest – not in chalk, nor in the fact that we were drawing on the pavement, but rather in fractions, the theme of the homework, talking about what she remembered about fragments from school. Her 2-year-old daughter, seemingly not knowing what chalk is, was intrigued by the coloured image and she walked around touching the figures drawn on the pavement and stroking them. Finally, Martin (9) stopped nearby seemingly struck (literally with his mouth open) both by the fact that we were doing the homework on the street by writing on the pavement, but also by the

complicatedness of fractions that he had not learned about in the school yet. When Maros tried to wipe our figures again, Martin grabbed him angrily and literally threw him away, yelling at him not to damage our work. Then he came back and further observed our work. (Extract from fieldnotes, January 2009)

Figure 7.1 Children drawing on the pavement with chalk

This story depicts a 'complex presence' (Mol, 2002) of things, environments and people with their individual histories, acquaintances and capacities, and the fundamental differences that chalk as a concrete material object simultaneously made to the actions of those present. I draw on this idea of things as having possibly multiple impacts simultaneously on different persons, while acknowledging Anderson and Tolia-Kelly's argument that 'new materialisms ... afford very different styles of "materialist" theoretical-empirical work' (2004, p.672), so setting a conceptual scope that would be realistic in terms of the chapter's range is necessary. In the first section, I discuss various ways in which children *encounter* things to begin with, drawing the topographic lines of difference between individual children (or groups of children) and the ways in which they come to engage with things. The second section then focuses on the diversity of ways in which things affect children's practices. Here, I relate to previous discussions of children's use of public space in Kopčany and of the immediacy in children's actions given in Chapters Five and Six, and subsequently I draw on Bourdieu's (1984, 1986) idea of different forms of capital as a framework that emphasises the complex role of things in how children develop their agency. Finally, the chapter draws topographical lines of differences and similarities among individual children and groups of children in terms of how their practices were constituted in different ways in relation to material things, and it outlines connections to Chapter Eight, where children's encounters with people as factors affecting their practices are explored.

Modalities of children's encounters with things

Very few children from Kopčany had regular access to money. While a few children used to go shopping and had money from their families so they could afford to buy something for themselves or for someone else, others had at most small amounts that they usually spent straight away on sweets or soft drinks, and most children I met had some money only occasionally. Many children had very few personal belongings and lending things – ranging from books through board games to outdoor equipment such as balls, ropes or skateboards – was a key service of the Centre.

With a relative lack of personal belongings, children spent considerable time and energy on *searching* for things and *creating* or *adjusting* things on their own. The neighbourhood was full of things on the ground, in the bushes, under stairways or near the rubbish containers. While most of the stuff that could be found would be considered as useless trash, many things that children could find in the neighbourhood served at least two functions.

First, children, especially given the lack of financial opportunities, often found ways to utilise even 'the most mundane throwaway bits and pieces' (Kraftl and Horton, 2007, p.1016) that most adults, but perhaps also more affluent children, would find pointless (I use this term from Horton and Kraftl as it refers to their discussion about the often negligible scopes of children's experiences that remain overlooked, or at least understated by adults, as the findings presented in this section support their claim that there is much in children's experiences that remains entrenched within such 'mundane' phenomena). At times this included finding and playing with rather dangerous objects, such as car-battery liquid, glass or cigarette lighters, but often children came up with quite interesting discoveries that helped them in their games, such as old buggies or carts. Utilising things they found included also reshaping them so they could be used in a different way, for example when children constructed a kite from thrown-away carry bags, or used old and rotten pieces of wooden pallets for swings by sticking it through a fence and leaning on a wall with up to ten children fitting in and swinging.

Second, encountering unknown things that had been disposed of allowed children to explore and scrutinise them. They thus often investigated things found on the street by touching, bending, throwing (on the ground to see if they break, or just at each other), spilling (such as car batteries or cleaning liquids and powders) or hiding them and exploring whether they change. One of my first encounters with the results of this attraction of some children was when Maros (5) discovered that when he stamped on aluminium cans, they remained attached to the shoes and made an additional slip sole that give an interesting clinking sound, and he could make rhythmic sequences of it. Especially younger children often explored unknown thrown-away objects just to explore their composition, shape, or how they felt and reacted to manual pressure, while older children tended to be more selective but still experimented with objects in order to create usable tools. Brothers Oliver (11) and Nikolas (7) thus showed me a swing they created from a small pole and seatbelts, while a group of 10-year-old boys used a wide range of things to reinforce a shelter they had created from mud on a nearby building site.

Several reflections come from these stories. First, Barnes and Kehily argue that 'toys are not necessary part of play' (2003, p.38) but their significance has dramatically increased through mass production, marketing, and what has been labelled as the 'commodification of childhood' (McKendrick et al, 2000). To contextualise children's practices in Kopčany in relation to their relative lack of money, I find MacDonald and Marsh's (2005) term 'disconnected youth' interesting, as in this context it implies not just the social disconnections that young people from deprived background experience, but also the material disconnection from everyday objects that more affluent young people can easily access. However, this section shows that children without money were not really 'disconnected' from things; only their ways of 'connection' were different from those of more affluent children and, instead of buying or receiving things from their parents, several children relied more on sharing or finding and reworking them.

Second, Maros's experience with aluminium cans emphasises the significance of acoustic, haptic and other 'touchy-feely' knowledges and interactions through which children engage with everyday objects of their practices (Gallagher, 2011; Procter, 2015). His acts exceeded any conventional and rational associations one would have with aluminium cans as everyday objects and were spurred by his bodily contact with the cans and the following sensuous reception. This echoes Woodyer's call to reconnect the cognitive and non-cognitive aspects of children's experience and to research more profoundly the relationship between 'the intertextual, semiotic culture' (2008, p. 358) of consumer toys and how material objects come to matter for children's embodied subjective experience.

This brings me to further two reflections. Third, then, and in relation to the discussions in Chapter Five, it was the spatial dispersion of children's activities driven by the lack of safe and satisfactory spaces in Kopčany, and by the ongoing contestations over the public spaces with other people there, that made children explore areas where thrown away items could be found. In parallel, it was the relative material deprivation that motivated them to explore and experiment with these objects, and this very motivation was an additional impulse for visiting and exploring unsafe and neglected areas where interesting objects could be found. As Ward noted, 'play is often *at the same time*, training in motor skills and sensory awareness, exercise and excitement, and *warfare* with the adult world' (1978, p.97, second italics added). What the word 'warfare' could refer to with regard to children from Kopčany is the process by which children reclaimed public spaces that were not designed for them, while at the same time they engaged with and reshaped for their own purposes a range of objects that abandoned by adults.

Finally, such spatial practices were crucial also for children's learning. Vygotsky's (1978) idea of the immediacy between thought and action presented in the previous chapter takes place within his theory of play as a cognitive process through which children learn about the world by appropriating it actively, and by engaging with the world through practice rather than through imagination or abstraction. When children found an interesting, even if unknown thing, they often explored it by poking it with sticks, touching it, pouring water on it and even tasting it, rather than making sure what the object was beforehand (for instance by asking someone older). This was my experience with Patrik, a seven-year old boy, whom I met carrying an obscure plastic object, probably found around the bushes:

Patrik: 'Look what I have!'
Matej: 'Wow! What is that?'
Patrik: (*sadly*) 'I don't know …'
(A dialogue extracted from fieldnotes, May 2009)
The dialogue is an illustration of how emotional experiences and learning through practice often preceded the cognitive or rational moments of children's experiences. Patrik happily showed me what he found on the ground but his excitement was disrupted when I made him (unintentionally) realise that he actually did not have any idea what this object was (and nor did I).

Especially in relation to the activities of the Centre, a setting that provided children with raw materials and supervision, *production* of things had its own important place in children's daily practices. Many of activities in the Club had children working on small crafts they could take home such as paper artworks or small items of jewellery (see Figure 7.2). Making things on their own, with resources, tools and instructions provided by the Centre, was a very popular activity, perhaps one of the most popular among children of all ages, both boys and girls. While many things had only a momentary significance and children often left them in the Centre, drawings being the main example, many others were taken away as a gift for their friends or parents. The Centre did not in fact offer organised craft workshops – making things was primarily the children's initiative and they usually also came up with ideas based on what they wanted to work on.

Producing things in the Centre is an example of an activity which was far less intuitive and much more structured through children's social contacts than the practices I have discussed so far. I took part in an event where a group of young boys shaped wax moulds in the Club. This idea came from one of the boys, Michal, after he did something similar in school. He mentioned the idea at one of the previous meetings, saying

Figure 7.2 Children doing craftwork in the Centre

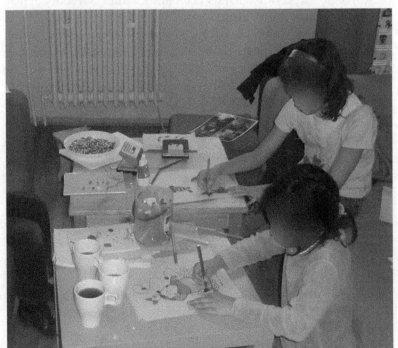

that he did not have enough time in the school to make more of them but he would like to. Michal was not able to produce moulds on his own at home as he did not have sufficient material and equipment. He also expressed his preference to make the moulds together with his friends. Later, we baked honey-cakes before Christmas with the same group, an idea that came from the boys themselves (with about 12 of them taking part) and for which the Centre provided ingredients, equipment and partially also the supervision. However, the boys were able to organise themselves and to share the roles, with older boys helping the younger ones, a level of collaboration usually not seen but at that time motivated by the effort to make the cakes.

Children could also get a little reward (usually a piece of chewing gum) for their participation in the Club activities, such as when they helped with cleaning or for their school work. Several children actually learned to *ask* for things and some did so even if there was no adequate context for which they should receive a reward. With the younger children, this often took the form of rather naive, though very seriously asked, demands such as "Will you give me something?" or just "Give me something" without any additional context, and some children even became angry when they were given a negative answer. Among older children, this practice meant more sophisticated negotiations, where children tended to ask for a reward for particular participation in the activities. The policy of the Centre was to be careful about non-substantiated gifts given to children so a certain sense of responsibility and independence would be nurtured among them, although the Centre possessed a vast store of small toys with a very small value that they had received from a donor. Still, children often negotiated opportunities for easy acquisition of a range of not really desired items, so the Centre had to monitor and negotiate children's willingness to participate in activities of the Centre without the additional motivation of being rewarded for this.

Gregson and Beale show that things can be seen as 'complex, fluid and tangled' spatialities rather than 'bounded, singular containers of materialised meanings' (2004, p.699). Examples of boys baking cakes and producing candles reveal a process where the children had a clear idea about what kind of things they would like to engage with, and this was itself based on their previous experience. This also required them to meet in the Centre, to meet the conditions for coming to the Centre, to collaborate with each other, and to negotiate and agree on what this collaboration would look like. In other words, the boys experienced encounters with the objects they wished to, but only within the premises of certain spatial and collective arrangements.

The second example, of children requesting things, shows how things become actors in social practices through their value and the perception thereof (see Featherstone, 1991), but also through the connections between the value of things and how children valued their own deeds. Even the youngest children began to recognise the position of the Centre as a collective subject that occasionally provided them with things. The policy of being careful about reinforcing the correlation between children's participation and the reward they receive reflected another stage of this experiential learning when children could define their motivation purely from the perspective of a material gain. The Centre was recognised by children of all age groups as a social partner that had the power to give things, and children experimented in this partnership from the earliest age. When they grew older, even broader recognition, not only of the status of the Centre but also of their own status of deprivation could be seen in their expressions, such as when some youth clients joked saying, "Hey, we are *from Kopčany,* we cannot pay for this" when they went to the cinema with the Centre staff, even if they actually had enough money for this.

An important mode of engaging with things in children's lives was *stealing.* In the neighbourhood, a number of young people were on probation or even imprisoned for thieving and things such as metal trash bins or benches often went missing in the past (having been stolen). Even the youngest children became involved in obtaining things illegally. While I tried to stand aside from experiences of children pickpocketing or stealing in shops, the issue of thievery was also common in the everyday running of the Centre, where things were often lost, many of them presumably stolen. This included marker pens or small toys, but also seemingly pointless objects such as miniature pieces of a board game. Stealing a thing was not just a manner of acquiring it, it was often also a moment of collaborative activity if several children were involved, and it sometimes served to get attention, either from the staff or from other children. The story of Marcel and the skipping rope from the previous chapter was an example of how he ceased stealing things, at least from the Centre or me personally, when the relationship between us and his position within the Centre reached a different status. I had similar experiences with Peter's young sister, who, at the beginning of our contact, stole a toy, pretended to return it, stole another one, negotiated about what she did, ran away and brought it back within 20 minutes, mostly in order to be in contact with the Centre staff outside the usual hours. Towards the end of my stay in Kopčany, however, I also saw her, when she thought she was alone in a room of the Club, reaching instinctively for a loosely placed marker pen, but she stopped and decided not to break the rules and the increased trust from the Centre she had at that time. This story suggests that children's lives are often embedded within multiple cultural worlds at the same time, and the simple dichotomy between 'child worlds' and 'adult worlds' is not particularly useful. With Peter's sister, there was the local cultural factor where she, but also her closest social acquaintances, found stealing as acceptable and thieving was locally a relatively common activity, but there were also other cultural aspects, such as her relationship with the Centre based on the mutual trust and respect, that she found more important at that moment. The significance of site-specific moments of encounters between children and things (see the references to Latour [2005] and Kraftl [2006] in this chapter's introduction) can be seen here as referring not only to material practices, but also to broader cultural constitutions of children's worlds.

I have already mentioned that many of the craftworks produced by children in the Club were subsequently given away as gifts. For many children in the neighbourhood, the ownership of things was seemingly not as important as just their temporary possession. With many children – though not all of them – things, often valuable items, were often lost or damaged. Lina (8), for instance, could be seen sometimes in very decent and decorous clothes, while at other times her clothes seemed to be torn or badly sized. However, she did not seem to differentiate between them when she went to the school or when she climbed roofs and trees and searched for things in dust and puddles. Similarly, it often happened that gifts that children received, but also relatively useful or valuable items (such as equipment for school), were damaged or lost within a couple of days, either by the children themselves or by their younger siblings.

While I discuss children's perception of relative financial value more closely in the next section, the focus on children giving things away reveals another aspect through which children were tied to things – their emotional value. The varied individual value of possessions and the significance of the diverse ways they were owned or acquired does not deny the importance of the value of possessions in the lives of children in general. On the contrary, I was impressed by the number of occasions where children actually gave things as a gift. I myself was often offered small gifts, mostly sweets and candies, but the most revealing context of gift-giving was when children prepared presents for their parents (see Figure 7.3). A range of products, from drawings, through bakery, to small items of jewellery were prepared very carefully and with explicit intentions to give them. When, after four months in the field, I told children that I would be away for the next three months, Martin, a 9-year old boy, played out a scene showing how they would not allow me to leave and eventually made me promise that I would bring him a small red-heart locket as a present that he could give to his mother. To my surprise, he indeed did not forget about this and reminded me at our very first meeting three months later in April, so I had to spend next the few days searching for such a locket.

Figure 7.3 Examples of things produced by children in the Centre

In the discussion of children's bodily acts from the previous chapter, I showed how children often struggled to express their feelings or attitudes in words and their actions often followed their thoughts or feelings without focused rational mediations. The importance of gifting as a material practice embedded within the local and symbolic emotional value of material objects (Rose, 2000, 2003; Tolia-Kelly, 2004a, 2004b) and in social relations that underpin the process of gifting (Gregson et al, 2002a; Silk, 2004; Isin and Uestuendag, 2008) adds to this argument and shows another example where materiality supplements children's practices in moments where cognitive actions become insufficient. Martin was a child whom I rarely experienced talking about how he felt towards other people, but his request for a gift to his mother, or the number of times he prepared gifts for her in the Centre (cakes, picture), illustrated his feelings towards his mother and how he 'practised' the emotional ties by expressing his feelings through giving a gift. A thing was thus a material mediator of Martin's social relationships and emotional ties that he otherwise did not reflect on through words or other practices.

In summary, several modes of circulation in which material things came to be present in the everyday lives of children from the neighbourhood acted in diverse ways as extensions to children's agency. Examples of buying, searching for, adjusting, producing, asking for, stealing, maintaining and giving things introduced a diverse and complex (and incomplete) register of social ties, spatial networks and located practices that children experienced, and which link the analysis to other socio-spatial extensions of agency. Having introduced the mobile nature of these associations, the next section will focus directly on the impact of engaging with things for children's agency.

Things and the formation of children's practices

During my fieldwork, a small group of young boys (the youngest was just 9 years old) from the neighbourhood were arrested and convicted of a series of robberies where young children had been assaulted and had their mobile phones taken. The police later gave a release saying that the boys used the stolen telephones only for playing games, something that was also confirmed to me by one of the boys.

This information, and the fact that the boys did not try to sell the telephones (and they did not steal for the purpose of selling the stolen telephones) or at least use them for calling, is an illustration of how children usually placed emphasis on using things to meet their immediate desires or needs rather than on their relative value in potential commodity markets. Using Marxian vocabulary, it can be said that the use value of things as the capacity of objects to be utilised for satisfying one's immediate needs was more significant in children's understanding of, and engagement with, things than their exchange value, that is, the relative significance of an object expressed by its relative value in comparison with other objects if they are to be exchanged. This finding is not surprising – it fits with the suggestions from Chapter Five about the importance of the use value of public spaces for children, which in Kopčany has its roots in the lack of adequate spatial opportunities for children's activities. Even more importantly, exchange value is a concept which is intrinsically dependent on the context of one's social networking and it cannot be contained within one's individual encounters with an object or within the actual use of an object. In Chapter Six, I argued that the immediacy between children's thoughts and actions becomes curtailed through the social experiences that children have of particular contexts. In a similar way, the experience of commodity market relationships, including plain exchanges with friends or neighbours, was largely absent among the children, and the reason for this was not just their age but also the level of their material deprivation. While it is usually the monetary exchange value of commodities that determines the value of one's assets in social relations, the economic role of things for children from Kopčany lay more in how they could be of use for immediate actions. The boys played games on the stolen phones because that was the most contiguous experience they had with phones, rather than one of buying or selling phones for appropriate financial amounts. Likewise, an old tracksuit might have been more appropriate clothing for Lina when she climbed trees or jumped over puddles, but she still wore an elegant and probably much more expensive skirt and blouse, one of the very few that she owned. It was the use value of these clothes – where a loose short skirt was as comfortable for climbing the trees as some old trousers – that meant that Lina wore fancy clothes for an activity where these could be expected to get damaged.

This does not mean that the level of comfort for climbing trees was the only value of the skirt for Lina. She liked the skirt also for aesthetic reasons and she was proud of it. This is an example of how the relevance of things for children was often based also on their symbolic value. One day, I met Hugo (9) with a huge glittery trinket on his neck with a sign '50Cen'. He made clear that he would prefer to talk to me alone and then asked me whether the sign was alright. I had to explain that the spelling was wrong (50 Cent is a US rapper) and the trinket was probably fake. Hugo seemed to be aghast and eventually put the whole trinket aside. I found it interesting that it was particularly Hugo who came with a really huge accessory which referred to a figure of a dominant and powerful male. From what I knew of Hugo, he rather lacked self-esteem while being confronted with the image of his uncle, a successful person who was one of his closest relatives.

The huge and visible sign of the 'gangster' fashion on Hugo's chest can be read as a material expression of Hugo's articulation of his desired social status. Bourdieu (1984) emphasises how the notion of taste indeed can mark a 'cultural distinction' and is one of the signifiers of social position of a person. While Bourdieu's analysis penetrates much broader segments of the society, the implications of his findings can also be applied to understanding children's practices in Kopčany, particularly those about how one's position in a relatively integrated social setting (or the aspiration to achieve a position) tends to determine one's inclinations and interests. Hugo's example thus illustrates how children's personal styles (including children styling their bodies, as discussed in the previous chapter) were embedded in their everyday practices, not just through bodily acts but also through affiliation with – or even dissociation from – material objects (such as when Hugo took the trinket but then threw it away when he found it to be a fake). The things (in the case of Hugo, a trinket) mattered for how the children presented themselves within a complex network of emotions (such as pride and consequently shame, anger and dissatisfaction), discourses and imaginations (about independence and strength), embodiment (by marking and presenting one's body) and daily practices (of wearing the trinket). The element of emulation, the projective attempt to impress others or potentially become someone else himself, as read through Bourdieu's concept of taste, can be a reference to children's social position, as well as a means of changing it.

This discussion leads to another of Bourdieu's concepts, namely that of symbolic capital (Bourdieu, 1984). For Bourdieu, capital in general is the set of assets that, in certain social relationships and systems of exchange, promotes social mobility and increases one's power, social status or other dispositions (see Bourdieu, 1986). Capital is not identical with agency but it has direct implications for the latter. Capital is always situated in, and contingent upon, particular social settings, but it is also a form of relational social empowerment that enables one to act and, as such, it is an extension of agency. Where the use value of objects referred to things as direct material utilities enabling children's practices, things as sources of capital enable children to act (or prevent them from acting) because of the effect they have on their social settings, essential or at least impactful for their practices.

Within such a context, symbolic capital refers to resources based on prestige and emblematic honour. Hugo's trinket could be an example of the source of symbolic capital, objectified within a representation of power associated with the popular artist, and thus a means for getting respect or recognition. While things could be expressions of taste (as a mark of social distinction) and thus develop children's capital through their intentional acts, there were also occasions when things built children's symbolic capital in a different way from what the children wished but also against children's will, creating a negative symbolic capital, echoing Eco's (1979) semiotic distinction between the 'model' and the 'empirical' reader, for whom the expected reception of symbols differs from that actually evolving once the audience encounters them. Robert (10) was a boy who seemed to have several fierce conflicts in the neighbourhood. While he owned some relatively valuable things – such as electronic games or CDs – he had had some experiences of negative reactions from other children, partly as they felt Robert was boasting about these. In his case, possession of material things led often to rejection by other children since he was seen as conceited. He then often decided to conceal his belongings. Things and their associations with particular people thus received local cultural meanings, often as a result of children's broader relationships or usual practices, and these could be negative and exclusionary as well as positive and encompassing.

The last example also illustrates that things were important in building or disconnecting social ties among the children. Things thus served as a means of developing children's social capital in terms of what Bourdieu calls 'the aggregate of the actual or potential resources which are linked to possession of a durable network of more or less institutionalised relationships of mutual acquaintance or recognition' (1986, p.248). Illustrations of how children's social capital is formed by material things can be found throughout the whole book. In the previous section I mentioned how Peter's sister aimed to get attention by stealing and then returning several things from the Centre. This is an example of social capital that is very instant and elusive, but taking the things enabled her to be in the Club as the Centre staff would allow her in so as to return the things. Examples of more substantive and steady relations and networks boosted by things would be football games, where having a ball was an asset that could induct boys into the networks of other children in the neighbourhood (see the previous chapter and Chapter Ten), or how engagement with other family members or even non-relatives was established when children gave them gifts, often made by themselves (see the previous section and Chapter Nine). In all three examples, things were media for establishing and maintaining social contacts through which children's capacity to act increased (by Peter's sister having contact with and recognition of the Centre workers, by the boys establishing new friendships, or by the children enacting relationships within their families).

Things had also an additional impact on children's agency in a way that was intrinsically individual but not immediate. For the boys who had a passion in football, having a ball was not just the means of developing social relations, but also an opportunity to develop their individual football skills. Bourdieu (1984) writes about cultural capital, a set of skills and abilities that an individual has in relation to others that can be used as assets in social interaction. Bourdieu (1986) also emphasises that one of the forms that cultural capital can take is 'objectification', that is, enactment of one's cultural capital through material objects that one owns or commands. The ability to perform because of one's personal abilities thus can be based on one's disposition of opportune tools. As a similar example, mobile phones served for many children not just as means of communication (or for games) but also for enhancing their individual abilities (see Holloway and Valentine, 2003). They enabled children to acquire more information or knowledge through being in contact with others – even very simple information, such as knowing where one is or when one will be back at home – but children more often used them for taking photos or listening to music. This could be seen especially among the older children, who stored a diverse range of information in their mobile phones, such as songs, short texts or pictures, shared them with their friends and discussed them, often approaching the Centre staff for explanations of the details of a song or idea they had in their phones. Children also borrowed things from the Centre, including games, books but also stationery items such as glue or scissors when they needed these for their homework or other activities. A lot of these experiences came from the contexts that children found through their involvement in institutional settings, but even this had effects on how they learned to recognise the cultural capital of things and the impact this could have on their activities.

While the immediate use value, often associated with intuitive exploration of everyday objects, was the main domain of how things affected children's agency, other forms of impact became more important, along with particular experiences, such as with different social settings or orderings or new physical activities. The symbolic capital that things established for the children was perhaps the next most imperative, and even the youngest children often worked with this, including mundane practices such as the choice of the colour of chewing gum that they received in the Centre. Through the symbolic capital that children developed because of the things they owned, social relationships were often unfolding and enabled the children to act in new ways (a theme that is developed further in the following chapters). Of the very least significance for children were those forms of impact that stemmed from more complex social and cultural patterns such as cultural capital (where things served children to develop skills they could use in particular social settings, while the experience of these settings was new for them) or the exchange value of things (a recognition of which came from children's experiences of commodity exchange that were for many children rather negligible, not least because of their material deprivation).

Conclusions

The very particularities of how children encountered material objects indicate differences in what children's encounters with things were even possible in Kopčany in relation to underlying factors such as children's material background, their everyday mobilities and spatial awareness in the neighbourhood, but also their moral strategies (such as whether to steal things or not). This discussion not only outlined the topographies of children's practices in relation to things and to children's aforementioned circumstances, it also showed that while children's encounters with things can be dependent on children's social connections, these social relationships can be themselves affected by children's possession, or at least disposition, of various material objects. Through things, children often built their social or symbolic capital, or developed their cultural and economic capital so their relative social position could have been adjusted. Hence, things did not only serve as an extension to children's agency, but through practices stemming from these extensions, children also affected their other circumstances and consequently reshaped their agency.

The particular modality of impact that things have over children's agency proved to depend largely on children's experiences with different contexts, a statement I link to the discussions in Chapter Six, where similar arguments were given for the discussion of the role of the body. I suggest that the more intuitive and immediate forms of capital, such as the use value of things or symbolic capital, were more significant for how children perceived and understood things than those forms that depended on highly intentional arrangements, such as the patterns of exchange value or cultural capital. The need to draw on the latter forms of impact that things have, but also the capacity to understand how they can be formed in an encounter with things, emerged with children's expanded social experiences and particularly with more standardised schemes of economic or cultural values that children increasingly encountered. While this pattern of difference can be related to children's age, there are other factors that impact the level of children's experiences, including their social and spatial mobility, affluence, range of social contacts and others. Together they outline complex topographies of children's practices in relation to everyday material objects as well as highlight the critical element of (material) inequalities being important factors in the formation of children's agency.

While people were present in the three empirical chapters so far as implicit factors in the formation of children's practices in relation to things, bodies and spaces, I have not paid any explicit attention to the specific differences that the presence of other people made. Before discussing more grounded children's relations, such as in the family, with friends or in formal institutions, Chapter Eight will focus on the immediate encounters of children with other people in the neighbourhood and their impact on their actions.

EIGHT

Everyday social encounters and circumscribed routines

I began Chapter Five by describing the first minutes of my first street work shift in Kopčany. I discussed this with a focus on spatial configurations of children's practices while the role that other people had in children's experience there was only implicit. And while various people appeared in Chapters Six and Seven, I have not really attended to the consequences of children's social ties for their practices. This chapter builds a link between discussions of spaces, things and bodies, and children's social lives. Simply put, I am interested here in how children's practices are related to their encounters with other people in Kopčany and in commencing the discussion about the role of other people in how children organise their activities in time and space. On a more conceptual basis, I explore these encounters and practices as relational performances of children's relationships to other people in particular spaces and times. While more grounded social relations of children are analysed in Chapters Nine, Ten and Eleven, it is the moment of their performative expression in children's activities which is discussed here as a source of understanding how the relational effects of other people on children's practices emerge. My rationale is linked to Law's argument that 'entities achieve their forms as a consequence of the relations in which they are located. But this means ... that they are [also] *performed* in, by, and through those relations' (Law, 1999, p.4).

Everyday encounters are here considered as specific performances of children's relations in and through which children come to act on a daily basis. Although the starting point of the analysis is hence located within the 'surfaces' of children's daily lives and not in their 'depths' (Laurier and Philo, 2004), following the 'particular moments or events in what [children] do and think' (Crouch, 2003, p.1945) – and many argue that these are precisely the moments where and when human subjectivities unfold (Dewsbury, 2000; Latham, 2003) – I am interested in identifying the ways and types of connections in which immediate encounters relate to children's broader circumstances, including larger social, cultural, economic or political formations. As Latham argues:

> The everyday should not be viewed as a world apart from more rationally grounded realms of social action such as 'the state', 'the economic', 'the political', or whatever. Rather, what needs to be recognised is how all elements of social life, all institutions, all forms of practice are in fact tied together with the work of getting on from day-to-day. (Latham, 2003, p.1998)

It is at the interface of the two – the moments of practice in an encounter with others (in a particular spatial and temporal setting), and the overarching relationships, routines or schemes, that is, in the '*circumscribed* everyday geographies, limited by an array of social and physical constraints' (Bondi, 2005c, p.5, italics added) that the empirical core of the chapter is located. However, this highlights the importance of children's actions as *affecting* their everyday circumstances and this aspect is also considered within the chapter. In parallel with Laurier's view, I aim to understand moments of children's practices as 'a setting reflexively tied to unfolding action, or equally [as] lines of action tied reflexively to an unfolding setting' (2001, p.499), considering children as reshaping the circumstances in which their actions happen.

Thematically, the chapter focuses on two overlapping but distinctive themes. The first section discusses children's 'geographies of encounter' (Valentine, 2008). I am interested in what effects children's familiarity with the people they meet has on their practices. Drawing on Simmel's (1950a) figure of the 'stranger', I re-emphasise the role of children's previous experiences in their practices and discuss the importance of 'low-level sociability' (Valentine, 2008) in children's everyday encounters. Then I target connections between the social contexts and constraints of children's encounters and the way they are situated within spatial and temporal settings. The focus is here placed on what ethnomethodologists call 'accountability' of practices (Garfinkel, 1967), on the ways that a sense of the immediate experience is important for the ways in which people act. I discuss the importance of routine and circumscribed events in children's lives and the ways in which they submit to these circumstances, evade, reinforce or challenge them. The second section explores ideas of tactics, submission and transgression in order to illustrate different modalities of intentionality in children's actions in relation to sedimented or, on the contrary, dynamically changing conditions in which their actions in the neighbourhood evolve. The end of the chapter situates the findings within the broader topographical analysis of children's practices and draws links to the discussions of children's most important social relationships in Kopčany that are provided in Chapters Nine and Ten.

Encounters with strangers and the role of children's experiences

> A few days before Christmas Eve, the Centre received a pile of books from a local charity within a project where people could buy a gift in local bookstores that would be given to children from a disadvantaged background. The distribution was usually problematic as the Centre did not know surnames of all children, even if they did, they did not know their addresses, and even if these were known, there was still the problem of access – all houses were secured by electro-chips as were often the staircases and elevators.
>
> At the beginning of our journey, I and a colleague met Simon (14), who offered us his company and to guide us. Simon proved to be invaluable. He knew everyone; he knew where they lived – even the particular flats. He knew which elevators were out of order and although some hallways were entirely dark, he guided us confidently to the right doors.
>
> What I found interesting was that it was particularly Simon who had such profound knowledge of the locals, including those kids that I expected he hardly knew at all. Simon had moved to the neighbourhood three years before and not so long ago – just about a year and something – he struggled heavily to integrate with other children, hardly making any new friends and remaining a loner. Now, Simon seemed to be on perfectly fine and confident terms with the local people and he had an expert knowledge about them. (Extract from fieldnotes, December 2009)

My story with Simon shows Kopčany as a locality that differed from what I knew to be the popular image of Petržalka, that is, a dense and anonymous area where people do not know their neighbours and everyone lives their isolated and alienated lives. Also, the way the Centre workers depicted the neighbourhood initially sounded more like a portrait of a close-knit rural community, with dwellers knowing each other very well, any news spreading around the neighbourhood quite quickly, and with just a handful of strangers visiting the neighbourhood that others would not know about.

It is precisely this idea of strangers appearing in the neighbourhood that will be central to my discussion of children's practices in their everyday encounters with people:

> During a shift after Christmas, I had a walk around the neighbourhood with a colleague. Three girls aged between 11 and 13 joined us for a while, when a car stopped nearby and another colleague came out, along with her fiancé. She hastily went to take something from the office while her fiancé stayed nearby. After a minute of silence, Marta (13), turning her back to the man asked quietly: 'Who is he?', and my colleague replied: 'Well, ask him.' Marta hesitated, and then, whispering, asked us again: 'Is he a new one [that is, a new Centre worker]?' The colleague replied with a smile: 'No, he's [colleague's] old one [a phrase for one's partner].'
> (Extract from fieldnotes, December 2008)

As we gave her no hint, Marta's question showed what she found to be the most probable explanation of why a man of an age similar to other Centre workers (most were between their middle and late 20s) would be on the streets of Kopčany in the company of another Centre worker during their street work shift. Reactions like this were not unusual and other children would have probably expected the same. As the staff members for some activities often changed, and also the one-off activities organised in the neighbourhood were often supported by outsiders, the presence of unfamiliar people in the Centre could signal that their involvement might matter for the children – this was possibly a new person affiliated with the Centre who would work with them.

Children's approaches to unfamiliar people who visited the Centre were very similar to children's routine attitudes to the Centre staff. If they had identified a new person through their affiliation with the Centre, they expected them to engage in ways similar to those of the staff – so children wanted to chat about their recent achievements, younger siblings, news in the neighbourhood, wanted to play football or just stroll around. The ability of the 'strangers' to meet the roles that the children had assigned them determined how 'strange' they would remain. For instance, a group of volunteers from a software company visited the neighbourhood to spend an afternoon playing with the children during a charitable project organised by a local foundation. Eight volunteers along with three Centre members were with children for a couple of hours and their programme was very similar to ordinary events of the Centre's shifts. During the afternoon, two younger men from the group struggled to find their role with the children and towards the end of the afternoon they just stood by and watched the others. While their colleagues engaged in a wider range of activities and were flexible about their roles with children – they talked to them, played different sports such as badminton or dodge-ball, jumped over the rope, or had a walk with them, still respecting and following children's preferences – these two volunteers played football at the beginning, but after the children lost their interest, they did not manage to engage in another activity. Their colleagues were not really initiating activities themselves – children decided what to do, mostly following the activities they were used to from their contacts with the Centre. Rather than being resourceful on their own, these other volunteers were just better noticing and addressing children's signals while the two young men engaged initially in the activity they were familiar with and comfortable in (football), but they did not cope well with children's changing preferences afterwards. As they themselves admitted, they had become rather nervous and moved outside the flows of interactions and they thought that the children had probably felt this and eventually did not seek the men's presence at all.

These two stories suggest that, for the children, the fact that they knew exactly who the people next to them were was often not as important as whether their presence could be accounted for. For example, workers from the hostel generally did not interact with other dwellers in Kopčany and the children knew very few of them personally. However, they could be easily identified – they usually wore overalls, had a different accent (often coming from other regions), walked in groups as they went to and from their work-shifts. Although their contact with the children was minimal and the children thus did not know them as individuals, they did not interrupt the routine of children's everyday encounters. As Simon said:

> 'They're [workers] ok. They come back from work, do the shopping, go to the pub for a beer. They say hi when you greet them and in the summer they sit at their balconies and watch the neighbourhood. We do not mix much.'

For the children, the workers became a part of the place, although a distinctive one from the children themselves, and, apart from a few exceptions with whom children had closer contact, they were present as noticeable figures rather than as specific persons. Although very few had any individual relations with the children, they were not strangers any more. Children did not raise their eyes when they recognised them, they did not observe them curiously, and they did not ask the Centre staff or other children who they might be – as they did with other strangers. Using Creswell's (1996) phrase, the workers were 'in place' for children from the neighbourhood, they had a rank within the children's sense of the neighbourhood.

The workers' presence in Kopčany was just one of the major patterns through which the children recognised the presence of other people. In Kopčany, a locality with only few visitors coming from outside, other similarly recognisable groups for the children were their peers, parents and other adult dwellers of the neighbourhood, or the gatekeepers and security guards of the buildings. Occasionally, people such as police officers or taxi drivers came to Kopčany. For all of them, the children had some expectations about who they were and what they were about to do in Kopčany. Children usually stayed at a reasonable distance from the police and observed what the reason for their visit in the neighbourhood might be. With taxi drivers, the children were often curious as to who might have called them, and they even remembered some of those who used to drive to the neighbourhood frequently. A difference was when really 'new' people arrived – whose presence in the neighbourhood could not be explained through the patterns of meaning that children were familiar with. In such cases, children suggested explanations linked to what was familiar for them.

Simmel argues that the figure of the stranger can be seen as a 'specific form of interaction ... an element of the group itself ... both being outside it and confronting it' (1950a, p.403). The figures of strangers from the stories (the colleague's fiancé, volunteers from the software company and workers from the hostel) provoked an interaction with children through confronting their ideas about people's presence in Kopčany. Even if the children did not know these people, they placed them within their sense of the social group that other dwellers in Kopčany, as well as their regular visitors (such as the Centre workers) formed. The fact that Kopčany existed as a relatively closed and transparent community (in terms of people knowing a lot about others) meant that children tended to identify most of the 'strangers' that passed by in this way. Paraphrasing Simmel's words, even if these 'strangers' were outside the social group in Kopčany, for the children it was more convenient to classify them as figures from within the group, at least until other explanations of their presence could be found.

Parr suggests that responses to difference can also bring an 'opening up of encounters' (2008, p.19) with others and she illustrates how 'spatial proximity weakens social distance between self and other' (2008, p.19, quoting Wilton, 1998, p.178). In the accounts from Kopčany, the active role of children as subjects representing the dwelling group in the neighbourhood is emphasised with a particular focus on the practices of reflection on what is known and present in the community routine and what confronts it from the outside. While the children searched for explanations for the unusual proximity of strangers through possible associations with the Centre or with the very general patterns of presence in the neighbourhood, there were also cases where children's sources of interpretation were more individual. Simon, for example, used to mention his concerns about and fear of the people who visited the harm-reduction centre for drug users that was also situated in the neighbourhood. Although even the staff of the harm-reduction centre had no knowledge of any troubles and conflicts that their clients, the vast majority coming from outside the neighbourhood, might engage in in Kopčany, Simon said that he found the visitors dangerous and he was afraid of the needles he said they were leaving around. In a different story, Nina (9) told a Centre worker about some bad experience with an exhibitionist near the neighbourhood and how this made her scared of unknown males who wandered around Kopčany. Children also assigned specific meanings to other people on the basis on their ethnicity, age or gender, such as when I, as one of very few male Centre workers for a long period, was repeatedly asked by the children whether I was a boyfriend of any colleagues, so as to explain my presence.

These examples relate back to the role of children's experiences for the shaping of their practices in encounters with other people. Experience with the Community Centre workers in Kopčany was relatively widespread, even among those children who did not engage with the Centre much. In a similar vein, most children accepted workers from the hostel – if they could be clearly identified as such – as a normal presence in the area that had very little relevance for them. However, particular experiences of children such as Simon or Nina made a difference for how strangers would be recognised individually and the source of these experiences was hidden in children's personal histories.

Some common axes that made a difference in children's recognition of strangers could be identified; age is one example. When I joined the Centre, I developed relations with younger children quite quickly, getting to hear about their lives, desires, or plans of some already during my first shift. Children understood me as a member of the Centre and gave me their trust, even before knowing me as a person. On the other hand, I did not have the same experiences with older clients, especially with those over 15. In my first shift, a colleague who was with a group of 15–20-year old boys called me over to join them so she could introduce us. Even though, as I was told later, the boys were interested in me and were asking about me before I joined them, one of the boys literally ran away and another two detached themselves from the group before I had walked the short distance between us. Even then, the conversation in the group mostly avoided me and the boys concentrated on my colleagues. This was a relatively usual experience with older children and young people as confirmed by other Centre workers. While the older children could develop even closer and more intensive relationships with Centre workers, usually it took a long time and the relationship often worked only with some of the workers, while the younger children were ready to open up to the majority of the staff.

In my conversations with young people from the neighbourhood, the issue of trust and of their expectations often arose in relation to the theme of relationships. Most of the young people mentioned a number of negative experiences of contact with other people – from frustrations in their families, through disappointments in their relationships with friends or various professionals, to experiences of harm or threats by total strangers. Even as a member of the Centre staff, I had to present my individual qualities (Moser, 2008) that would persuade them to consent to a closer relationship between us.

An interpretation of this difference between the younger and older children in relation to the comparative lack of social encounters (long-term as well as momentary) that can be anchored in most experiences from the field can be again informed by Simmel's sociology of difference. Simmel (1950b) argues that 'hiding from others', that is, not opening oneself to others, is a way of negotiating the too-diverse and too-hectic nature of everyday encounters with difference. Even if the context of Simmel's work relates to modern metropolitan life, the range of difference in the presence of new people that the older young people from Kopčany experienced in comparison to younger children mirrors the structural difference Simmel's argument comes from. Detachment and social distancing can be interpreted as a mechanism of coping with the amount of pressure resulting from the everyday social interactions with a range of people that bear potential risk in relation to individual past experiences and that are too non-transparent and confusing to make the opening of one's self safe. In the case of my fieldwork, such a mechanism would explain the difference between the older children, whose often troubled experiences were more intense and/or frequent, while most of the younger children were still spared to a greater degree issues such as violence, health concerns, crime, financial troubles or addictions. Using Simmel's framework, to open up to a stranger would thus mean a lesser risk for the younger children than for the young people from the neighbourhood, who were more aware of their vulnerability if they opened themselves to someone unknown, as based on their previous experiences.

The everyday encounters of children with other people were affected not only by how the spaces of their practices were populated by others, but also by how children themselves thought about the processes of social ordering and how they tried to make sense of the presence of other people (see Lee, 2001). Various commentators have labelled everyday encounters in shared spaces as the field of 'living with others' (Laurier and Philo, 2006, p.193), 'a being together of strangers' (Young, 1990, p.240), 'throwntogetherness' (Massey, 2005, p.181) or living with difference (Valentine, 2008) that is central to how shared social spaces can be politically and culturally imagined and shaped. For children from Kopčany, encounters with unknown people were shaped by their experiences, which, in turn (as I argued in Chapter Five), were greatly fashioned by their activities in the neighbourhood. There is a strong spatial factor in this process of understanding – the sense that what the children made of strangers' presence was linked to the fact that their encounters happened in a neighbourhood where the social actors came from a relatively closed community. This on the one hand opens an interesting question about children's encounters outside Kopčany that this book cannot answer. The finding that children's experiences from Kopčany are crucial for their understanding of the unknown in their social lives is itself still important though, in relation to the social potential of children in the future, especially in relation to arguments that 'low-level sociability' (Valentine, 2008a, p.324), that is, the mundane everyday interactions between strangers and semi-strangers underpinned by how they mutually recognise each other, can be absolutely pivotal for children's learning to live with difference and with the unknown in everyday social interactions, either formal or passing (Laurier et al, 2002; Amin, 2006; Bannister et al, 2006). This argument may have the following implications for counter-topographies of children's agency in Kopčany: children tended to form explanations about the people they met and these were based on their previous experiences. For children from Kopčany, these experiences mostly came from their lives in the neighbourhood and, while some were relatively positive, the older children especially often accumulated negative experiences with friends, neighbours, families but also with unknown people, so a negative attitude was widespread was widespread in the neighbourhood. This, in turn, opens up the question of what is the impact of children's individual experiences on their future lives, a theme that I will revisit in Chapter Eleven.

I will now follow the discussion of children's everyday encounters by focusing on how factors beyond the familiarity with other people mattered for children's practices. Key themes that will be discussed are the spatialities and temporalities of these meetings, and they will be developed through the ideas of routine and recognition in children's practices.

Routine, transgression and the focal points of practices

> As the holidays started, the number of children on the street in early afternoons was lower. Those few I met could thus receive more time and attention. Lina (8) suggested having a walk at the outskirts of the neighbourhood and climbing on trees there. She did very well while I was making sure she would not fall down, and I saw that this might be an activity that she would flourish in. As there were still just few children outside and they were mostly busy on their own, I suggested taking a rope and climbing with it.
>
> We spent almost an hour coming up with new challenges for Lina. Meanwhile, some other children joined us, partly being interested in climbing, but many of them drawing me away with them. I could not leave Lina on her own climbing the trees with the rope so I suggested it was time to have a rest. Lina refused and I did not feel that the argument that I should be also with other children would help. Eventually, I suggested that in my next shift, three days later, I would take the rope again and would come with some 'exciting' ideas about the things we can do on trees. Lina hesitated, but then checked the agreement (when and where), turned on her heel and left. (Extract from fieldnotes, July 2009)

My story with Lina was in some ways exceptional. The children only rarely agreed to a meeting at a certain time and place, especially if it was a few days in advance. Arranging a meeting was usually hopelessly uncertain. Children forgot about our appointments, gave me afterwards reasons why they could not come or came at different times or even on different days. Younger children did not fully understand clocks and dates, but whatever the reason was with the older ones, I had the same troubles arranging a meeting with them. Work in the Community

Centre was thus based mostly on incidental occurrences and the staff could rely only a little on pre-arranged encounters with children.

I met Lina on the day of our meeting. I was not sure whether she realised it was the time, but she was outside the lodging house when I came and she immediately recollected our arrangements about the rope and checked if we would go climbing. In other words, our encounter was marked by Lina's explicit care and recognition of it. She recollected our previous agreement and she cared about the upcoming encounter happening in the way she wished and how we had agreed about it. Even if she had indeed forgotten that it was the time of my shift, she had not forgotten about the meeting in general, and she expected the awaited encounter with me to take the form of climbing up trees.

Lina approached me because she had expected me to come (even if she was not aware that it would happen at that time) and she had made me promise her this meeting. Latham argues that activity is 'central to the self's ability to recognise and care about the places it inhabits and the people encountered within those places' (1999, p.161), and Lina's interest in climbing trees (as one of her most favourite activities in the neighbourhood) was the factor that inspired her actions – insisting on me being on the street as quickly as possible with a rope and requiring my attention to be given entirely to her for the duration of the shift, as I had promised at our previous meeting.

Within the context of street work in Kopčany, this kind of children's enthusiasm and planning was mostly linked to only certain types of encounters with the workers. Only rarely did I meet such enthusiasm for meetings outside, where the attractiveness of the place and activities were less than in the Club. Here, to be in the premises and to have the privilege of using the equipment of the Club, but also the more concentrated attention from the workers (who would not leave children alone in the Club) made children care more about just being there. One day, Mario (8) who was usually very keen to spend as much time in the Club as possible, knocked on the door and asked if he could borrow a book from the Centre's library. I allowed him in and let him choose from the books on the shelves. There were not many, but Mario spent a long time with each, eventually placing them back. When he had already leafed through the books he had previously seen and I felt that he wanted to be in the Club rather than really being interested in books (and he had not brought his glasses without which he could barely read the books), I insisted that he hurried up and as it was quite late and I had to go home. Mario asked what time it was and after I told him, he cried "I must see *Rex*" and ran away from the Club. *Rex* was Mario's favourite TV series and at that moment the importance of watching the show was even more pertinent than his desire to be in the Club (or to borrow a book).

In Mario's but also in Lina's case, an interesting way of recognising the temporal ordering and the care about certain types of experiences can be seen. Although neither Lina nor Mario had a clear sense about time (they struggled to understand clocks and dates), they recognised the daily routine through other means. They were aware of some landmarks on which this was focused, such as "Thursday when we would go out with a rope" or "5.30 when *Rex* starts". They assessed their routine experiences in terms of their significance, and they were still able to link them to other associations. For Lina, the connection was not so much with Thursday coming as the day of our activity – she associated the forthcoming event rather with my current presence in the neighbourhood. For Mario, knowing what time it was did not mean much in itself, but he knew that the show started at certain time. If he was in general told what time it was, this did not say much to him, but there were some specific associations – such as that to wait for 'an hour' before the Club was open was quite a long time and that he could go and do something else meanwhile, but not so much if the time was '15 minutes'. The information about time was often given to children in this way by the Centre workers – the numeral information accompanied by an explanation of what it meant for them in terms of their activities.

Mario's recognition of his present temporal contexts determined his action in space (leaving the Centre and going back home). Stories like this suggest the existence of certain organisation of children's practices in time and space in regard to how they recognised them. On the one hand, their recognition of temporality and spatiality was partial and related to only some focal moments of their lives (such as climbing trees or watching a show); on the other hand it helped them to organise some of their practices in a similar way that, for instance, diaries provide for adults. There were other domains of routine in children's lives – those related to their daily regimes, such as attending the school, but also some that were less periodic. Most children had to be at home before nightfall, but some stayed outside until late at night. Most children woke up every morning and went to school, but several stayed at home when they wished and their parents did not push them much to adopt this kind of routine. Even children's encounters with the Centre were routine in a way – children complained if a shift was cancelled without any prior notice or even if we were a few minutes late; they also pointed out if we were on the street after the shift was over; I even experienced shifts on windy and rainy days when children, although freezing themselves, stayed outside to keep me company as they knew I had to be there to complete my shift.

Children's reactions to the Community Centre's routine are examples of situations when children awaited routine events keenly as they found such events associated with mostly positive experiences. However, as Gregson et al (2002b) argue, everyday practices might be less likely to evolve from choice than from the necessity that is a result of broader social relations and commitments. Using the example of being at home in the late evening or going to the school every morning, the necessity of children's practices in encounters was diverse and related to their age, or to the size of, and individual rules in, their family. An example of this (although more about family patterns is given in the next chapter) is a story from a project in which I interviewed children from the neighbourhood on behalf of the Community Centre about their needs and experiences with the Centre. The children responded quite positively and, although they were a bit nervous about the interview, they were mostly happy to have individual attention from a Centre worker as well as to be in the Club where the interviews took place without other children. It was very difficult to arrange a meeting with the younger ones but the older ones also often did not turn up when they should. One of the most difficult cases was Olivia, a 12-year-old girl. Although she was very keen about a meeting and although we often talked together during our outdoor shifts, she struggled to turn up at the Club for our appointments. The main reason was that she was caring for her young nephew with whom she often had to stay when she was told, often without prior arrangements (see Blazek et al, 2015). Because of this, Olivia's time was neatly organised – not through an ordered and established schedule, but rather through the principle of being flexible in helping her family in the first instance, and only then spending the rest of her time with her own activities.

Many authors have argued that constraints and boundaries, social and spatial, are particularly strong signposts of the social construction of childhood (Sibley, 1995b; Matthews et al, 1999). While some are structured through rules and limits over children's practices (Matthews and Limb, 1999; Kraftl and Horton, 2008) or imposed through children's perception of potential risks in transgressing 'safe' spaces and activities (Nayak, 2003a; Pain, 2006), my discussion highlights also the significance of affirmative routine activities as constraints to children's practices. This gives a different meaning to the word routine for this context. Olivia's organisation of activities and whom she could meet was not a matter of repetitive events, but rather of an ongoing submission to the instructions given by her family. Family commitments had very specific implications for children in Kopčany and I discuss them in detail in Chapter Nine, but it is crucial to note at this point that while Olivia's activities and encounters were framed around certain focal points, as Lina's or Mario's were, the stories with the latter demonstrate their practices as a result of their ongoing choice while for Olivia this focus was instead a matter of necessity and decisions made by others that she had to follow.

Importantly, children were not just passive participants in their encounters. In the case of routine encounters (that is, those where they had had some previous experiences of the contexts and when they formed expectations about the nature of the encounter with particular persons in these contexts), children contemplated deliberate actions by which they challenged the settings of their encounters. Jakub (5) was about to attend an appointment with an educational psychologist who would evaluate postponing Jakub's school enrolment. This was not enthusiastically met by Jakub's mother, for whom this meeting was an additional burden in her everyday child care duties, and his father did not seem to care about Jakub's enrolment in school at all. While he assigned this aspect of child care to Jakub's mother, he also expected her to fill other household duties while he was at work. For the meeting with the psychologist, a Centre worker volunteered to accompany Jakub and his mother. When she went up the staircase to meet them in their flat, she found Jakub at the top of the staircase waiting for her and raising his finger towards his mouth, asking her to be silent and to stay where she was so they would not be seen from the flat. My colleague then heard Jakub's mother explaining the departure to her husband, not telling him the real purpose of her journey, and then she met the colleague and Jakub at the staircase. Jakub's mother explained how his father would not approve of the visit to the psychologist so she had to make up a reason why they were about to go out and Jakub, when hearing this conversation of his parents and expecting the Centre worker's arrival at any moment, went to wait for the colleague so she would not appear while his mother was telling the story to his father.

Jakub did not really know when the colleague was about to come so he waited at the staircase for quite a long time. Yet he had realised that an encounter of the Centre worker with his father at that specific moment would have caused trouble and possibly would put his visit to the psychologist into jeopardy. Although he did not fully understand the purpose of the meeting, he was looking forward to it, partly for the experience of something new and of a journey out of the neighbourhood with his mother, and partly because of the enthusiasm of the Centre worker about the meeting. His understanding of his father's presence in his daily activities was mostly associated with regulations and restrictions – for example, several times I have seen Jakub asking his sisters when their father was going to come home from work so he would know how much time they had left to be outside before they would have to go home.

Jakub's account thus can be read along with the arguments such as those given by Tivers (1986) who claims that everyday routine establishes social and spatial constraints for the daily scope of individuals, especially of those whose social dependence is highly structured and sedentary. In Jakub's case, the expected manner of his father's reaction was what he supposed to be a constraint on what he was looking forward to so he had developed a practical response based on preventing an encounter of the Centre worker with his father. Yet, the formation of children's agency in the context of highly structured everyday circumstances is different from that of other groups. Drawing on Heidegger, Schillmeier (2008) and Schwanen et al (2012) argue that, for older people, the formation of agency is about adjustments to the 'always changing social and material arrangements' (Schwanen et al, 2012, p.1315) and looking for routines that facilitate independent everyday action. Children from Kopčany looked to establish some routine elements that would guide their practices, such as when Mario focused on his TV show, but more often their actions were shaped by subversiveness and opportunism due to highly circumscribed conditions, unfolding in the vastly uneven power relations of children and adults and constraining children's practices spatially and temporally (Kallio, 2008).

Jakub's act can be thus seen as what de Certeau (1984) labels everyday 'tactics', as a framework for the practices that explore 'the imposition of power through the disciplining and organisation of space' (Crang, 2000, p.137) and at the same time 'take the predisposition of the world and make it over' (2000, p.137). Although de Certeau's writing analyses more extensive and stretched structures of social power, and Jakub's story is an example of the power relations concentrated within a single family unit, the underlying principle is not essentially different where the established power mechanisms and more opportunistic and spontaneous 'ruses' in actions of the children are concerned. Jakub's action can be also understood as a 'mobile' practice, which is for de Certeau characteristic of the everyday transgressive behaviour that aims to identify and exploit 'gaps' in the mechanisms of structured necessity that power relations impose over everyday life, again, different in comparison to older people's agency in the accounts of Schillmeier and Schwanen et al Jakub's action was not repetitive, an act by which he would resist his father's dominance on a regular basis continuously. Instead, it was an opportunistic deed formed at, and limited to, a precise moment and using the specific spatial configurations of the forthcoming encounter (or its absence) between his parents and the Centre worker.

Jakub's story, but also children's spatial practices discussed in Chapter Five, or the way they engaged with things explored in Chapter Seven, suggest that they did not just accept the given established order nor did they internalise it and take it for granted entirely. However, this does not mean that Jakub's action was a part of his everyday routine through which he would regularly and repetitively challenge his father and the ordering that he established. Rather, Jakub reacted to a routine (that is, known-to-him) context of his father's behaviour as based on his previous experiences that he recognised at that moment. Jakub's story shows interesting intersections between his experiences of social settings (his family relations and his relationship to the Centre workers), space (the proximity and visibility in the narrow hallways and staircases in the lodging house) and time (the succession between Jakub detaining the worker and his mother leaving the father and joining them) as they informed his further action. This lack of open and systematic resistance against the, even if symbolic (Warren, 1996), order established in the family does not mean that Jakub or other children did not challenge or even oppose institutional mechanisms in the family, but also in school and elsewhere. As Scott (1985) shows, resistance and transgression can be individual and immediate rather than always organised and premeditated, they can be opportunistic rather than principled, and they can partially accept the nature and mechanisms of domination and not negate them entirely.

To understand better the ways in which children recognised their everyday settings (social, spatial or temporal), the term 'circumscribed geographies' (Bondi, 2005c, p.5) is helpful. Where Bondi uses it to describe the constraints imposed by social, spatial and temporal structures, I see circumscribed geographies of children from Kopčany also emerging through children's own understandings and expectations about these structures, and informing, or even 'circumscribing' children's practices. As ethnomethodologists (Garfinkel, 1967; Leiter, 1980) argue, 'social order ... refers to a *sense of social order*' (Leiter, 1980, p.159) and children's sense of their circumstances is what drives them even to transgress the rules and norms given by adults. However, the traditional ethnomethodological perspective also tends to overemphasise the 'rationalisation' or 'accountability' of people's 'past experiences, present circumstances, and future prospects' (Leiter, 1980, p.188) as the means of 'the maintenance of stable routine of everyday life' (Garfinkel, 1967, p.185) by situated performances. As the previous chapters showed, not all children's actions were rationalised outputs of their experiences and recognitions of the circumstances, and not all of them could be fully accounted for by the children as several pre-reflective or even pre-cognitive factors were relevant. However, where the ethnomethodological perspective provides additional ways of understanding children's practices is in its focus on children's efforts to seek explanations and a sense of their experiences.

Practices and interactions at the reception of the lodging house that children had to pass if they were to reach the Community Centre can serve as an example of the relationships between children's actions and their complex spatial, social and temporal circumstances. After passing the reception, children had to cross a short hallway. This area was a common source of noise as children liked to negotiate their access to the Club out of the designated hours, but also because there was just one other flat in the wing of the building on the first floor where the Club was situated and no other adults used to cross the hallway so children often gathered there. Encounters with the neighbour from the flat were often unpleasant as he disliked the frequent and loud presence of children around his flat. Children were often told off by the receptionists if they made noise in this area, leading to arguments and conflicts. The hallway was a relatively safe space because of other residents passing nearby – as it was located directly after the reception and next to elevators – and also a relatively comfortable space, especially if children could not stay outside because of bad weather or darkness. However, children were often also expelled from the area as a result of encounters with the neighbour and with some of the receptionists. Yet, the regulation of the hallway by adults did not only take the form of exclusion, and neither were children's expectations from encountering an adult necessarily formed as such. Most adults passing by did not really care about the children making noise or even damaging the walls in the hallway. The Centre staff kept asking children to be silent in order to prevent conflicts with the neighbour and the receptionists, but they did not really seek to move the children away. Children often had to wait in the hallway when they wanted to talk to the staff outside of the designated hours, and on a few occasions, some children were even given a small desk, chair, paper and other tools to paint or do their homework in the hallway. Even among the receptionists, attitudes varied, and there was especially one very patient one who often allowed children to play or just to stay around the reception area if the weather was bad. Around Christmas, when a group of children started to sing carols in the hallway, instead of telling them off for making noise, he even joined them in singing.

The example of the hallway shows the importance of children's experiences within a specific spatial setting, but also the difference that the presence of *particular* people and the way they behave, as well as other factors such as the time of the day, can make (more tensions happened in evenings than in the middle of the day when people were away from the building). Analogically, the constraints and circumstances arising from encounters with other people varied depending on the particular contexts of these encounters. Meeting a Centre worker on the street, for example, could be a pleasant opportunity to talk or to receive support, such as when children were playing games, experimenting with things they found, looking for someone or something, or if they were just hanging around. On the other hand, meeting us in situations such as when children were smoking, fighting each other or doing something illegal could make them expect the community workers to intervene, to avoid the children or at least potentially to worsen the children's image in the eyes of the workers.

Conclusions

This chapter explored what can be labelled as the circumscribed geographies of everyday encounters, drawing on Bondi (2005c) and Valentine (2008). Taking from the ethnomethodological tradition, I discussed how children's experiences of past events, recognitions of present settings, and possibly also contemplations of future happenings, all mattered for the evolution of their practices. Against the ethnomethodological notions of rationalisation and practical accountability, the discussion, in connection with previous chapters, emphasised also often unreflected, limited and immediate aspects of such experiences and recognitions, and the ways in which they drive children's actions.

Understanding practices in routine interactions, or in what Valentine (2008) labels a 'low-level' sociability, is arguably important for seeing children's practices in Kopčany as more than just the sum of individuals' practices, that is, as contributing to the formation of place. As Parr et al argue, 'communities are very much "made" by routine, mundane and highly visible social practices' (2004, p.414), and as she adds, 'altering ... the micro-social practices' can be a highly significant moment for relatively closed socio-spatial groups that can lead to attraction and pleasure, but also to rejection and disappointment.

My discussion began with the theme of children encountering other people in the neighbourhood. The key argument presented was that children's understandings of encounters, even with strangers, were mediated by their experiences with familiar people and with familiar situations with them. Using Simmel's ideas for understanding the age-axis of difference in children's and young people's openness to unknown people, the debate highlighted the role of increasing negative experiences in social relationships among the young people – and especially of their consequent attitudes – that had an impact on how they built their new social relationships. The age factor was, however, discussed as situational, and examples of younger children with individual negative experiences with strangers (but also familiar persons) were also given that illustrate the significance of safety and trust in the paths of growing up (see Chapter Eleven for the continuation of this theme).

However, this chapter also raised another theme, one of the socio-spatio-temporal contexts of children's immediate experiences and of the significance of children's own perception of these factors. Focusing on the idea of routine, I have argued that it mattered for the children more as an aspect of being familiar with the present settings than as a notion of repetition and regularity. The field examples illustrated how children's recognitions of time, space and social dynamics, were not always explicit nor did they unfold in the same way that adults organise them. However, this is not to question their existence or importance, and the chapter also gave examples from the field practice of the Community Centre where communication about time or space was adapted to children's own frameworks and capacities.

The third theme of this discussion was the role of children's own actions in challenging their existing circumstances. My argument – making conceptual connections to Chapters Five and Seven – was that children did not just conform to their overarching settings, but they were also capable of challenging and contesting them, even if their actions were not always deliberate, organised or premeditated. The significance of spontaneity and opportunism in everyday practices that was apparent in the discussions of children's engagements with spaces, things, or bodies thus begins to appear also in relation to children's placement within established social forms in the neighbourhood and elsewhere.

This will also be one of the underlying themes for the next three chapters. There, I will explore modalities of two key patterns of children's social relationships in the neighbourhood – family and friendship – as well as the relational impact of children's notions of social identity, focusing on the significance of 'growing up', 'being a girl or a boy' and 'being a Roma or Gajo'. Discussions in Chapter Eight drew links between these investigations of children's established social connections that have an impact in particular daily situations, other factors underpinning these situations (such as spatial or temporal settings), and children's own recognition and active involvement in the links through which their practices emerge.

NINE

Family life

As the previous chapter shows, exploring children's everyday encounters with other people indicates that other factors existed behind the passing moments of the encounter. In some cases, children's attitude towards other people was formed through the prism of expectations rather than through actual knowledge, while elsewhere a long-term history of contact and the sedimented nature of experiences with the other person shaped children's practices in the encounter. Chapter Eight raised the question of other people's significance in children's everyday actions, and in this and the following two chapters, I will focus on children's long-term ties with other people and the ways in which they affect children's practices. This chapter explores one of the children's most important relationships – with the family and family life – significant because of their frequency, intensity, and relevance to other everyday circumstances, but also because of children's own views about them.

The literature on childhood, the family and intergenerationality is too extensive to be reviewed here (Holt, 2011; Musgrove, 2012) and, perhaps more than before, I need to be careful about setting the scope of the chapter. Therefore, I am interested in the relationships between family patterns and the dynamics of children's everyday acts in which family (as a legal framework as well as a set of routine arrangements and emotional ties) comes to act in children's practices. In other words, family itself is not the subject here. The chapter is structured around two themes: in the first section, I discuss the composition of children's families in Kopčany, depicting the patterns of the relationships that stem from children's family lives and meander through their everyday activities. Tracing the most sedimented circumstances of children's everyday experiences as they are rooted in their families, I then focus on two types of dynamics in children's family relations – children being cared for by other family members and children being responsible for other family members. I also uncover the link between the latter and the configurations of children's peer relationships in their families, and with the question of friendship and its importance for children's everyday practices that is further discussed in Chapter Ten.

Family patterns

Previous chapters emphasised children's spatial marginalisation in Kopčany but factors of social vulnerability that resulted from children's family patterns were also notable. Three factors – the size of family, housing arrangements and the socioeconomic circumstances of families – are discussed later, eventually outlining their combined impact on the patterns of children's practices.

Table 9.1 shows family demographic data for Kopčany and reveals structural differences of families from the neighbourhood in comparison to the surrounding areas as well as to the national average.

Table 9.1 Selected family demographic data for Kopčany, Petržalka and Slovakia

	Kopčany	Petržalka	Slovakia
Proportion of families with three or more dependent children among all households	10.0%	2.9%	5.6%
Proportion of families with three or more dependent children among the families with dependent children	21.9%	6.7%	14.7%
Proportion of 'incomplete family units ' (*dependent children and one or both parents not living in the household – in Kopčany usually children living with the mother or grandparents*) amongst all households	30.5%	26.6%	17.7%
Proportion of households with two or more dependent children among the 'incomplete family units'	49.8%	31.5%	36.2%
Proportion of households with three or more dependent children among the 'incomplete family units'	9.5%	4.1%	7.9%

Source: Census 2001

These numbers suggest that Kopčany was demographically distinctive from the rest of Petržalka for other reasons apart from just the high proportion of young people (see Chapter Two). This factor is important especially in combination with the housing arrangements of children's families, and particularly of the larger families, as it amplifies the impact of the limited spaces that children had for themselves and which they had to share with other family members. While I mentioned the factor of 'overcrowded homes' as important for the amount of the time that children spent on the street in Chapter Five, Tables 9.2, 9.3 and 9.4 illustrate these figures more closely.

Table 9.2 Proportion of all households according to the number of bedrooms in their flat

	Studio	1	2	3	4+	0–2	3+
Kopčany	16.1%	9.0%	72.6%	1.8%	0.4%	97.7%	2.2%
Petržalka	9.7%	12.8%	55.8%	19.7%	2.1%	78.2%	21.8%

Source: Census 2001

Table 9.3 Proportion of all households according to the number of persons living in the flat

	1	2	3	4	5	6	7+	1–4	5+
Kopčany	27.4%	15.7%	17.9%	21.1%	13.0%	2.7%	2.2%	82.1%	17.9%
Petržalka	20.7%	18.3%	23.0%	28.3%	7.0%	1.9%	0.8%	90.3%	9.7%

Source: Census 2001

Table 9.4 Proportions of households with five or more persons living in flats with two bedrooms or fewer

	Among all households	Among households with five and more persons
Kopčany	17.5%	97.5%
Petržalka	5.6%	57.3%

Source: Census 2001

The key implications from Tables 9.2–9.4 in regard to children's family circumstances are that the overwhelming majority of children from Kopčany lived in flats with two or less bedrooms, that almost one sixth of the households in Kopčany consisted of five or more persons, and especially that almost all households with five or more persons lived in flats with two bedrooms or fewer – all numbers differing from those for the rest of Petržalka. Not all larger households consisted of parent/s and their children – other adult relatives, such as grandparents, uncles, aunts or cousins quite often lived with them. However, only very rarely (if at all) did such numerous households consist of adults only. In other words, a considerable number of children (even if the exact figures are unknown) lived in highly overcrowded home spaces, sharing premises often even with their wider-family relatives, and commonly sharing their room with their siblings or cousins.

Housing arrangements can be partly attributed to the economic circumstances of the families. Although there are no accurate statistics for the average income, unemployment rate, or incapacity benefits in the area, Kopčany was considered among the most deprived areas in Bratislava and the financial situation preventing the children from using other services and leisure time facilities was cited as one of the reasons for establishing a community centre here. I have not met a child or a family that would be considered affluent according to relative standards for the Bratislava region, and in the few cases during my stay in the neighbourhood when families could afford to take a mortgage or buy a new flat, they moved away from Kopčany. According to the 2001 Census data, the proportion of residents without secondary education was 60% higher than in Petržalka as a whole, and the proportion of residents with a university education was four times lower. Still, there were families with an income higher than the national average who travelled abroad for holidays, several families had cars or their children attended organised (paid) activities. This proportion was not significant – for example, the proportion of families with a car in Kopčany in 2001 according to the Census was 17.9% while in Petržalka it was 42.1%. The local social geography was variable, with differences between the families from the lodging house, the two buildings with rental council flats, and the two buildings with mixed ownership that included private flats. However, even within the latter two buildings, there were families with very few possessions, including basic objects such as furniture or clothes, while some families in the lodging house owned a car.

Family and neighbourhood ties are important in the economic strategies of low-income residents in Petržalka (Smith and Rochovská, 2007), especially regarding household economic practices (such as informal labour for relatives or commodity exchange) and child care (Blazek et al, 2015) as areas of cooperation within family networks that help to fulfil everyday needs through the social capital existing within families. People often rely on the involvement of their relatives from distant regions in economic activities and, to a much lesser extent, on their neighbours for child care. On the contrary, extensive family networks existed directly in Kopčany, which was untypical for a housing estate of this kind. Numerous family ties and networks existed within the relatively small population of Kopčany, and many children had their cousins, uncles and aunts, or grandparents living in the same area, building, or even flat. One of the reasons was the low socioeconomic status and unattractiveness of the area, where some long-term residents with experiences of the life in Kopčany encouraged their relatives to move in, benefiting from the lower demand and their knowledge and experience of the local housing situation – all of this not really typical for the residential strategies in Petržalka. Several young people who were born in Kopčany also remained in the area, often establishing their own families there, mostly in rented flats. In Kopčany, 42.9%

of residents were born in Bratislava, while the average number for Petržalka was just 11.8%. This confirms the relative youth of the population in Kopčany (the second generation of the residents), low in-migration into the area and the presence of a relatively residentially immobile population, at least among a significant part of the residents of private and council flats.

Children from Kopčany were thus growing up in diverse and often complex patterns of care and support (Figure 9.1). Many lived only with their single parents, grandparents or uncles/aunts, while others were growing up in families of several children, not just siblings but often also cousins. Examples from Kopčany included very complex families – such as when several cousins lived with their grandparents while the mother of some of them along with her other children, as well as their several other family members, lived in the lodging house. But there were also children growing up in traditional nuclear family units with mother, father and one or two siblings. Only a small minority of the children that I worked with had no siblings, however. And while many children had a number of relatives in the neighbourhood, there were some families with very few social contacts at all.

Figure 9.1 Gathering of children's carers during one of the community events

These family patterns were important circumstances which framed children's relationships with their family members and from which daily family practices emerge. Relating to them, I explore the place of children within familial agency next as well as children's own agency in family life.

Children's place in family

Children as recipients of care

> 'After six months in Kopčany, we had established contact with *over one hundred* children and young people and with *three* parents.' (One of the Community Centre Managers when she described to me the beginnings of the project)

My early work with children in Kopčany was notable by the absence of adults in our interaction and this was a result of the relative absence of adults in children's everyday activities more generally. In Chapter Five, I introduced Peter, a very young boy, who, as well as his siblings, spent much of his time on the street and he was also one of the most frequent users of the Centre's services. In Peter's case, several key factors in why the adults in the neighbourhood spent only relatively little time with their children could be seen, such as long working hours (Peter's father) or a large number of children in the family and the amount of domestic work necessary (Peter's mother). Other reasons why children spent a lot of time on their own included, in some cases, the lack of parenting skills or (very frequently) the transfer of responsibilities for care from adults towards other siblings (see later in this chapter). In several cases, I noticed that parents were strict about setting the rules for their children and they tried to control or organise their activities, but working in the evenings and on weekends, or simply not being consistent or persistent enough (or a combination of the two), meant that many children did their own things anyway, spent time outside until the late evening, met with friends their parents did not wish them to, or engaged in other types of activities that their parents forbade them while doing little to prevent them (such as truancy, smoking or thieving).

In contrast to these two types of family circumstances – little parental intervention because of the lack of effort or because other daily commitments took them to the limits of their capacities – there were some exceptions when parents were actually children's key partners in their everyday activities. There was a group of girls in Kopčany who did not interact with the Centre very much and their mothers told us that they deliberately kept their daughters away from activities of the Centre, not because of the Centre itself, but because they had concerns about some of the children who spent a lot of time with the Centre. While for several other children, the Centre was a favourite social space, these girls interacted with the staff mostly just to borrow things and then went to play with their parents, who actively regulated, but also engaged in, the girls' daily lives. Protection was the key motive for this attitude, and, in order to keep them away from the children the girls' parents perceived as 'uncivil' or 'dangerous', they chose to spend their time with the girls. Several of the mothers were on maternity leave with their younger siblings so they also had more time to spare with their older children.

This kind of relationship was also interesting in terms of how girls' other social contacts were restricted because of their mother's preferences (see Chapter Ten), how this division had its explicitly spatial patterns (as these girls and their mothers usually spent time in one of the playgrounds [Area 6 in Map 3]), while the hub of the contact between the Centre and most other children was in front of the lodging house, that is, at the very opposite end of the neighbourhood (Area 3 in Map 3), but also how this had an impact on girls' own individual embodied practices. For example, children from Kopčany usually did not pay much attention to injuries or illness, so they were outside in the winter even with flu, a high temperature and intensive coughing, or strolled around Kopčany with crutches after they broke their leg. On the other hand, I was told that when Stela (11), one of the girls from this group, broke her leg, her mother carried her around in a buggy even several months after the accident, a kind of indulgence that was rather uncommon among other parents.

Even though I emphasised the relative absence of adults in children's everyday activities, this does not mean that a sense of family did not exist among the children. This included negative experiences and perceptions (see the story of Peter and his visit to a psychologist in Chapter Eight), but the majority of expressions I witnessed from the younger children about their parents and family members were positive. In some cases, they were very explicit when children recognised their family patterns but also expressed their feelings about family life:

> 'My mom is the one who is more tolerant and allowing me to do things, while dad is usually more directive and stricter. If there is a trouble, I prefer to talk to mom as she will be milder, while dad is very stern. But I like it, I think

it is important to hold a child on a leash. I know they care about me and perhaps know better than me, so it is how it should be.' (Extract from my conversation with Marian, 13)

In most cases, however, children's engagement with their families, and especially their parents, could be seen from their practices rather than heard in their words.

Yesterday I took part in a conflict where Alan (10) and Viktor (9) attacked Peter (6) and Norbert (8). I did not really understand what was going on and the older boys told me it was none of my business. They did not even respect my presence, as the children in conflict usually do, and tried to punch Peter, four years younger and half their size, even when I protected him with my body. They just ran around and hit from all angles. Eventually, when I demanded an explanation urgently, Viktor told me: 'This is not your business. He insulted my family.' (Extract from fieldnotes, July 2009)

In this situation, emotional ties of Alan and Viktor towards Viktor's mother (the family member who had been 'insulted' by Peter) could be read, particularly from their anger with Peter and their commitment to and protective feelings for Viktor's mother. For both Viktor and Alan, commitment to the family was of a crucial importance – Alan was Viktor's cousin, so his part in the conflict was not just to support his friend as he was standing up on behalf of his own family too. In such a context, Viktor felt it as his duty to avenge his mother and his other family members, and the boys even threatened Peter that their 'uncles would take care of his father'.

This story is not unusual and it demonstrates how the children who did not usually talk about their families still 'practised' their feelings in a daily *ad hoc* situations. My very first contact with a child in Kopčany was when Martina (12) jumped at my colleague after we left the building and she yelled at her for some discourteous remark that the colleague supposedly had said to other children about Martina's mother (which proved to be a hoax). However, I have never noticed Martina *talking* about her mother again, or about her feelings towards her. In both examples, the children, who rarely talked about their feelings for their families, and who probably would struggle to articulate explicitly their attachment to their parents or siblings, demonstrated their recognition of their families in a complex mix of verbal and non-verbal performances.

On the other hand, in situations like Martina's, children's expressions about their families could be seen partly as a challenge against other children as well. One day, I was in the company of three or four younger children and an older boy (17) and we were talking in the lodging house hallway as there was rain outside. The older boy teased Nina (9) about her father, who had been seen drunk and fighting, until Nina left the group. She returned after a few minutes and when the theme of her father was seemingly forgotten, Nina began talking about how her father had taken her and her siblings out to the town a couple of days ago, how he had bought her new boots and ice-cream and then had taken them all for a lunch into the McDonald's. While saying this as a passing remark in our conversation, the reply felt to me like a response to the recent unpleasant dialogue about her father.

The story of Nina links to two other questions of the children's relationships with their parents. First, such an expression of children's feelings through narratives of their previous experiences rather than through characterisation of the parents was very common, especially among the youngest children. One day, I was introduced to Anna (5) who was on the street with her younger cousin Nikoleta, and her father was sitting nearby and watching them. I spent some time with the girls and when I wanted to leave, they asked to join me and their father agreed. During the walk I mentioned how "kind" their father was for allowing them to join me outside of his view. Anna consented this, saying that her father was "indeed kind", and then she commenced a long speech about him. Instead of using adjectives to describe him, Anna focused on stories and events that she had experienced with her father – what he says, what his voice is like, how he drives the car, what her mother says about him, what his friends are like, how he greets her every morning, how he gives her presents, and so on. Thus reproducing the experiences of her world was, for Anna, also a way of expressing her feelings about the world, and about her father in particular, another example that links to the discussion from Chapter Six about the immediacy of children's actions before the process of abstraction or rational translation takes place.

Another theme that emerges from the story of Nina is that of children's stigmatisation in reference to their families. In several cases, the images of children's family members, such as them being drunk or involved in fights or illegal activities, were transferred to the children. While Nina was just teased for her father, there were also examples when some children or their parents avoided other children because of their family background. While this was relatively less common in relation to the parents, children were quite often excluded by their peers because of their association with their older siblings.

Traditionally, the place of children in families has been explored by social scientists in relation to the functions that family is supposed to fulfil for children, such as protection, provision, regulation or support. The traditional roles of family in the lives of children from Kopčany can be seen in some ways to have been eroded. Parents were still the main providers in the families (or other adult family members were, such as distant cousins or uncles), but, as demonstrated in Chapter Six, material deprivation in several of the families drove the children into obtaining material belongings actively on their own from the earliest age, including activities such as stealing, exploring or sharing. Most parents definitely tried to regulate children's activities and the majority of them were certainly concerned about their children's protection and safety, but the level of their control over children's actions was often limited, either because of the limited amount of time they could spend with their children, but often also because of the lack of parenting skills or persistence. Children often made decisions about where to go and what to do on their own or together with their friends and the parents had only limited amount of control over this. Also, family was not always a safe haven for children and they often challenged their parents' rules and explored alternative opportunities for everyday actions (see Chapter Eight).

Qvortrup suggests that one of the paradoxes of childhood nowadays is that 'adults argue that it is good for children and parents to be together' perhaps more than ever before, but 'more and more they live their everyday lives apart' (1995, p.191). Regardless of the parents' intentions, in Kopčany, the majority of children's activities remained outside of their direct control or even awareness. While Connolly and Ennew claim that 'to be a child outside adult supervision, visible on city centre streets, is to be out of place' (1996, p.133), in the spatial setting of Kopčany, where the majority of children's activities took place, this was very ordinary. This set of observations, then, raises the question of the importance of children's agency within the families, against the notion of children as only passive objects of parental care and regulation (Horton and Pyer, forthcoming). In the next section, I will discuss this opposite view of the place of children in their families – one of children as active agents, first in the practices of (child) care, and second in the formation of peer relationships, as ways of expanding children's agency.

Children as active agents in family life

The social and economic circumstances of the families, such as the long working hours of the parents, the size of the family, or the lack of accessible social support services in the area, often required children to be involved in various family duties from the earliest age. While children contributed to an extent to domestic work, their key contribution was care for younger relatives, that is, siblings, but also cousins, nieces or nephews, as the age difference across generations in wider families was often low (see Figure 9.2). Responsibilities included taking care of children when their parents or guardians were away from home, and many young children were allowed to spend leisure time outside their home only in the company of their older (child) relatives. Older children thus often involved younger relatives in their own activities or took walks around the neighbourhood with them. Some children also studied with their younger relatives or accompanied them to educational (and other) activities in the Community Centre.

Figure 9.2 Children's collective play in front of the lodging house (the children's youngest relatives, who do not take part in play, are on the right side of the picture)

These relationships had a gendered character. While young boys often spent time with their younger sisters, engaged them in joint activities, introduced them to their own friends, or were given direct responsibility for them by their parents when going outside together, deliberate care for children outside one's own activities was prevalently a domain for girls, with just very few exceptions, and with an increased gap between the boys and girls as they grew older. Evans (2011a, 2011b) demonstrates how particular roles of young carers are not just gender- or age-related, but are often constituted by the complex ties between the two factors and as aspects of the life-transition of the young people as well as of their families. Many girls in Kopčany were required by their families to take care of their younger relatives – staying with them at home when the parents or other guardians were away, taking them out and keeping watch over them, or helping them with their homework. Whereas the boys were usually responsible only for their younger siblings (if at all), the girls did not care just for their younger siblings, but they were often asked to spend time with their cousins, nieces and nephews as well, or even with children of their family friends, within the close and intensive ties and networks in Kopčany.

Smyth et al (2011) argue that many young people do not identify themselves as carers and they understand their domestic duties in caring for other family members as a 'natural' aspect of the bonds and reciprocities that characterise family life. Contrary to this idea of 'hidden carers', older girls, in particular, recognised their roles in their families explicitly and in contrast to what they perceived to be the responsibilities of their brothers or male cousins. A group of children aged between 13 and 14 and of mixed gender took part in producing a short video about the key aspects of their life in Kopčany (see Blazek et al, 2015). When they brainstormed the key themes for the video, child care resonated with the group's experiences as one of the very key aspects of their individual experiences, with the girls from the group laughing and giving 'high-fives' to each other, expressing the mutual recognition of their family commitments. Eventually, only girls took part in the group that produced the video and they limited the focus of the whole video to the lack of play and leisure opportunities in the neighbourhood, especially for the youngest children, a problem that was related to their daily experiences with their younger relatives. Some girls even had to take their young relatives along during the actual video production in the neighbourhood, so they included them in the video in order to fill their time (Figure 9.3). They also managed to assemble several other young children from the neighbourhood, and to obtain spoken as well as written consent from their parents, thus demonstrating their strong social ties with other parents and guardians of the youngest children in Kopčany.

Figure 9.3 A shot from the video that girls from Kopčany produced about the lack of play opportunities for the younger children

However, such a 'formalised' organisation of child care was not the only mechanism of protection or support among siblings or young relatives and more mundane or even situational acts of familial engagement could be seen among the children. Even those siblings who usually did not spend time together, or were even hostile to each other quite frequently, were protective of their brothers and sisters in encounters with other children:

> Richard (7) and Filip (8) were provoking each other and they started a fight on the stairs to the building. They had fun really, though, and the conflict was not really a conflict. Simona (13), Norbert's oldest sister, was on her way home when she was passing the boys. She slapped Samuel twice, cried 'What you're doing to him, ha??!', and not waiting for his reaction, she entered the building. (Extract from fieldnotes, April 2009)

'It is important to know someone who is older than you, if you have an older brother or sister, that's the best case.

You get some respect then.' (Conversation with Jano, aged 14, about children's relationship in Kopčany, July 2009)

Arguments have been made that it is other children on the street that children are most likely to be harmed by (James et al, 1998). Protective actions such as Simona's were quite common among the children, irrespective of their age difference and even if only in passing encounters such as the one presented here. Even the youngest children cared and made a stand for their younger siblings (and also for the older ones as much as they dared), as did the older, even adult siblings. On a weekend trip organised by the Centre in summer 2009, a 10-year-old girl lost her cell phone. She was very distressed because of the expected reaction from her father. A couple of days later, her older brother who was in his mid 20s approached one of the workers. The worker asked him whether his sister had talked about the trip and he reacted very aggressively, asking the worker whether she was on the trip, and then blamed her for the loss of the phone, yelling and even threatening her. Interestingly, the information that he was a brother of the girl was completely unknown to the Centre until I was told this by another boy just a couple of weeks before this incident. This was despite several years of contact between the Centre and the girl, and the Centre and the young man respectively, showing how little actual interactions between the two could be normally seen on the street. Still, he took up his protective role and stood up on behalf of his younger sister very firmly.

Several authors who explore the dynamics of family life in households without adult carers emphasise how sibling relationships constitute complex dynamics of care, protection, support, but also of structured patterns of power, as well as of horizontally organised bonds comparable to the patterns of friendship (Evans, 2011a). While siblings in Kopčany were protective of each other, authoritative power relationships were very frequent between older and younger siblings. The older ones often took things from their younger brothers and sisters without asking (and while the younger ones did this too, the older ones did so overtly), commanded them to do things, or used (mild) violence if the others resisted. Especially when there was just a small age difference between the children and they spent their time together in Kopčany, a remarkable 'coalition' was often formed: on the one hand, the older child was protective of his/her sibling and took him/her into the company of his/her friends; on the other hand, the relationship between the two was not equal and the younger sibling had to respect or obey the older child. The whole process was a constant negotiation of power between the older siblings who provided care and protection but in turn required respect and compliance, and the younger ones who benefited from this privileged position of being protected by their older siblings and at the same time resisted being entirely subordinated. Often such relationships followed parental instructions that the younger children could be outside only with their older siblings and the latter were given the responsibility formally, and at such times the power relationships were expressed most clearly:

> During a game, me and a colleague came into a conflict with Mariana (7) who refused to return the sheet with which we played and she eventually used very bad language against us. We could not get to talk to her at the moment as she was just spitting curses, so we left as another colleague came and approached her. While Mariana was not hostile to her, she still refused to apologise and we heard more swearing towards us. The colleague eventually took a bottle of water from Mariana and said she would not return it until she would apologise. Mariana began to cry and ran to her older sister Erika (9), telling her about the bottle. Erika approached the colleague, screaming at her that Mariana needed the bottle for the school and asked how the colleague dared to take it. After the colleague explained the situation, Erika turned and slapped her sister, yelling at her for her behaviour so Mariana cried even more. Eventually, Erika took the bottle and said she would deal with this and with Mariana. (Extract from fieldnotes, October 2008)

Stories such as this were a frequent theme in children's family lives and they were also an important agenda of the Community Centre. While there were cases when asking older children for help in dealing with the challenging behaviour of their younger siblings would probably have saved the workers some time and effort, the strategy of the Centre was to minimise such involvement and address the younger children directly in order not to reinforce the power mechanisms within the families.

The later stories suggest that 'hidden carers' among the children indeed existed, and that their contribution to the family life was important (see Robson, 2004), even if the practices of care in such relationships were different from those of the girls from the story about the video, whose roles were more explicit (see Aldridge and Becker, 1993). With the majority of children largely spending their time outside of any adult control, the parents relied at least on the more 'accidental' practices of care and support, meaning the fact that the younger children were spending time in the same limited space of the neighbourhood as their older siblings, and that the latter would stand up on behalf of the former if needed. In Chapters Five and Eight, I emphasised the high level of mutual knowledge in the neighbourhood, where children (but also adults) were often able to advise where someone could be found, or explain what had happened in the neighbourhood recently. The lack of parental involvement made the children from Kopčany relatively more resilient to everyday difficulties or conflicts – almost no children even mentioned their parents in mutual conflicts and attempted to deal with everything on their own – but the frequent presence of their relatives (as well as other friends, see Chapter Ten) meant that children often received even unexpected support, such as in the story of Simona discussed earlier in this chapter.

These discussions suggest that the relationships between siblings or other relatives often closely resembled friendship. For many children, their relatives indeed were also their most important friends. Samo (5) and Lenka (7) were among the children with whom I had most contact. Living with four other siblings in a small flat, the children seemed to be on the street as much as possible. Lenka had just started school, but Samo had not obtained a place in a kindergarten (see Chapter Two) and he stayed at home with his mother and their younger siblings. When I met them for the first time, Samo spent most time in the company of Lenka and her friends. These were primarily three girls – two of them were of Lenka's age, and the fourth was Samo's and Lenka's older sister, Lucia. They usually played around the lodging house, often skipping over the rope, with Samo holding the rope or staying near the girls and looking at them. I left Kopčany in January 2009, and when I returned in April 2009, there was a change in Samo's and Lenka's company. Now, they still spent much time together – although less so than a few months before – but it was now more often in the company of Samo's friends, boys of his age or just a little bit older, that is, younger than Lenka. The nature of their activities had also changed – now they usually strolled around the neighbourhood, explored bushes and corners, and climbed trees and roofs.

The story of Samo and Lenka was typical of children from Kopčany. Both children grew up in a large family where children were responsible for their younger siblings. When I came to Kopčany, Lucia was responsible for both Lenka and Samo when they were outside, so they had to spend most of their time with her, and this is how Samo found himself in the company of other girls. While I was away, the friends of Lucia and Lenka moved away from Kopčany, and Lenka was meanwhile allowed to spend time in the neighbourhood on her own (without Lucia's supervision), although she now had to care for Samo. As Lenka's best friends moved away, and as Lucia found a new best friend, a bit older than Lenka, she found herself without the company she had been used to. Her new best girlfriends spent much less time on the street than she did, and as she mostly had to be in company of Samo anyways, she began to engage in games with his friends, boys a bit younger than Lenka, and the nature of her activities changed as well.

As Punch (2005) demonstrates, sibling ties are a specific type of relationship that retains several features of the differential power distribution on which family life is based (similar to the intergenerational organisation of families), while at the same time it creates attachments based on reciprocal performances whereby children accompany and complement each other (Mauthner, 2002; Punch, 2007). Understanding children's relationships with their young relatives (not just siblings because of the complex family background of many children) situates this part of children's family life between the structurally organised practices of care and responsibility in which children take part as formal carers with explicit responsibilities grounded in specific practices, and more spontaneous opportunistic practices of engagement in which children act primarily as friends. Neither of these positionalities should be understood as preferred by the children over the other in principle, however. Several children and young people expressed how they actually liked taking responsibility for their younger relatives and how they enjoyed the time they spent as carers, while for many this constrained their own activities considerably (see the story of Olivia from Chapter Eight; see also James et al, 1998). At the same time, while many children enjoyed and benefited from the company of their siblings, the sibling relationship was not something they could choose, and there were children who complained about the level and frequency of their contact with their siblings that was unavoidable because of the housing arrangements or the limited spatial range of the neighbourhood:

> 'I just want them [the younger siblings] to leave me alone
> … I need to reserve some space for myself and not always
> have to bump into their moods …' (Veronika, 13)

Veronika lived with two younger siblings and one older one in a small two-bedroom flat and, although she was not explicitly responsible for her younger siblings when they were on the street, they often bothered her, both outside and at home. In her case, the sibling relationship was one that she could neither escape nor that she would particularly enjoy.

Conclusions

In the stories of this chapter, family life was shown as circumscribed in multiple ways by the socioeconomic factors experienced by many families from the neighbourhood, while at the same time circumscribing children's everyday contacts, activities and agendas. I have presented Kopčany as a neighbourhood with several larger families, mostly with a relatively low income. Family circumstances in Kopčany were highly diverse, but one of the hallmarks was a considerable number of broader networks of relatives and neighbours who cooperated in several areas, particularly child care, an arrangement untypical of Petržalka and surrounding neighbourhoods. However, and in contrast with this, a number of young children grew up isolated not just spatially, but also socially within the neighbourhood.

In these circumstances, family often served as a socially inclusive mechanism in which some children's social capital increased and their engagement with other people became broader, extending also the scope of their activities and acting as an extension to agency. In relation to care, children joined social networks through being cared for by adults, not only by their parents but in many cases also/rather by their grandparents, uncles and aunts, as well as older cousins, siblings, and other distant relatives, and sometimes also by neighbours. At the same time, many children were also involved as carers, flattening the intergenerational gaps (Bosco, 2007) in everyday family roles through their active role in child care with their commitments ranging between highly structured ones (especially among older girls) and more spontaneous everyday practices of care, recognition and responsibility towards their younger relatives. Family ties also contributed to children's inclusion within peer networks in the neighbourhood and the presence of older siblings was often an important mechanism through which they developed further contacts with children but also adults. Families further often served as gatekeepers to the neighbourhood so that children who moved to Kopčany found their place in the local social networks more easily if they had family connections.

While some children found material and emotional circumstances for their practices in their families (such as Stela and her friends), very often it was the lack thereof that had an impact on children's actions. As children sought to obtain material things (by looking for them, stealing them or sharing them, see Chapter Six) or searched for everyday companions outside their home, their practices were often developed in the unexpected spaces and social ties they encountered in highly opportunistic events in the neighbourhood (see also Chapters Five and Eight). For several children whose family life was unpleasant (they did not receive much attention from their parents – including because they were from big families – or even experienced neglect), the neighbourhood, street and contacts with other children (or adults, such as those from the Centre but also with neighbours and members of their wider families) were the main domains of social activities and emotional attachments. Family life also shaped barriers and constraints for children's everyday activities. While most children were highly autonomous in their daily practices and many parents struggled to enforce rules and limits even if they wished to, duties in child care were a particularly apparent cause of the restriction of some children's activities in time and space. This included especially several older girls with extensive duties in their families. This time being spent with/for their families meant they could spend less time with their friends. Importantly, then, the material presence of family was often as important an extension to children's agency as its absence.

An obvious theme that this chapter raised is the question of the difference, boundaries or relations between family and other types of children's grounded relationships, particularly friendship and peer ties with other children. Considering the empirical examples that show how family dynamics often served a similar role as children's bonds with their friends, this leads towards an understanding of the role of family in children's practices as a complex institution with multiple functions and mechanisms that are individualised in the everyday arrangements of particular children (Aitken, 1998, 2000b), 'affirmed, confirmed and reaffirmed through social action' (James, 1993, p.215). This challenges the idea of universality in the family function for children's everyday lives (Holloway, 1999; Aitken, 2009). The topographical analysis showed a variety of factors that differentiated the impact of family life on children's practices, depending on children's age, gender, family structure or socioeconomic circumstances. However, it also showed family as a dynamic and situated pattern in children's social lives whose impact in many ways overlapped with other children's relationships.

The role of friendship directly ties in to the issues of family, so a relational framework that understands children's relationships through the performances in which they are materialised can be seen as more useful than thinking about families as existing 'in principle'. Chapter Ten will thus develop this perspective and will analyse children's relations with their peers, while Chapter Eleven will focus on children's broader relationships to society through the notion of social identity.

TEN

Friendship

'Hi, I'm Matej.'
   'Hi, I'm Ronald. Will we be friends?'
   (My first meeting with Ronald, aged 9, October 2008)

I was taken aback by the easiness of Ronald's question but, not seeing any better reaction, my answer was "Yes, we will." I also made a mental note to find out what exactly Ronald meant by "being friends" (if anything specific at all) – that is, what commitment I had just made – and whether this would be a meaning widespread across the neighbourhood.

Ronald was a boy who struggled to engage in more complex or sophisticated conversations, but he often surprised me with straightforward and unexpected remarks or questions. Over the next couple of days, Ronald asked me further questions, such as the very frank "Will you protect me?" or a more mysterious "Will you be here?" No further context was given and I was now more careful about replies to these questions, trying to ensure that I first understood what Ronald meant.

I never got to talk to Ronald about what he meant by "being friends", but we talked a lot about "being here" and "protection". Ronald was very attached to the Community Centre and he was one of the children whose attachment to me as a worker I felt was perhaps too intense, as he claimed my attention for whole shifts or required physical contact regularly. He often came into conflict with other children and usually left them bruised, but he also struggled to prevent such incidents, often adding fuel to the fire. Hence, while Ronald repeated his request for protection several times, I tried to raise the theme of the behaviour that would prevent conflicts instead.

With experiences such as these, I began to understand (or to think that I understood) what Ronald meant by "being friends" at our first meeting. The theme of safety and protection, but also the very fundamental ongoingness and stability in the relationship, were very important to him due to the number of his conflicts with other children, his lack of skills in coping with such situations and the lack of support he usually received. I guessed that issues such as safety, consistency, support or acceptance were what he expected when he asked about being friends and which I could provide him as a Centre worker. And this partly contradicts James's (1993) arguments that durability is often absent from children's friendships and it is not as important for children's relationships as for adults. While most children's friendships in Kopčany were rather turbulent (discussed later), children often valued stability or constancy in any type of relationship very highly, partly as a result of their experiences of stability and its absence, both with their friends and in their families.

I have emphasised several times the significance of what could be labelled as the 'being-together' of children in the limited spatial area of Kopčany. The notion of friendship, as Ronald expressed it (in words as well as practice), was just one form of expectation that children had of their peers and it was also related to individual factors, such as Ronald's personality, age or activities. In this chapter, I explore what kind of grounded affirmative relationships emerged among the children from Kopčany, and what impact the diverse ways of 'being-together' had on their everyday practices. Similarly to the discussion of family, I explore friendship as a complex and dynamic domain of social ties among the children that has different meanings and is performed in various ways by individual children (James, 1993). Whereas the scope of the previous chapter was delimited by the legal ties and housing arrangements that defined family and from which everyday performances of bonds evolved, this chapter will be focused on the social dynamics formed by children themselves in their own social fields.

Although friendship has been recognised widely as an important domain of everydayness, it has eluded a sustained interest from social scientists for some time. Yet what interest there is seems to be moving from formalised forms of social relations and/or relations based on subjugation and hierarchy towards everyday grounded interpersonal relationships that are, at least at first glance, based primarily on social bonding and positive affirmation (Allan, 1989; Bell and Coleman, 1999); in a shift from the field of social and developmental psychology (for example, Erwin, 1998; Schneider, 2000; Dunn, 2004), the focus is primarily on the impact of friendship on children's immediate wellbeing and on their transitions to adolescence and adulthood. I draw on some of key debates in social studies of friendship, especially those related to ideas of friendship as a performative device, as a medium of both social affirmation and segregation, and as a social domain reproducing and contingent upon other social factors.

Empirically, the chapter explores three interrelated themes. First, it will expand on the debate about the meanings of friendship for children from Kopčany in order to show the impact of these notions on their practices. Second, the discussion will look at how peer relationships among the children are constituted, what types of inclusive or exclusionary formations they cause, and what performances emerge from these processes. Finally, the chapter explores the mutual links between the constitution of friendship, children's everyday practices, and place.

Sense and practices of friendship

> Hugo (10) met me on the street and asked whether I had seen XX and YY (he mentioned a couple of names). He said that he was organising a birthday party and would like all his best friends to be there. (Extract from fieldnotes, May 2009)

When I asked Hugo why he decided to invite these children and not others, he re-emphasised that he wanted his "*best friends*" to be there and we began a short conversation about what he meant by friends. Hugo mentioned Silvester (11), a boy with whom he spent a lot of time, including at school, doing martial arts training outside Kopčany, time in the Centre, but also on the street. He said that he could trust Silvester as he was someone who would not lie to him or gossip and throw dirt at him behind his back. I knew that Hugo often presented his friendship with Silvester openly, saying on several occasions that he would do something only if Silvester would join him or explaining how they were "a crew".

Such an explicit account of friendship was largely untypical for the children and Hugo was also one of the very few children who also talked very openly and directly about his feelings towards his family members. More often, children's understanding of friendship and their accounts of their peer relations were tied to their practical experience of other people.

> I asked Michal about the summer camp, co-organised by the Centre, that he and some other boys from the neighbourhood had attended. His first reaction was short – "it was great", he said. Then he added more, telling me some short stories. However, although he mentioned positive experiences, he rarely talked about himself and described instead what his friends did, how they behaved, what fun it was with them, or how they annoyed him. He

mentioned Emo and his stuttering, Daniel and the troubles
he had caused, or Simon and how they had got along very
well and supported each other. (Extract from fieldnotes,
July 2009)

Children often talked about the character traits of their friends and
usually could provide a link to an actual experience that would illustrate
these traits. Although some used terms such as 'friends' in order to
describe their relationship with other children, more often they
described the other person and the activities they shared (including
even what they did *not* do, such as when Silvester would not tell others
about Hugo's personal troubles). In a similar way, in Chapter Nine, I
mentioned stories of Nina and Anna who expressed their relationship
to their fathers by telling stories of activities they shared rather than by
describing their feelings – in the case of Nina, it was a direct reaction
to a boy who expressed his opinion about Nina's father by telling the
stories of him being drunk.

Several authors argue that while friendship is an important domain
for the development of children's identities, it is the practices of
friendship and the everyday embodied interactions with one's peers
rather than the attachment among children, or 'a cognitive relationship
of affectivity' (James, 1993, p.215) that effectively form children's
relationships (Goodwin, 2008; Dyson, 2010). This claim does not mean
that emotional ties among children do not exist, but rather than having
a form of attachment to an individual person, they are linked closely
to children's everyday experiences of events in which their 'friends'
take part. From positive experiences, children in Kopčany were then
capable of extracting key values that marked what their expectations
and appreciations of their peers were – such as loyalty, support, or just
simple fun. For many, it was the very presence of other children in
their lives which was valued – especially as children and their families
often moved in and out from the neighbourhood (Chapter Two) and
several children had thus experienced losing their best friends suddenly
(Chapter Five).

The significance of the performative aspects in the formation of
friendship raises two more themes. First, the processes of establishing
relationships between children were themselves situated within the
fields of other social or individual factors and these backgrounds were
crucial for what kind of individual or collective performances could
take place in Kopčany and trigger the development of children's
relationships (Morris-Roberts, 2004; Goodwin, 2008). Second, the
performances of friendship also had an effect on children's identities

and on their social positions within the children's cultures in Kopčany (and beyond), and reshaped the social landscapes of childhood in the neighbourhood. Both these themes are explored in the next section.

Formations of friendship and their social circumstances

In the previous chapters, I argued that Kopčany, an isolated and spatially constrained area with a high number of children living in small flats, was a place of frequent interactions and mutual engagements between children because of the proximity these factors caused. Children met other children on the street regularly and they engaged with each other routinely. Even though children's ties were complex and heterogeneous, several overarching factors of differentiation in the formation of children's friendships could be seen.

Age was an important axis, even beyond the similarity in interests or physical capacities or experiences among the children of the same age. The majority of children from Kopčany attended one of the two elementary schools in the nearby neighbourhoods and many children of the same age were in the same class. The everyday contact in school meant that the children spent considerable amounts of time together, as well as sharing experiences (but also problems) and activities (such as programmes in the school or homework). For the children who visited the Centre, several activities were designed for certain age groups. As most of these took place in smaller groups and required social interactions (through a deliberate focus on the development of social skills), children of similar ages met together frequently. There were also certain differences among children of different ages in what activities they most usually engaged in. While the youngest children particularly enjoyed exploring the neighbourhood, searching for new objects, climbing roofs or trees, or often just digging in the ground, older children spent more time hanging around and chatting together, or playing games. Older children tended to have more interests outside the neighbourhood and they had higher mobility than the youngest children as these were often only permitted to stay in the front of the building they lived in.

However, several peer connections were established among children with a considerable difference in age, most often when children spent time with their siblings. I mentioned already a couple of stories of children whose best friends left the neighbourhood and what impact it had on their daily practices. In the story of Samo and Lenka (Chapter Nine), Samo initially spent time with his older sisters and in the company of their friends. After two of his sisters' friends left the neighbourhood and his sisters spent less time together (Lucia, the older one, found a new best friend), Samo found new friends before Lenka did. As they had to spend time together because Lenka had responsibilities for her brother, she joined his brother's new company (of younger boys) and usually spent time on the street with them. Another similar story was that of Alena (9), whose brother, and also her main companion, left the neighbourhood. Alena initially was not seen on the street for a couple of months and then appeared in the company of her oldest sister and her friends. In both cases, older but also younger siblings acted as children's key or at least most stable peers and partners in their everyday activities. They often joined peer groups of their siblings and, while many of the newly formed relationships ceased to exist afterwards, in some cases the friendships established through the company of children's siblings persisted or even surpassed (in frequency or intensity of the contact) existing ones between the friends and siblings.

The factors of having several siblings and spending time with at least one of them frequently, either because of the responsibility assigned by the parents or out of children's own choice, were crucial in how mixed children's groups of different ages but also gender were constituted in Kopčany. Even if groups of the same age or gender existed, children very often integrated their siblings into the groups, so contacts between children of various ages and between boys and girls were formed and the children spent their time together. Children's residential mobility in terms of moving to and from the neighbourhood was also an important factor. A sibling or a cousin was often the closest social contact that children had after their best friends (often unexpectedly) left the area.

While children did not necessarily prefer single-gender groups of friends at all times, gender was another axis of difference in children's friendships. There was not much gender difference among the younger children in the amount of time they spent on the street and with whom. The most frequent and most routine activities, such as just hanging out and exploring the area, or chatting together, involved both the girls and boys of different ages, and indeed, mixed age and gender groups existed among the children. Also, activities at the Community Centre, often aimed at encouraging cooperation among the children, helped to integrate them. The children did not express any sustained tendency to separate from the other gender either, as boys and girls interacted together and mixed contacts were sought and initiated by the children themselves. Within the Community Centre, separate group meetings of the girls and the boys existed initially, only to be merged after children's demands. Even before that, children asked for joint weekend trips that had previously been organised separately for the girls and for the boys. After I left the field, the groups, as well as the weekend trips, were organised for mixed groups of boys and girls, but during my stay, the children attempted to negotiate the mixed access, arguing for their friends to be allowed to participate, or simply spent time in the Club by looking from the window and talking to their friends of the opposite gender on the street. There were even cases when children tried to sneak in the Community Centre to join the other group, often with help from their friends, and sometimes even in disguise. I discussed already (especially in Chapters Six and Eight) children's use of their bodies as a means of action and communication. Whereas gender was articulated as a regulatory component of the rules in the Centre by separating girls and boys on various prescribed occasions, it also worked as the children's embodied tool of resistance and transgression (Renold, 2006; Kallio, 2008; Kallio and Häkli, 2011).

Only a small number of practices in Kopčany divided pre-adolescent boys and girls. For boys, it was primarily football, an activity that formed intensive engagements often across different age groups. As there was not a suitable site on which to play football in the neighbourhood, boys sometimes travelled together to a nearby pitch outside the area. While some girls also played football, they only occasionally joined the boys, or joined them only if there was just a small number of boys. For boys, football was a social environment through which they developed relations with each other and it triggered social networks among them (see also Chapters Six and Seven). This line between boys and girls was not based on the matter of physical activity itself. Girls from Kopčany, usually up to the age of 12 or 13, were often as keen on physical activities as boys. Where football provided a collective environment and group interactions, however, physical activities preferred by girls were more individual or involved just small groups. Younger girls engaged in skipping over the rope, but usually no more than four or five children took part (some, usually younger, boys occasionally participated too), whereas there were very few limits for playing football. Older girls preferred physical activities such as roller-skating, cycling, swimming or dancing, that is, those that could be done individually or in just very small groups (see Figure 10.1). Engaging in small groups (or pairs), the contact in such activities was more intensive although the networks among the girls were also considerably smaller.

The gaps between boys and girls increased as children grew up. As older children were allowed to spend time on their own and not necessarily in the company of their siblings, this gave them a chance to

Figure 10.1 Girls' friendship (this time 'practised' around play with a volley ball in a small group, or rather around chatting while having borrowed a volley ball)

find new contacts and establish new relationships. An important factor was the increasing mobility, that is, the fact that older children could spend more time on their own outside the neighbourhood. However, while older girls did this often in the company of their friends from school, or with their boyfriends (from outside Kopčany), boys spent time outside the neighbourhood usually with their friends (boys) from the neighbourhood. Groups of older boys (over 15) were more open to their younger peers joining them in their regular activities, such as sport, visiting swimming pools (in the summer) or shopping centres (in the winter), drinking, or just spending time in the company of others in the course of their affairs both within and outside the neighbourhood, thus experiencing new everyday mobilities together. Addressing similar themes, younger boys first took part in the activities of the older ones that went beyond the spaces of Kopčany and they later developed closer relationships. On the other hand, older girls developed their peer relationships primarily outside the neighbourhood, and their relationships within Kopčany were linked to their duties in family. Older girls often engaged with other young women, especially young mothers from the neighbourhood, with whom they spent time together when caring for younger children (siblings, other relatives, or neighbours). Girls' contacts within the neighbourhood thus came from family and caring activities with neighbours, and their friendships with young people of the same age from the neighbourhood were now more individualised.

These new dynamics also affected the gendering of public space of the neighbourhood. One of my first impressions after coming to Kopčany was the presence of groups of older boys (over 15) on the street, with very few girls (or none at all) among them, and only a minimum of the girls-only groups regularly showing up on the street (see Figure 10.2). Several reasons were outlined earlier – girls' responsibilities in their families, their relationships outside the neighbourhood, or smaller and often closer relationships even within Kopčany. However, the increasing dominance of boys over the spaces in the neighbourhood was also important. For instance, I was told that the decision to organise girls-only meetings in the Community Centre (a few years later followed by boys-only groups after some requests from the boys) was partly the result of girls' exclusion from the initial programme of the Community Centre indoor activities. Here, the split of the children into various groups (due to the limited space in the Centre) was initially based on age. However, the number of the (older) boys who visited the Club was much higher than that of the girls, and even those girls who entered the Club felt uncomfortable in a male-dominated space and ceased to visit the Community Centre. Moreover, some older girls had responsibilities for their young relatives and could only come to the Centre in their company, which was against the rules that set a minimum age threshold so they were consequently disqualified from the spaces of the Community Centre. Parallel patterns of gendering space could also be seen on the street, where older girls, especially those caring for young children, occupied different sites than older boys. As a result, older girls and younger women spent more time in domestic spaces or caring for their younger relatives on the streets of the neighbourhood, a spatiality that can be seen as extending the domestic caring space into the street.

Figure 10.2 A shot from a video that young people (over 15) produced about their everyday activities in the neighbourhood (Blazek and Hraňová, 2012). This was supposed to be an example of an ordinary activity, for which a football game was chosen, including only boys.

Social background also played a limited role in differentiating children's friendships. However, unless children's families intervened and forbade children to meet their friends, younger children interacted with almost everyone else on the street and contacts became established across all social groups. As children grew older, more segregated peer groups were formed according to their social background (including issues such as ethnicity, see Chapter Eleven), but for younger children, a family's affluence, image, or the ethnicity of their peers was rather irrelevant. If some friendships emerged across social differences, this was primarily as a result of particular *activities* that children shared. For example, attending organised activities outside Kopčany (such as playing football in a club) was not accessible (because of time and financial reasons) to all children, so contacts among them transferred to their everyday activities in the neighbourhood. Similarly, some contacts were established through activities based on material things that only some children possessed – such as riding a bicycle or playing computer games. In a similar fashion, quite intensive contacts and ties arose among children who spent time in activities such as pickpocketing or stealing in shopping centres – this included children from relatively more as well as less affluent families.

This extended discussion leads me to two themes. The literature on children's friendship usually emphasises the importance of support, trust and often even mutual reliance in children's peer relations from which their friendships emerge. On the one hand, several studies, particularly from the global North, highlight the cultural autonomy that children and young people are able to achieve through peer relations, that is, how they are able to form their 'own social worlds which revolve around friendship' (Skelton, 2000, p.82). Such aspects can be clearly seen in the emotional dimensions of children's friendships, such as when Ronald seeks protection or Hugo appreciates Silvester's honesty. On the other hand, there is a strand of research that reveals how friendship or other forms of informal peer relations among children and young people, particularly in the global South but not only there, are crucial even for their 'pragmatic concerns over livelihood' (Dyson, 2010, p.495), including their daily strategies of survival. Authors exploring experiences of street children (for example, Lees, 1998; van Blerk, 2005) emphasise mutual protection as a key factor in children's relationships. This can also be seen as a highly significant aspect for children from Kopčany, who did not stay on the street overnight but for whom the street was the main social domain of their activities. Accounts of children's experiences in more complex and difficult social situations often emphasise friendship also as a strategy of daily survival activities, including its role in the organisation of begging and other forms of access to resources (Stevenson, 2001; Swanson, 2009) or in children's work activities in their communities (Katz, 2004a). Again, while children from Kopčany by and large did not beg or work for money, friendship can be seen as instrumental in their daily wellbeing activities, such as when they were looking for things around the neighbourhood, or went stealing, activities that often took place in groups and in which children supported each other.

However, many authors also argue that friendships are constituted through the reproduction of established social structures and cultural differences such as class, gender, sexuality or subcultural belonging (Hey, 1997; Nayak, 2003b; Thomas, 2009; Sutton, 2009). The debate in this section highlighted the intersectional relations between family and friendship (Punch, 2005), and age and gender (Hey, 1997;

Hopkins and Pain, 2007), through which children's daily dynamics emerge. Younger children engaged in mixed-gender activities and groups, but as they grew up, the gender gap in social contacts and in children's regular activities increased, partly as a consequence of children's family arrangements. This also affected the patterns of their friendships in which children's gender identities and gendered practices were consolidated (see Chapter Eleven).

In all these accounts, the role of siblings was important. Siblings, even if of the opposite gender or of a different age, often filled the main roles of friendship as they provided support, reliability, protection, company in everyday activities, or material belongings to their fellow young family members. A deconstituted division between family and friendship can be seen through the focus on children's daily activities and on the role of siblings. On the one hand, friendship filled several expectations that children did not find in their families – children's friends helped them in acquiring everyday objects they used in games, or protected them on the street where children's parents were absent. On the other hand, children's siblings were often also their main friends. Not necessarily their best friends, but as children's best friends often left the neighbourhood unexpectedly, siblings then took the role of being the main company, at least for the time children spent on the street, and this relationship worked in both directions between older and younger siblings.

Place of friendship

> I was walking around the neighbourhood with Robert (9) and every time we passed Hugo (9) and Marko (8), the boys yelled something at Robert, once or twice they even threw a twig or a little stone. I asked Robert what was going on and he said nothing and urged me to go on. Eventually, Hugo and Marko stepped in our way and stopped us, assaulting Robert. I insisted that they at least explain the reason for this. They refused but after I insisted again, Hugo told me that Robert borrowed something from him and did not return it (Robert said he had lost it) and that he also bad-mouthed him in the face of other boys. (Extract from fieldnotes, May 2009)

This story with Hugo relates to some of the themes that have already been mentioned. The formation of friendship between Hugo and Marko, but even more the formation of hostility (as the opposite of friendship) between Hugo and Robert, was marked by the local circumstances. In Kopčany, where borrowing and debts were important and very sensitive issues of everyday life, especially among young people, Robert's act – failing to return the thing and thus breaking the agreement – was considered as something very detestable, something that initiated Hugo's repulsion and anger. Similarly, badmouthing someone behind his/her back was something that children perceived very negatively. In this situation, Hugo and Marko pointed out Robert's particular actions that made them angry and Hugo also mentioned how "it was not a decent thing that Robert did". Such a characteristic was in opposition to what Hugo would expect from his friend – loyalty, trust and safety – but it also referred to Robert's very particular act.

Apart from arguments about friendship constituting inclusive structures, several studies also suggest that they are instrumental in the production and reproduction of exclusionary patterns among children (Hey, 1997; Skeggs, 1997; Goodwin, 2008). In the story with Hugo and Robert, two quite young boys, the process of detachment came from a particular experience rather than from a cultural pattern between the two boys, something that again highlights the performative nature of children's friendships. The story however also relates to Dyson's critique of the institution of friendship because of its 'capacity ... at some moments to generate critique and novel practice and at other moments mirror and reinforce dominant structures' (2010, p.484). The theme of friendship as not just a mechanism of alliance and affirmation, but also as a device of exclusion and separation, thus opens up the question of the relationship between children's friendships and place, one I will illustrate with the story of Simon (13). Simon had moved to Kopčany less than two years before I started my fieldwork but it was only at the time that I arrived that he began establishing relationships with children there. He mentioned the history of being bullied that accompanied him in the past and because of which he changed school a couple of times. Although he was not a belligerent type, my first experiences with Simon were with the troubles he had with other children. With several, the conflicts seemed to be ongoing: a couple of younger boys attacked him frequently, partly making use of the fact that Simon did not defend himself. However, there were a number of situational conflicts triggered by Simon's unintended actions – such as how he joined conversations or activities of other children without asking, which made them angry. Simon's way of dealing with conflicts did not help the case either, as he often added fuel to the flames by his words and reactions and it was too late when he realised the seriousness of the problem.

We [me and my colleague] had a nice long talk with Simon, Alexandra and Michal after which they left us and met another group of children. We had a short walk around Kopčany that might have taken not more than 10 minutes and after returning to the place of our departure we saw a surprising turn of events. Where a while ago the children were in a friendly talk and joyful game, Simon was now standing alone on the roof of a small switch-house and about ten children were throwing chestnuts at him, Michal and Alexandra among them. Nobody could explain how this started. We argued that the ratio is quite unfair and maybe someone should join Simon if it was a game, but the children were really too busy throwing nuts to reply. Simon was standing on the roof, throwing nuts back and teasing other kids about how they could not hit him. While Simon seemed to be having fun and many children were perhaps too, some were evidently getting furious and the situation could escalate. A couple of boys now threw stones and one or two attempted to climb the roof from the other side so they could strike Simon from behind directly on the roof. Simon was still laughing, and escalating the situation even more. (Extract from fieldnotes, October 2008)

We talked to Simon about situations such as this and suggested that he needed to think more about the boundaries between having fun and getting into serious conflicts. He often argued that it was the fault of other children who were plainly wrong and did not understand him. Unlike the majority of children, Simon attended a school on the other side of the city and claimed it was a much better environment, with other children whom he described as "much more normal [than those in Kopčany]". He admitted that he did not really have friends in the school, however he felt more accepted and safe there, partly because of having his older brother attending it too.

About ten months later, I talked to Simon about his experiences in Kopčany and with the Centre. Simon declared that he "loved" Kopčany and "would not like to move anywhere else [as] ... it was the best place he had ever lived in". Our talk turned towards the theme of inclusion and Simon emphasised how he had made several friends that he could rely on. Quite importantly, some of his friends were generally popular and respected also by other children, and they also had the capacity to negotiate mutual conflicts among other kids. He also mentioned how he had become more familiar with Kopčany and knew "what to expect" from the people. I outlined some past conflict events with other children and Simon admitted how he had learned to "read" others' reactions better, and how he had become more sensitive in ordinary interactions and more assertive in conflicts. While still experiencing tensions with other children, for example as he was very responsive to other children making fun of his family, he also said that he had learned how to react in such conflicts, not taking them further, often relying on those friends who took some notice of his discomfort and supported him.

Simon highlighted the role of his best friend who supported him constantly and helped him to integrate with other children. He also acknowledged how his life was improved by having a good relationship with other children, being able to maintain (for instance by playing football regularly with other boys) and not damage these relationships (acting calmly in conflicts) in routine everyday interactions. Simon explicitly emphasised friendship as the matter through which his attachment to Kopčany was also formed and enacted. Similarly, when I asked him for a feedback on the Community Centre services, Simon highlighted the role of the Centre in establishing children's relationships through group activities and the safe social space that the Centre provided, either through its indoor spaces, or through the presence of the staff during the street work shifts. As he said, he experienced the Centre as a space where the children could meet without any risk of being harmed, and where they were also stimulated into mutual interactions, although not forcefully so they could digress if they wished. As Simon said: "I would recommend to anyone new to Kopčany visiting the Centre so as to have a chance of meeting new people, and thus to get established here."

Simon's story began situated in a social field of children's peer relationships in Kopčany with relatively high exclusionary potential. However, this field, as a resource from which children's relationships were constituted and unfolded, was also highly dynamic and intersubjective (see Scourfield et al, 2006), reflecting the diversity of individual children and the complexity of their ties (Kjørholt, 2003). Over the course of time, Simon learned more about other children, about their reactions, and the differences among them. While he learned more about his social environment, he also transformed his daily performances that had led him into trouble in the past and now he became accepted by others. Holt (2010) emphasises that social capital among the children does not have only a representational fabric but also has ultimately an embodied and performed nature, as the discussions from Chapter Seven about the role of embodied performance against the rational domain of language also show. For Simon, it was important to adjust how he acted in relatively mundane circumstances, such as not interfering in other children's activities without asking, in order to find acceptance among them and a chance to develop ties with others.

Several factors thus contributed to Simon's involvement with other children increasing over the course of time. His social capital was expanded and maintained both by his performative actions, but also by his relationship with a key friend or with the Community Centre staff. Simon's path towards other children was not guided by an older sibling, as was the case for several children in previous paragraphs, but he found different resources locally – a good friend who was respected by other children and the safe space in the Community Centre. Along with improving experiences with other children, Simon's attitude towards the whole place also changed and he became fond of Kopčany. This, in turn, increased his motivation to spend more time here and to engage in activities in the neighbourhood with other children, deepening his relationships there.

Conclusions

This chapter followed on from discussions in Chapter Nine about family life and further explored what circumstances affected the formation of children's key relationships and how they, in turn, affect children's daily practices in relation to friendships. Because of the amount of time that children spent on the street and the extent of their activities within a relatively limited spatial radius, their mutual relationships were crucial for the range and type of their practices in the neighbourhood. I have discussed examples when the notion of friendship resonated among the children and the conclusion was that, rather than existing 'in principle', children usually recognised friendships through specific experiences with their peers, or through the identification of specific traits they appreciated about their friends in these situations. Rather than being a separate entity, children's friendship can be seen as a domain of routine social practices along with children's personalised expectations on their peers (Hey, 1997; Skelton, 2000).

Children sought a range of things in their relationships with other children: trust, support, protection, stability or fun being the most prominent. The emergence of friendships happened in relation to children's other relationships, particularly in their families (although the role of the Community Centre, for instance, was also mentioned in the cases of Ronald or Simon). Siblings often took the role of children's main friends and filled their expectations for support or company. Especially among the younger children, whose best friends often left the neighbourhood suddenly, the presence of siblings was a stable domain of social engagement.

I have argued that several social factors, such as age or gender, had an impact on how children built their relationships, but also that, because of the fluid dynamics in children's lives and the significant role of sibling relationships, children often formed friendships with older/younger children or in groups with children of the opposite gender. These patterns were most notable among the younger children, who actively sought the presence of children of the other gender (less so of different age), while older children, mainly as a result of the difference in their everyday activities, split more into friendships within the same gender.

Friendship was shown not just as an inclusive and supportive device, but also as a mechanism of exclusion and separation. This came primarily from the differences in children's regular practices, or from their mutual experiences, not so much (especially among the younger children) from their social or cultural backgrounds. Due to the complexity and intensity of children's everyday encounters concentrated within the relatively small area of Kopčany, the place, as an overall source of spatial opportunities, social contacts, or material equipment, became an important factor in how children developed their relationships, while children's experiences of friendship shaped their attachment to the area.

In this chapter, the notion of social or cultural difference has in some cases appeared as an important cornerstone of the topographies of children's daily practices. Also, the question of how notions of social identity based on gender or age were formed as a result of children's everyday activities was touched upon. In the next chapter, I explore this theme in more detail, leading to wider conclusions connecting Chapters Eight, Nine, Ten and Eleven in a thread addressing children's social relations as I draw out the mutual links between the circumstances of children's daily practices and broader notions of social identity.

ELEVEN

Notions of social identity

'I will leave the school when I'm, well, 15 or 16. [And then?] I'll be working with my uncle, he has a company, works with cars. He earns pretty much money and he'll give me a job.' (Martin, 9)

Martin's statement introduces the last empirical chapter of the book where I explore how several aspects of children's social positionality and their perceptions thereof intertwine with their everyday practices. While in the previous chapters the significance of children's age or gender was among the key circumstances that affected what the children did, this chapter primarily explores how such notions (and ethnicity) emerge in discourses among and towards the children, how children performatively negotiate the social constructions of their identity traits, and how both the discursive and embodied negotiations of social identity act as extensions to children's agency. I am interested in how issues such as children's relative age, gender and ethnicity emerge through everyday discourses, but also how such discourses circulate and affect children's embodied actions, and how they are contested, negotiated or reinforced both in children's understandings and practices.

Theoretically, the chapter is inspired by what Foucault (1985) called the 'practice of the self', a reflective set of practices that establish a human subject and which are both situated in a dynamic set of conditions and actively seek to re-shape them. Sharp et al (2000) argued that in Foucault's later work: 'something of *a gap does* open up between discourse and practice, between scripted invocations of what embodied selves should be like and the particular performances of selves that individuals fabricate in their everyday lives' (2000, p.19). The view that the contacts between discourses, power relations and individual embodied practices are constituted through everyday performances, and therefore that to acknowledge them adequately requires understanding their spatial and temporal dimensions, is central also for how I employ this framework and how Chapter Eleven connects with the rest of the book. I will explore the moments when children establish and perform a sense of themselves against the notions of identity which they are assigned within their social relationships and within discourses produced by other people. The purpose of such analysis is to consider children first as gendered, ethnic and aged subjects in Kopčany in 'performative social situation[s]' (Thrift, 1996, p.41) that are constructed through the array of children's social contacts (already discussed in previous chapters), but then to shift the focus onto how children 'effect ... a certain number of operations on their own bodies and souls, thoughts, conduct, and way of being, so as to transform themselves' (Foucault, 1988, p.17) into new social subjects through their everyday practices. The interface of the narratives of children's identity, collectively constructed and imposed through children's social relationships, and of children's embodied actions as individual human beings, is the extension of agency that is the subject of this chapter and it is also the juncture where previous analyses of material and imaginative circumstances of children's practices meet.

I am interested in exploring the everyday positions that children adopt in complex relationships with other people as social subjects, possibly accepting and reinforcing some, but challenging and reworking others, and in the practices these points of contact instigate. Against the noticeably rationalist view of 'practising the self' advocated by Foucault (see Thrift, 2007), I explore a broader range of connections between children's positions as social subjects in power relations and everyday discourses, and their embodied practices, many of which are essentially unreflected or unaccounted for (see discussions in Chapters Four, Six and Eight).

The discussions in this chapter build on the previous narratives where, for instance, themes such as gender norms or practices were presented in relation to other thematic areas (such as family life). Although the chapter is structured in three sections according to the themes of age (or 'growing up'), gender and ethnicity, the previous chapters already made it evident that 'childhood, as a variable of social analysis, can never be entirely separated from other variables' (Prout and James, 1997, pp.8–9) and these variables intersect in a number of changing and unique ways. This chapter thus continues to argue that children's social positionalities need to be understood in relation to each other through the lens of intersectionality (Hopkins and Pain, 2007) but also a constant problematising of singularity and of social categories. Different notions of social identity very often affect each other, and together they form a heterogeneous and fluid basis for children as dynamic social subjects (Evans and Holt, 2011).

In the first section of the chapter, I explore the idea of 'growing up'. Linking back to Katz's (2004a) views on the immediacy (see Chapter Six) between children's thoughts and actions, I investigate the relative autonomy of children's agency in its relation to the spatialities of children's activities and to temporalities in their lives. The next section examines how ethnicity was a factor in children's activities in Kopčany and I argue that discourses about ethnicity, while present in children's everyday actions, are projections of discourses about other aspects of society, particularly discourses about civility. Finally, I draw on the debates in the last two chapters and I focus on the notion of gender in children's everyday lives, examining the connections between institutional formations of gendered patterns in children's lives, and children's own embodied performativities of gender. The chapter concludes with a short discussion about how the notions of social identity can be thought of as aspects of children's relationship with society but also with themselves as constituting individual subjects.

Children's autonomies and the temporalities of 'growing up'

Autonomy of the youngest children's practices

> Two days ago, Jakub (6) and Patrik (6) broke a window in the Community Centre when they were throwing stones … A colleague visited their families today and told their mothers about this. Both apologised for the window and explained how the other boy had a bad influence on their son, and how they forbade their son to meet the other boy, but they still *"do their own things anyway"*. (Extract from fieldnotes, June 2009)

The last statement was more than just a sigh from Jakub's and Patrik's mothers. Rather, it relates to the level of independence that even the youngest children from the neighbourhood had in their everyday activities. Neither Jakub nor Patrik went to school yet and their parents had very little time to spend with them as Jakub's mother and Patrik's father were working, and Patrik's mother spent much time with his youngest siblings. Although the responsibility for the boys when they were on the street was given to their older siblings, the boys often challenged this control and pursued their own interests, while their siblings were often happy to leave the boys on their own.

With the amount of time that the youngest children in the neighbourhood spent either on their own, or in the relatively loose care of their siblings, they became more independent in terms of their decisions and actions, and even the children aged 5 or 6 formed their own sense about their everyday experience, seemingly not just adopting the order of things proposed by others. In the summer months, the Community Centre organised an educational programme for children of pre-school age (Figure 11.1). I noticed that some children were recruited through the contacts that the Centre had with their parents, but many found out about the programme on their own through their other forms of involvement with the Centre or with their friends. Although parents had to sign and approve children's attendance at the programme, they were not present. In some cases, there was very little contact with the parents besides the written permission and, in one or two cases, I believe that the children might have been even discouraged by their parents from attending the programme, but they did anyway and managed to persuade their parents to give them the consent.

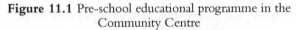

Figure 11.1 Pre-school educational programme in the Community Centre

Aitken argues that scholars writing about activities and experiences of younger children too often 'adopt ... a unidirectional approach wherein focus is on how adults direct and control interactions, while there is a conspicuous lack of interest in the infant's contributions' ((2000b, p.106). I agree with this statement, particularly insofar as it suggests that a popular view on the everyday life of younger children is that they lack agency beyond the practices that are scripted, controlled and enforced by adults (see also Holt, 2013). On the contrary, even the youngest children I worked with (that is, aged 5) did a lot on their own. I have seen the youngest children doing things that nobody else in the neighbourhood did and in places that were unknown to others, such as when 7-year-old Richard asked me to join him in catching frogs in a puddle of water near the neighbourhood. Nobody else in the neighbourhood knew about the puddle that Richard had found himself, nor about the frogs there. The youngest children explored places that others would not (such as wedging themselves into the space under stairways where interesting piles of litter could be found) or experimented with things, places and activities that others would not (such as playing with the liquid in a car battery and exploring its consistency). They worked with certain moral norms, so in the case of conflict (see the story of Samuel and Norbert in Chapter 6) they would attempt to deal with this on their own and only exceptionally asked adults to intervene.

The youngest children were aware of their needs and articulated them, but they also took actions in order to meet them. They even had an active sense of responsibility and care for each other, including their friends beyond the family, and pursued this with the experiences they already had:

> Peter (6) knocked on the door of the Club and asked if he could borrow a bicycle pump. I asked him to return it when he finishes and he left. He came back about twenty minutes later and asked me to help him, saying that he was unable to inflate the tyre. I asked whether it was really soft, remembering that we had inflated it a few days before. Peter explained that it was not himself he asked the pump for, but his friend, Milan, who was two years younger than Peter. When I went out, I found Milan with his grandmother standing near the bike and Peter showed me which tyre was soft and where the valve was so I could do it. (Extract from fieldnotes, July 2009)

In this situation, it was not Milan who came to ask for help, nor was it his grandmother, although she knew the Centre and its staff. It was Peter, who had the knowledge about the equipment in the Centre and also the experience of inflating the tyre with me a few days before. Peter also demonstrated his knowledge of bicycles (knowing where the valve was), a sense of care for his younger friend, but not least also his communicative skills, as he asked politely for help and explained the problem very accurately and in detail.

Prout and James claim that 'children must be seen as actively involved in the construction of their own social lives, the lives of those around them and of the societies in which they live' (1997, p.4) and not just from the perspectives of more 'powerful' adults determining their lives entirely (Mayall et al, 1996). Yet, in the burgeoning debates in the social sciences on children's agency, the youngest children remain largely excluded (Kraftl and Horton, 2008; Holt, 2013). With regard to children's lives in Kopčany, two interrelated perspectives could help to contest this neglect. The first is the decentred view on agency developed by Holt (2013) in her discussion of babies and their activities. Rather than thinking about agency as corresponding to a premeditated agenda for one's actions, there are broader connections between babies' usual activities such as sleeping, eating or crying, and the circumstances that enable and trigger those on the one hand, and the effects these activities have on other social actors, on the other hand. Through this prism, even babies or toddlers can be seen as relevant agents within certain social spaces as their activities have a huge impact on the economies, time management or emotional wellbeing of their parents or households, despite not being the same type of (rational) agents themselves. In this line of thought, relatively autonomous activities of children from Kopčany aged between 5 and 7 can be seen as having impact on people around them, even if these children were as yet only rarely involved in household duties or support of their families in other ways. However, children's requirements, the occasional damage they caused, but also their emotional affections and expressions (such as when Peter showed everyone in the Centre a Christmas gift he bought for his family) show that the youngest children's daily activities had effects on the people around them.

Another explanation of why the youngest children's agency is disregarded in popular discourses (including the academic ones) can be found in the context of what is called the 'Dionysian' view of childhood (Jenks, 1996). This understands children as naturally savage and lacking the awareness of, and respect for, social norms, making them potentially dangerous for civilised society. This view intrinsically expects that even the youngest children *do* have agency, but this agency represents a risk for society, so it needs to be repressed and controlled before it can be replaced by a more socially appropriate agency acceptable by adults. Katz, for instance, contests the Piagetian view that what is 'childish' about young people's actions is 'banished in the teleological march toward reason' (2004a, p.98), that is, banished as a part of the natural developmental process. Instead, she supports Benjamin's claim that this is rather what gets 'drummed out of children in the course of bourgeois education' (2004a, p.98), In other words, children's agency exists, but it remains rejected and excluded by adults until it resembles the conventional social norms.

In times when childhood is said to be 'the most intensively governed sector of personal existence' (Rose, 1999, p.123), the importance of adults controlling particularly the space and time of children's activities has been noted (Sibley, 1995a, 1995b; Kallio, 2008), so children's everyday practices are becoming standardised and commoditised (Katz, 1993; Aitken, 2000b) in order to facilitate adult control over childhood. In contrast to this view of constant and all-day monitoring and control of children's activities that involve not only their parents but also other institutions or (indirectly) other adults as they attempt to maintain the 'purity' of the spaces where children spend their time (Jones, 2000), the relatively limited area of Kopčany, along with the amount of time that children spent on the street, granted them a higher level of spatial and temporal autonomy in which their activities evolved with only very little adult interference or governance. And this is where the sigh of Jakub's and Patrik's mothers reveals not just their sons' lack of obedience, but also the configurations of control, or rather their relative absence, that the younger children in Kopčany were subjected to, and through which a significant portion of their daily activities could evolve.

On the other hand, children's lives can be seen as determined by adult agencies because of the level of provision that they cannot obtain on their own. While in Kopčany children's adult family members were their main economic providers (unlike cases mainly in the Global South; see Aufseeser, 2014), the previous chapters showed that in several areas, such as emotional support or obtaining objects for everyday activities, children relied to a great extent on their friends or siblings, or even on themselves (such as when they were looking for things or stealing them). Despite the relative material deprivation and spatial isolation (or because of this), children's everyday practices were still rich as they explored new objects and spaces instead of receiving access to them from others, and their agencies were shaped through these encounters.

Future and present in 'growing up'

The introductory quotation of this chapter, where Martin talks about his 'plans' to leave school, raises the question of how children's agency, existing even among the younger children, is constituted in relation to the course of growing up. There were a small number of life-course transitions that the youngest children recognised and explicitly articulated, such as when their milk tooth popped out, when they went to school for the first time or when their younger siblings were born. All these events, implicitly containing a notion of 'growing up' or 'becoming older', including some sense of adopting features associated with being older (being more responsible, for instance), were mentioned by children themselves as important moments. However, the children showed very little recognition of these events in terms of their self-perception. They did not present themselves as a 'schoolgirl' or 'not a baby any more', and they did not reproduce having heard such terms from other people, parents or friends.

Some of the previous examples seem to contradict this. In Chapter Six, I mentioned an experience with Peter (5), when, after being allowed to attend the Centre activities for boys of school age, I appealed to him ("you are a big boy now") when he tried to steal a skipping rope. Peter stopped and returned the rope, even challenging his sister for taking it. However, even in this situation, his attitude seemed to be more associated with having permission to attend the activity than with his symbolic status of a being a 'big boy'. In a similar situation a couple of weeks later, when the Club activities were suspended because of a holiday, this appeal did not work and Peter said he "did not mind not being a big boy". This story reflects the connections between the institutional disciplining to which I subjected Peter and the formation of discourses about age that confront children (Aapola, 2002). Peter's reaction to the notion of 'being a big boy' also reflected his refusal to be subjected to the discursive meanings of the term, so he accepted the game only insofar as it made a difference to what the Community Centre allowed him to do because of the way he bahaved.

The difference in Peter's behaviour between 'aspiring to be a big boy' and 'being a big boy when it is convenient' again raises the question of immediacy in children's action. In the discussion about the youngest children's agency, all the circumstances that contributed to the constitution of children's actions came from their focus on the present. Jakub and Patrik broke the window because they found it funny at the time and, in the story from Chapter Six, Norbert encouraged Samuel to hit him because at that moment he found it to be the best way to make him calm. In this respect, Martin's statement about leaving school and working with his uncle is clearly different as it reflects the increasing orientation towards the future that could be seen among the older children. For instance, older children engaged much more in economic activities. Even if the youngest children recognised the value of things or activities, they rarely kept things in their possession or exchanged them. Younger children tended to ask "Would you give me something?" without any particular reasoning about what it is that they would like or why they should receive it. Older children were more sophisticated – they were able to recognise different values of objects or the different weight of deeds and negotiate the reward they should receive (see Chapter Seven). Their economic negotiations were more rational – younger children often asked for things even when they were not entitled to them while the older ones were cautious about asking if they did not expect to receive, but straightforward when the claim was justified. The economic rationality and sophistication of the older children was apparent in more areas. Some children began to steal things at this age – not just small items from the Centre, but also from shops, sometimes with an order from their older friends who would be legally responsible if caught thieving and who paid younger children for this. Despite having limited funds from their parents (and no job or other source of income), children's agency was thus increased through economic activities and the amount of commodities they could command.

That some young people from the neighbourhood who would be legally responsible if caught for thieving after they turned 15 asked their younger peers to steal for them is a mechanism that opens up the theme of a structural difference between the circumstances of younger and older children already raised in Chapter Ten, namely one about peer connections with individuals of different ages. Stealing is an example of how some activities of older children were shaped in contact with their even older peers. For thieving, even patterns of reproduction existed when older youth residents gave ideas or hints to younger teenagers while the youngest children (younger than 10) were spared from this. There were also several other ways in which children formed their lives through interactions with the lifestyle of older persons (including older teenagers). For some boys, encounters with martial arts were one of the ways they shaped their growing up and while in some cases they had relatives with experiences in martial arts, for some it was the presence of older boys that introduced them into this activity.

> Silvester (11) was one of the first children I met and perhaps the first with whom I had a longer talk. While we walked around the neighbourhood on a rainy day, the main theme was martial arts and weapons. Silvester asked

me whether I was trained in any martial art and whether I had a knife or knuckleduster with me, and although seemingly discontented by my negative response, he went on talking about his experiences. (Extract from fieldnotes, September 2008)

A lot of what Silvester told me was not so much about his present experiences but related also to his future plans, desires and expectations. Silvester was fascinated by martial arts and he had vivid imaginations of becoming a skilled fighter. His activities and priorities were directed towards *becoming* a fighter *in the future*, towards a change that would come with age through his martial arts activities, a vision for which he found a number of adult male role models around him.

While in Silvester's case, growing up was associated with developing into a particular adult role model, other children were growing up aiming to differ from their older peers and, in their everyday practices, tried to avoid being the same as them.

['What concerns you in the neighbourhood?'] 'Hm … drugs. There are people who take it and they are unpredictable then. I mean, not everyone … There are guys such as [few older boys from the area mentioned] who are alright, and although when they smoke [marijuana] you can't really talk to them, it's still fun with them. But sometimes, with others, it's dangerous.' ['So drugs are a problem only at times?'] 'No, they are problems generally, really. Even for [the same boys mentioned again], it's a shame they do it, it would be much better with them if they don't.' (A dialogue with Michal, aged 13, July 2009)

For Michal and his friends, older boys from the neighbourhood were not really friends, nor were they role models. They interacted and younger boys even occasionally joined the older ones in some activities, such as football. Although Michal generally seemed to like and respect the older boys, he was concerned by their smoking of marijuana and despised it. Even though he was not afraid of them, as he was of some other adults who took drugs, especially of those whom he did not know very well, he disapproved of this and found the boys unlikeable after they smoked marijuana. On the other hand, Michal usually talked about the boys positively, emphasising their positive attributes such as their skills in football, sense of humour, or good knowledge of the life in the neighbourhood. However, experiencing them and their behaviour after smoking marijuana shaped what he was trying to avoid as he declared his ambitions to avoid drugs when he was older. As theories of role models' function in identity formation suggest, the influence of admiring one person does not have to follow all traits of this person and some characteristics can be ignored, or even critically assessed and their adoption can be rejected (Nauta and Kokaly, 2001). While Michal's 'self-thematisation' (Beck, 2000) was affected particularly by his contact with the older boys, he applied only some of the traits of their personalities for how he thought about his future and developed his visions as negating what he experienced with the boys.

Experiences from the family were also important for examples of how, and to what extent, the children thought about their future life paths. Martin's statement about how he would follow the path of his uncle was a relatively common picture presented by the boys from Kopčany, one I heard from four or five other boys. With just one exception, they all lived with their single mothers, and their uncles, who did not live in Kopčany, supported the families. Even in the case of one boy who lived with both his parents, the uncle was in frequent touch with the family and often came for family events, supporting the family. Uncles who were independent and distant, but still interested in their broader families and providing assistance to the boys, thus turned into role models that partly shaped the future aspirations of their young nephews.

As Picchio (1992) or Bezanson and Luxton (2006) show, social reproduction in families does not follow only material routes but it is also marked by children's expectations resulting from symbolic experiences with their parents' life paths. In this context, a connection can be seen between how post-secondary education was quite rare among the residents of Kopčany and how I heard a mention of this path just once or twice, even among children aged between 12 and 14. In a similar manner, children's discussions about high school (which they should move to, usually at the age of 15) mostly focused on vocational training rather than on general educational programmes that emphasised continuation to higher education. While children's visions about their future careers were generally uncertain and indistinct, occupations common among their parents were often mentioned. Here, while the younger ones tended to think about professions different from those of their parents or other family members – such as doctors or IT specialists – older children linked their plans more with the professions of their adult relatives. Even among them, boys could be more commonly heard talking about particular plans – such as becoming a car mechanic or other highly skilled manual labour professional – while girls' visions were usually less clear. This social reproduction of (imaginary) career paths was especially significant in families with multiple children where mothers (and often also other female family members) tended to spend much time at home with children, or/and taking additional low-income manual part-time jobs. As Rawlins (2006) shows, not just children's recognitions but also the actual intergenerational relationships between parents and children (in Rawlins's study particularly between mothers and daughters) mediate children's formation of 'identity'.

Benjamin (1978) developed the idea of 'mimesis', which understands children's action materialistically as the immediate appropriation and manipulation of the objects of their experience, 'releasing [simultaneously] new possibilities of meaning' (Buck-Morss, 1989, p.264), through which children learn. From this perspective, forming consciousness through embodied actions is dependent on the range of features that are present in children's immediate experience (see Katz, 2004a). In terms of the social positionality that situated children's daily practices in Kopčany, the difference in age, as a varying circumstance for these practices, can be seen to be connected to the amount and type of social contacts that younger and older children had. While younger children primarily engaged with their peers, and even their contacts with older individuals (children or adults) were framed by the latter being expected to provide care to the younger children, older children were better connected with their older friends but also some adults. Through these configurations, they were more often confronted with visions about the future and changed their perspectives accordingly, often incorporating these visions of their future into their present practices.

While the relationship between childhood and temporality is often theorised through the lens of generations or through childhood as a life-course period (James et al, 1998), the view presented earlier opens up a different perspective, which reveals childhood as a temporally specific set of attitudes towards the elements around human subjects as well as a specific attitude to the temporality of individuals' realities. These are of course intertwined with other factors that determine the constitution of different domains of childhood, such as the social configuration of experiences that children can have and which also modulate also their aforementioned attitudes. However, this perspective also maintains a high regard for children's agency and the complex formations of their practices as it accepts that children are networked with a range of circumstances that enable them to act. I will revisit this idea at the end of this chapter, after the discussions about children's positionalities in relation to their ethnicity and gender.

Notions and performances of ethnicity

During my third month in Kopčany, I was walking around the neighbourhood and heard someone shouting: "You fucking filthy gypsy!!!" While this was not unusual on its own, what made this event interesting was that it was Adam, a young Roma boy who screamed, and Erik, a young blonde boy with blue eyes who had been the object of Adam's outrage.

This story is an example of how the term *gypsy* (*cigán* or *cigáň* in Slovak) is used in ordinary discourses in Slovakia. While *Gypsy* is a word traditionally used to ascribe ethnic background, *Roma* (*róm* in Slovak) is a word that means 'a man' (both as a male and as a person) in the Roma language and has been introduced into the official Slovak language in the last couple of decades in order to replace the negative connotations of the term *Gypsy*. The term *Roma* initially designated a subgroup of the Romani population living in East and Central Europe, some of whom are also Slovak Roma (a different context from the UK or Irish context; see, for example, Holloway, 2005). However, the term is nowadays often used generally for all Romani people. These ethnic differences within the larger geographical scope are not really important for this study (cf. Ryder et al, 2014) and my references to the social situation or culture of Roma are highly situated, so I use the term *Roma*. Still, it is used quite infrequently in everyday Slovak language while the word *Gypsy* is dominant both among Roma and non-Roma people, and *Roma* is used mostly in official contexts and when the awareness of negative connotations is demonstrated as a political act. The verb *cigániť*, for example, is still used in Slovak as a synonym for 'to lie/cheat'. Children in Kopčany (both Roma and non-Roma) used the term *Gypsy* almost exclusively, and the word *Gajo* (*gádžo*), or *Gorgio* in English, was employed from the Roma language to name a non-Roma person, which is also used in informal Slovak.

Slovakia is a country with a high level of tensions between Roma communities and the non-Roma majority, evolving since well before the fall of the Iron Curtain in 1989, but accelerated and amplified during the uneven development of the post-socialist period (Stenning et al, 2010), when the social exclusion of Roma and ethnic antagonism have become central political topics. The position of the Roma population and the issues of discrimination have been outlined elsewhere in the literature (Vermeersch, 2003; Ringold et al, 2005). Themes such as segregation in education through placing Roma children into special classes for children with learning disabilities, a high level of Roma children's truancy (particularly in rural areas), poor living and housing conditions of Roma communities and their segregation (for example, by building walls between Roma and non-Roma neighbourhoods in Eastern Slovakia), and children's involvement in illegal economic activities (such as theft or begging) are among the prominent themes in discourses about Roma's children's position in the Slovak society.

For the scope of this study, however, I will explore how specifically the *notions* of being a Roma or Gajo affected children. Adam's use of the word 'gypsy' (intentionally written without capitals) represents the negative connotations of the Roma ethnicity that are present in Slovak society. Adam (who used to refer to himself as a Gypsy, through his ethnic background, and his older siblings mentioned this quite often and used the Roma language at times) used the term in anger as an insult routinely used in the neighbourhood, despite the exceptionally high (for the region) proportion of Roma residents.

> Ria, a 7-year old girl, has been very hostile towards me for some time. Today, she was quite nice, but after I gave my attention to other children, her behaviour became rather difficult – she tried to steal some things from my pockets, shouted insults, kicked me and said that she would spit at me. Meanwhile, Monika, a 12-year old girl joined me, and after few assaults from Ria, she jumped hard at her in order to protect me, screaming and saying that Ria is a 'dumb gypsy cunt'. (Extract from fieldnotes, November 2008)

The meeting of Monika and Ria was an encounter of two different backgrounds that the area of Kopčany embraced. Ria, a young Roma girl from a family with several children and a very low income, did not receive much attention from her parents, especially the father, struggled in school, and had very limited contacts and scope beyond her everyday activities in the neighbourhood. Monika, on the other hand, was a young white girl from a family with a moderate income and with both parents working, so they could afford to spend money even for a summer holiday or camps for the children. She had moderately good results in school and had considerable social and communicative skills. In the first months of our contact, Monika complained about the neighbourhood, mess and filth, explaining that it was "Gypsies" who were responsible for the majority of the problems, while families such as hers "had to live with it".

This contrasting view does not mean that children's friendships were normally ethnically segregated. On the contrary, friendships (dynamic as they were, see the previous chapter) were formed among the younger children across the whole neighbourhood and there was perhaps no Gajo child in the neighbourhood who did not have at least one Roma friend at some point, and vice versa. Still, particularly among the older children, some of the closest friendships were formed within individual ethnic groups. Many Roma residents in Kopčany were of the distinctive Vlachi ethnic group, with a culture based on strong family cohesion and patriarchal rules, and on the significance of family life over education, paid labour or civil life. Younger Vlachi children usually interacted with other children in the neighbourhood and they also regularly took part in activities of the Community Centre, but their families remained detached and engaged more with their relatives outside the area, as did the children usually, when they were older.

The issue of ethnicity was more prominent among the older children. I worked with a group of Roma children aged between 11 and 14 whose recognition of their Roma background was very explicit and they articulated it openly. They often used Gypsy words, even in conversations with other people so they could have fun when these did not understand. Especially in the group, the children were often noisy, at times insolent, and usually very explicit in their words and deeds. They raised the theme of ethnicity explicitly – singing Gypsy songs, discussing traditions and norms, or asking the Centre staff about their ideas and experiences with Gypsy culture. I was thus asked whether I had some Gypsy background myself (because of my dark look), whether I knew any Gypsy songs, whether I had been to a Gypsy wedding, or whether I knew any (racist) skinheads. They raised also some themes that were quite unusual among other children – such as spirituality, both in terms of religion, but also superstition and themes such as life after death or ghosts.

An important factor in the behaviour of these children was how they performed their ethnicity explicitly. When they were older, they were often detested by several other children who did not wish to spend time in their company. Some of them were even asked to stay out of the Centre for a period as their behaviour there was unacceptable (they damaged some objects in the Centre and were very disrespectful towards the staff) and some other children refused to attend the Centre in their presence. This incident was later discussed by the children through the dichotomy of being a 'Gajo' or 'Gypsy' in relation to who was allowed to visit the Club. Some of the children struggled with social norms elsewhere as well; for example, they truanted frequently. While this was also the case for several other non-Roma children, for this group of children, their view on such behaviour was encouraged by their presence in the group, and consequently also shaped in relation to their cultural values. The children presented themselves as different and expressed their different views on social norms explicitly. The notion of ethnicity was thus present to some extent as a cultural factor in children's activities. For several Roma children, it became relevant through their family lifestyle, language use or spirituality, while for several Gajo children it served as a synonym for uncivil behaviour and style of life. While these Roma children often performed their ethnicity through everyday practices such as singing or being noisy, others labelled particular kinds of performances (especially those considered as uncivil) with the notion of being Roma.

Associations between the construction of civility and the construction of ethnicity have been discussed in the literature elsewhere (Lee, 2006), along with the process of how they emerge through the connections between individual experiences (or prejudices) and the patterns of group behaviour and its cohesion or perception (Allport, 1954). The ways in which children thought about being Roma or Gajo and how some of their performances related to these notions (or their oppositions) explicitly do not suggest that children's views of ethnicity were necessarily determining their practices. The ethnic labels rather served to articulate particular expectations about socially acceptable behaviour with reference to the collective background of children's ideas about what was appropriate (Burney, 2005).

My argument is that while several cultural factors of being Roma or Gajo were present in children's practices, the ethnic identity of children from Kopčany was primarily built on the basis of their everyday collective experience of their own as well as other people's embodied performances. These were consequently classified through the lens of situated cultural meanings and everyday social ties associated with the ideas of being a Gypsy or Gajo. The notion of ethnicity thus crystallised hand in hand with the enacted networks of social capital built through children's embodied actions (Crawford, 2006; Holt, 2010), that were later negotiated, reformulated and overturned through children's reconsiderations about what was acceptable and what was not (see Fyfe et al, 2006). Meanwhile, the labels of ethnicity that children attached to themselves or to others were used in order to advocate or challenge these considerations. The notion of ethnicity crystallised *along with*, rather than *as*, the image of civility as children perceived it. The fact that children engaged together in everyday activities without considering the supposed underlying differences of their ethnic identities in the first instance was, then, a key factor in why especially the younger children got along together relatively well on a daily basis, resembling what Amin calls 'solidarity woven around the collective basics of everyday urban life' (2006, p.1009), the material circumstance of togetherness in a particular spatial context.

Notions and performances of gender

The previous chapters revealed children's gendered experiences as constituted in complex socially structured circumstances, including their family arrangements and roles, or the patterns of their friendships. Rather than repeating myself, I will link these discussions to the reflections on children's gendered performances and discourses.

My first impression in the neighbourhood corresponded with existing studies suggesting that children are clearly aware of various gender norms and expectations, even if they perform them in diverse ways, and that this includes even the youngest children (Kehily et al, 2002; Blaise, 2005; Youdell, 2005). At the start of my work in the Community Centre, I was frequently asked whether I was the partner of some of the colleagues (being the only man in the team). Several young boys asked me whether I had a knife or any other weapon and if I had been trained in martial arts (or rather, in which arts I had been trained), seemingly an ordinary thing I was expected to have or do as a male. My arrival was also met with pleasure by some boys who at once asked me to join them in playing football and kept suggesting it for a few months until my ongoing apologies discouraged them (see Chapter Eight on the role of football in friendships). I experienced some children wondering why I, as a man, worked with the youngest children, or, more specifically, why I *played* with them (cf. Horton, 2008). Children had several expectations also of my role as a male street worker. Older children expected me to be with them rather than with the younger ones and younger boys expected me to be with them, and particularly to play football or other sports with them, rather than being with girls. While at the beginning many children approached me to join them in physical activities, only very few asked me when they needed help in the Centre with cutting something from paper or with drawing, asking my female colleagues instead (see Barker and Smith, 2001).

Renold (2006) suggests that children's performances of gender begin as soon as they enter gendered social spaces and this is when they also begin to form meanings about gender. My ethnographic work took place in children's spaces that had a gendered nature and I had to negotiate children's expectations about the norms of masculinity carefully, balancing between my own comfort and what would be accepted by the children. This process involved constant exploring and learning about children's gender expectations and at times I was caught in situations where I did not expect children's ideas about gender norms at all and they shook their head or laughed at me over issues that made no sense to me at first. Sometimes children laughed at or criticised my clothes or shoes, or they often had fun when I was sitting with crossed legs, saying that it could not be a comfortable position for a man.

During an activity with a group of boys and girls aged between 12 and 14 in the Community Centre, the children were asked to write examples of activities which men and women must/must not, or can/cannot, do because of their gender. Both the boys and girls (working in separate groups) agreed on certain ideas – that both men and women should take responsibilities for their families; that men should be responsible for the material provision and should have a good enough job; and women should be more involved in family care and domestic work. Although the children were very confident about these statements at first, they found themselves challenging some of their visions as they reflected on their own experiences. One boy stressed how he was regularly given the duty of care for his younger brother (living only with his mother) and other boys admitted they helped with some domestic tasks (shopping, baking) though they refused others (vacuuming). Actually, from my experiences in the Centre, boys were as keen as girls, or maybe even more, to help with cleaning up after the programme (Figure 11.2), or enthusiastically took part in activities such as baking and craftwork. Irrespective of gender, children in Kopčany helped their parents with shopping outside the neighbourhood or even did some small shopping on their own in the local store.

Especially among the younger children, the awareness of gender was particularly situated and immediate, rather than based on naming convictions about the nature of these roles. Ester (11) was the youngest member of the group mentioned earlier, and when she was asked to complete the sentence "As girl, I can ...", her answer was "... I can read". It took extending the sentence to "As girl I can ... and boys can't" before she focused on gender differences when illustrating her point of femaleness, and some other children also did not immediately understand the first sentence as referring to gender differences. Even then, the children started the list of gender attributes with physical features such as pregnancy or menstruation, or with legal differences between men and women such as the military service men have to

Figure 11.2 Boys engaging in cleaning windows in the
Community Centre

do. In other words, children's conscious articulation of the notion
of difference between men and women (or boys and girls) stemmed
in first instance from the physical/structural differences between the
two, and even though their notions of gender were formulated quite
explicitly, especially among the older children with a knowledge of
socially reproduced gender norms, the children were able to confront
these expectations with their personal experiences.

Gender thus can be seen as a simultaneous mixture of established
expectations, circumscribed activities, but also of open, playful and
often transgressive performances (Thorne, 1993). Before my first
meeting with Michal (12), I heard a rumour about him saying that 'he
wants to be a girl'. I asked a colleague what it meant and she replied:
"He just *wants* to be a girl, that's it." Michal mostly spent time in a

group of girls a couple of years older than him, and he was one of the most vocal children among those who argued for joint activities of boys and girls. Michal used to talk about gender and femininity often, declaring how he wanted to do the same things as the girls did. In the group activities of the boys within the Centre, Michal asked to do the same things that he heard from the girls they had done at their meetings (such as creating a bracelet or a photo-album), or he chose a book about menstruation from the Centre library. Michal also helped with cleaning the Centre more keenly than other children and I heard about a weekend trip where he basically refused to leave the accommodation in the lodge for outdoor activities and remained inside cooking and cleaning. While other boys also took part in cleaning or were keen to take part in baking, Michal added also a performance of the 'scrubwoman' stereotype, through his body movement, change of voice, or his language. On the other hand, Michal could be very aggressive and offensive, keen to be in the centre of attention and enjoyed acting and playing roles in general.

For Michal, working with gender was crucial in how he presented himself towards others. His female friends accepted Michal, along with his noisy and pushy behaviour and his feminine performances. Michal's gender performances were usually not emphasised within the group and he became one of the girls. Still, there was some recognition of his difference. For instance, I saw a conflict between Michal and Rebeka, his 13-year-old friend from this group. I witnessed only the final part and at this stage the children were just yelling insults at each other. To finish the clash, Rebeka screamed "Fucking faggot!" at Michal and went away. This story shows how children's performances, even if continually transgressing the expected heteronormative and gender norms, still remained under close scrutiny of deep-rooted expectations by their friends and others. Even within the fluid and vivid milieu of Michal's friends, who accepted and even encouraged him in his performances, the underlying notion of acceptable norms of behaviour was nonetheless adhered to and, under tensions, it could burst out. Rebeka's act was also a performance of gender: of gender expectations and norms that she was perhaps fine with being overturned at various moments by Michal, but she still remained aware of them and pulled them into their conflict.

In Butler's writings (especially Butler, 1993), gender subjectivities are shown to be constituted after acts of gendered performance. However, Butler also argues that the process of becoming a gendered subject through everyday performance cannot take place outside of the existing social gendered patterns and the existing discourses about gender and sex. Children's claims about gender usually corresponded with dominant discourses they knew from home, school or peer groups. However, their everyday experiences often contested these views and children's performances often crossed beyond what they themselves recognised as appropriate gender norms. Gender was a factor that had strong impact on children's practices but it was only rarely reflected upon as children's rationalised understanding of gender became highly habitual. The stories from this chapter (but also from the previous chapters) further indicate that gender affected children's practices through a range of moments. While some were highly circumscribed by children's roles and duties in the family or by their contacts in their peer groups, themselves formed with the patterns of the social life in Kopčany in the background, others negotiated children's expectations about gendered norms, and many were results of experiments and play through children's individual performances. Rather than accepting gendered patterns in their social life or discourses about their social position, children's gendered identities evolved in practice, although this practice was affected by the broader material and discursive structures.

As a result, the notion of gender in children's lives can be seen as coming from a multiplicity of sources corresponding to children's complex social positionalities (McCall, 2005; Shields, 2008). On the other hand, gender as an effect on children's practices can be seen as emerging in a highly fractured and unstable way through children's everyday experiences, encounters, and intersections between their expectations, habitual routines and circumscribed social relations, or as Butler calls it, 'as a constituted *social temporality*' (1990, p.141). The effect of the notion of gender on children's practices was precisely this – a site- and moment-specific complex relationship between children's prior experience, social roles, habits and cultural understandings of their everyday lives, and the immediate spontaneous copings with a range of other factors, people, activities or things. The discussion also shows that children's own peer groups were particularly capable of devising gender dynamics that continuously switched between dramatically transgressing the established gendered patterns of behaviour, and being subjected to those very same 'coercive' (Renold, 2006) rules and norms. Within such collective dynamics, children's accounts of themselves were then produced in a compound of discourses, social relationships and children's individual experiences of their embodied practices.

Conclusions

The scope of this chapter is situated along with the last two chapters focused on children's social relationships. While Chapters Nine and Ten investigated patterns and practices of children's most important relationships, in this chapter I explored what kind of social positionalities were emerging in children's overall relationships in general, discussing in turn the notions of age, ethnicity and gender, and their impact on children's activities.

Working through these themes from different angles, the key findings in each area provide additional perspectives on how social positionality works as a broader mechanism impacting on children's practices, effectively becoming an extension to children's agency. In the first section, I emphasised the existence of active and prolific agency even among the youngest children, even if its constitution may have been different (and therefore often rejected) from that of adults or older children through its focus on the present and immediateness rather than on broader schemes, networks or visions of future. How children were departing from 'being children' was related to how much the scope of their practices reached beyond their immediate ideas, events, things or people. In the second section, I argued that while the notion of ethnicity is a cultural factor that affects children's performances, it is constructed in multiple ways and its impact on children's practices is consequently diverse. While children often used ethnicity as a label for their expectations about what performances were appropriate, and for affirming their own performativities, they also negotiated their views on ethnicity in practice through sharing the social bonds in relationships that spanned across all social groups of children from the neighbourhood. In a similar sense, the discussion of gender showed how this is constituted in complex dynamics of connections between institutional arrangements, discourses about social norms and expectations, children's individual experiences, the ways they rationalise them, and the situated and often disruptive embodied performances of gender within complex matrices of the previous factors.

These findings relate closely to some arguments about the notion of social identity in childhood given by others. Sutton (2009) shows how children's understanding of social differences is for the most part fluid, dynamic and often rapidly transformed along with the changing context of social ties, discourses or activities that children encounter. Janssen (2009) highlights how children's own sense of identity is framed by dominant institutional patterns, but how their individual experiences confront this continually. In relation to these claims, I have argued (particularly in Chapter Eight) that children's practices are driven by the search for sense in their experiences, and emerging contexts can therefore challenge what children perceive as an established order.

The impact of social positionality on children's practices that I was particularly interested in lies in the moments when children form an attitude towards themselves as social actors – even if this often happened through forming an attitude towards others and identifying themselves in relation to these others (such as when Monika talked about "Gypsies" who were "responsible" for the "mess" in Kopčany and her non-Gypsy identity surfaced through this procedure). This moment is not necessarily cognitive or rational. As the examples showed, it contains an entanglement of habitual embodied actions that are negotiated through tacit experiences, circumscribed social spaces that structure children's practices, circulations of discourses about social positionalities, but also children's reasoning about the events they experience. In the examples presented in this chapter, some of these factors were shown as breaking through into children's ideas more intensely than others, but ultimately the presence and impact of all of them could be seen.

Foucault's (1985) idea of practising the self signifies the moments when social subjects establish relationships with themselves by locating themselves experientially in entangled contexts of being objectified by others, objectifying others, and performing against particular notions of subjectivity such as age, gender or ethnicity. The key conclusion of this chapter is that children, through a wide range of vectors (which build topographies of children's subjectivites), shape understandings of themselves through complex and often contradictory experiences with others and with their own actions. The ways in which such understandings leak into children's practices are also enormously diverse and include rationalisation of their behaviour but also more subtle, subliminal, habitual and unconscious mechanisms that form a hybrid structure of children's practices rather than a homogeneous pattern of performing gender, age or ethnicity.

Chapter Eleven concludes the empirical analysis of the formation of children's practices in the neighbourhood, even if the range of themes that could be approached is not definite. In the final chapter of the book, I will connect the findings and return to the book's rationales of drawing a counter-topography of children's agency.

Part Four

TWELVE

Rematerialising children's agency

The book explored children's practices in Kopčany as relationally constituted dynamics emerging from intersections of a wide range of elements present in particular moments of children's lives. With the choice of areas being field-driven, the thematic chapters explored in turn the neighbourhood public spaces (Chapter Five), bodies (Chapter Six), things (Chapter Seven), children's encounters with other people (Chapter Eight), family life (Chapter Nine), friendship (Chapter Ten) and notions of social identity (Chapter Eleven), as they take place and make a difference in the formation of children's everyday practices.

The relational view is not a deterministic one and children's practices are not univocal and immediate outcomes of particular circumstances. The presence of individual circumstances in children's lives prefigures some ways of how children act, but the book also showed how the range of factors (such as the presence of other people, children's long-term relationship with them, children's momentarily embodied states or the tangible context of children's practices) contribute *together* at individual moments, making the formation of children's practices complex and individualised. For instance, in my very first empirical note from the field (the hide-and-seek game in Chapter Three), I illustrated how the factors that mattered for children's practices during a few seconds of our run through the neighbourhood included our prior relationships, recent experiences from the game, embodied contact and moral codes about it, age differences among the children, and the physical environment (that allowed us to hide) among others.

The ontological relationship between children's practices and their circumstances has two important implications for how the 'methodology' (even though I problematised this term in Chapter Three) of the book is significant for what knowledge the research could produce. First, the range of factors that matter for the formation of children's practices is exceedingly open so to focus only on one domain of the circumstances, such as children's psychologies, economic circumstances or power relationships would take away from the rest. Discussions about family life in Chapter Nine, for instance, give an example of how regulatory family patterns, material opportunities of the families, or gender expectations of girls and boys contribute to the practices of child care in which many children from Kopčany, and particularly the girls, took the central role. Second, while children's practices are themselves spatially bounded within the extents of children's bodies and temporarily bounded within the moments of the practices' durations, their circumstances can be stretched across both time and space (though they are not necessarily) and any research methodologies need to include this aspect.

Starting the research in the moments of children's practices and then tracing their broader associations (Latour, 2005) meant that while not every significant circumstance relevant for the formation of children's practices could be identified, I avoided overlooking some before the inquiry even started by prefiguring *a priori* what domains of children's circumstances should in theory impact on their actions. My key interest was not in children's experiences, accounts or representations of their practices, but rather in the embodied acts themselves, while accounting for my role in them. My positionality as an ethnographer was embedded in the role of a practitioner, a youth worker. I explained that the pivotal reason for taking this role was the access to the children's lives and the ability to attain a richer insight into their practices, but in order to mediate my contact with the children and to take ethical and professional responsibility for my actions with children, the Community Centre required me both to give 'something back' to the organisation by contributing to the youth work activities in the neighbourhood and to commit to the Centre's code of practice. Yet, the practitioner role had also crucial epistemological implications in relation to the connections between practices and circumstances implied earlier. While the practices of the practitioner approach began in the direct contact with children, they were expected to depart towards exploring broader realities of children's lives. The practitioner approach is fundamentally holistic in placing individual children, their situations, needs and actions at the centre of attention and thus suitable for inquiring into the broad and heterogeneous range of circumstances that affect children's practices. My practitioner work also involved drawing on a range of professional skills of inquiry into, and contact with, children's lives and thus broadened the range of fieldwork aspects I could include in the research. Combining the two roles helped me to bring together the curiosity and analytical mind of a researcher and the attentiveness and ethics of care of a practitioner (Blazek, 2013; Blazek et al, 2015).

This is an outline of what the book did. The last three sections of this chapter respond directly to the initial objectives and I am setting out do what the title of the book implies: to propose a rematerialisation of children's agency. First, this requires bringing together the findings and ideas about what children's capacity to act is and where it comes from. By rematerialising, I mean looking at approaching children's agency beyond the idea of the independent, fundamental subject. Instead, I have been mapping connections (some of them indeed intangible, see Chapter Four) to individual children which, in manifold ways, impact on – trigger, constrain, foster, boost, interfere with, prevent, sustain, amplify, eliminate or negate – children's practices. Second, I look to move the focus from how children's practices are impacted to the impact they have, using the notion of place as a conceptual instrument. I will assert that this is probably the most challenging task of the three – to acknowledge the 'impactness' of children – and I will make a case that the 'rematerialisation', an empirically grounded account of the consequences of children's actions and capacities to act, needs to be focused on, highlighted, and investigated in a much greater deal. Finally, I turn towards a rematerialising of the connections between adults and children from the perspective of the political action that we, as adults, can adopt. Again, I find the word rematerialisation important, and more apt than, say, reconceptualisation, as I argue that such politics needs to acknowledge children's agency as coming into being, here and now, and in turn urges to do more than just thinking about it. As suggested in Chapter One, this is where my inquiry into agency turns towards an explicit theory of action.

Children's agency as extensions

A key theme that emerged particularly strongly in relation to the question about the relationships between children's practices and their circumstances was the role of immediateness in the formation of children's practices. Children in Kopčany tended to respond to their immediate experiences more directly than adults would have (been expected to), not necessarily arbitrating these moments through abstract patterns of behaviour, behavioural norms or complex and conscious (or even rational) strategies (see particularly Chapter Six). This aspect, for instance, highlighted the role of embodied practices in children's activities as opposed to verbal acts (Chapter Six), the precedence of use value of material objects for the children over their exchange value (Chapter Seven) or the sense of friendship among children as shaped by everyday embodied practice rather than through cognitive attachments (Chapter Ten).

Katz, drawing on Benjamin (1978), Vygotsky (1978) and Taussig (1993), cites 'an immediate connection between thought and action' as 'one of the key attributes of children's consciousness' (2004a, p.100). Katz adopts from the aforementioned authors the instant 'fusion of knowledge and action in children's practices' (2004a, p.100), a medium that embraces children's experiences (past and present) and involves them in action before they are scrutinised by societal norms and orders that children learn. Stories of children from Kopčany revealed how children's engagements with previous experiences, through their resemblance with the current circumstances, invoke the formations of practices, some of which children rationalise, while others they reflect on habitually and tacitly.

Lee (2001) offers an explanation for such a characteristic. Thinking about human subjects as 'assemblages' and about human agency as a series of extensions that affect individuals' capacities to act, he argues that children simply have fewer extensions, and the process of growing up is a process of 'an increase in the range and number of extensions available to us' (2001, p.142). This has two important implications. First, children's and adults' actions are equally 'real', play or other children's activities are not 'as if', but unfold from real extensions to agency and create new arrangements, the 'value' of which, in comparison to outcomes of adults' actions, is just an arbitrary matter, not a matter of ontology. As I showed on the example of boys engaged with football, the outcomes of playing ranged from established friendships and a sense of belonging to the neighbourhood to the handling of boredom. Second, however, Lee's view on agency also suggests that children's agency entails easier arrangements with fewer extensions. As a result growing up is also an increase 'in the range and stability of our action' (2001, p.142), where 'stability' refers to the fact that changing any arrangements in the world of adults is more difficult and takes more time because adults' lives are attached to a wider range of (mutually connected) extensions.

A similar view but a different terminology on such a relational-materialist view of agency can be found in Deleuze and Guattari's (2004) concept of 'lines of flight', a term that characterises the paths of change. Deleuze and Guattari differentiate between 'relative' and 'absolute' lines of flight, where the first refers to re-turning to pre-established settings while the latter stands for abandoning the existing connections and linking to new ones, creating new orderings in the process. This again has implications for what the promise of agency might be. If the difference between adults and children is seen as adults simply being more powerful and capable of acting in more ways, then their agency emerges clearly as superior – they are able to do more than children and change the world to a greater degree.

However, the perspective of relational materialism suggests that the referential frame also matters and children can actually make a change in *their* frames more easily, because their context, and the range and complexity of connections in their lives, are more fragile and prone to be affected.

This idea opens up two areas that I will discuss in the next sections. First, I look at the relations between children's agency and place. I will attempt to reframe the idea of place not as an objectively approachable entity, given that it would always have to be approached from an adult perspective (the model perspective), but as a situated relationality between particular individuals, including children. Finally, I will revisit the idea about the constitution of agency with a direct focus on politics, asking 'What can be done?'

Children's agency and place

What does this framework imply in relation to children's practices being located in Kopčany? What I labelled as counter-topographies of children's practices is a comparative analysis of the factors that impact on children's actions, and it revealed that multiple axes of difference exist among children living in the neighbourhood. The ways in which children come to act cannot be attributed to a single set of factors such as social categories (age, socioeconomic circumstances, gender, ethnicity or family circumstances), their spatial, historical or cultural settings, biological factors, or children's personalities. All of these matter significantly, but the formation of children's practices itself remains multifaceted. However, some factors that affect children's agency *can* be attributed to the place where children's activities happen.

In Chapter Two, I introduced Kopčany as a deprived neighbourhood negatively affected by housing policies, particularly from the perspective of children and young people as those from families with low incomes were provided with housing in an isolated and neglected area without adequate access to facilities. One reading of the relationship between children's agency and place could be taken from political-economic analyses of contemporary neoliberalism, as a significant element of post-socialist transformations. Restrictions in welfare and public support for children and their families experiencing social and spatial exclusion can be linked with the expanding project of neoliberalisation in East and Central Europe (ECE) that has been characterised by ongoing 'benefits cuts, attacks on "dependence", public sector rationalization, [and] fiscal austerity' in the last decade (Stenning et al, 2010, p.2). Stenning and her colleagues argue that 'the "transition" from communism to capitalism in ECE represents perhaps one of the boldest experiments with neo-liberal ideas in the world today' (2010, p.2), using Petržalka as an example of such patterns. They also emphasise that:

> [Neo-liberalization] is more than a political-economic project; neo-liberalization is a social project too. It is predicated on a rejection of 'society' and on a promotion of the individual – most particularly, the entrepreneurial self …' (Stenning et al, 2010, p.2)

Emphasising competitive individualism as the fundamental social philosophy of neoliberalism leads to an inevitable reflection that '[t]he ascendency of neo-liberalization … constructs a landscape of winners and losers' (Willis et al, 2008, p.1) and 'by lifting the constraints on the exercise of unequal power, increase[s] injustice and trigger[s] a downward economic and social spiral' (Kitson et al, 2000, p.631). If social justice should be defined in terms of 'capabilities – what people are able to do' (Pattison, 2008, p.107), then the consequences of thorough neoliberalisation in ECE, many of which children of Kopčany experience, raise not only questions regarding the uneven experiences of emerging social relationships under neoliberalism, but also of what the possibilities to 'detract from the violence of neoliberalism' (Stenning et al, 2010, p.229) are, as this violence is manifested through disrupted material and emotional paths of social reproduction.

In her analysis of social reproduction under neoliberal capitalism, Katz (2011) offers the metaphor of 'childhood as waste'. It represents the material and discursive continuities that, from the earliest age, dispossess children from disadvantaged backgrounds of assets such as access to high-quality education, training, social facilities or provision of social services that would enable them to achieve a higher life standard, and instead turn them towards low-paid jobs, lack of motivation and self-esteem in their capacities, or illegal activities. All these factors were present among children's older peers or adults in the neighbourhood, with exceptions on either side being quite rare. Katz's work shows that constructing the landscapes of 'winners' and 'losers' (see the previous paragraph) is an inherent element of social reproduction under neoliberalism as the neoliberal 'global expansion is riddled with and enabled by intimate dispossessions' (Katz, 2011, p.50) experienced particularly by children who are socially or spatially marginalised.

I have argued that while it would be unfair to label children from Kopčany ultimately as disqualified from the socioeconomic landscape of contemporary Slovakia (and they would themselves probably object to this), there is nevertheless a range of disadvantaging factors characterising the landscape of growing up in the neighbourhood. Katz's reading of childhood with regard to social reproduction gives an argument that children lacking access to high-quality education, social facilities or networks become more prone to '*further* dispossession – that is, *for a willed wasting of lives constituted as waste*' (Katz, 2011, p.58, first italics added) by the neoliberal landscapes of individualism and entrepreneurship for which these children lack training, social capital or other assets. Many children from Kopčany enter the neoliberal landscape of contemporary Slovakia disadvantaged by their history of social and spatial isolation, changing livelihood circumstances (moving to a new area, changing patterns of care or provision they experience), lack of success in education, difficulties in the family or neighbourhood, or lack of motivation and positive future prospects. Despite this, and the fact that societal arrangements are partly accountable for the development of the neighbourhood and the place-specific factors that surround children's growing up, the children are expected to cope with the insecurity of the neoliberal demands for segmented competence and flexibility.

I have shown that a range of children's practices must be read as actively challenging the impose processes of neoliberal transformations of land use (such as children's re-engagement with, and remaking of, the public spaces in Kopčany) or institutional services (such as their practices of child care and friendship against the lack of access to services), but also that other forces affect children's lives in a highly significant manner, including children's friendships, family values, or the cultural and social reproduction of gender role expectations. While many children from Kopčany experienced material deprivation, environmental discomfort or lack of institutional engagement or parental time, their agency was then built around other assets, some of which were shaped as a direct response to these factors, so the deprivation generated new opportunities. For instance, many children became quite independent in their everyday activities, with little control or supervision from their parents, but also in their social contacts, not relying on their parents or other adults in dealing with difficulties (see Chapter Five). They had very intensive and intimate contact with their everyday environment and widely explored, but also experimented with, objects and spaces in the neighbourhood because there were very few spatial restrictions on their activities and because searching for new objects compensated for the lack of possessions (see Chapters Five and Seven). Several children formed their agency largely through taking responsibilities in caring for younger relatives, and children's practices often evolved through peer relationships in groups of relatively mixed age or gender (see Chapters Nine and Ten).

I have adopted the empiricist approach that explores such a broad range of facets in children's lives in order to examine new possibilities of emancipatory approaches. The second reading of the relationship between children's agency and place will thus stem not from the perspective of how broader processes juxtaposed in the neighbourhood impact on children's practices, but rather from prioritising the broadest range of the potential in children's agency to transform the place. Benjamin (1978) argues that children's immediate consciousness and their capacities are repressed by societal education so they can be shaped and replaced by the principles and values preferred by adult society (see also Lee, 2005). In the language of Lee (2001) from the previous section, it could be said that such socialisation is *slowing* children's agency down in order to make it engage with a wider set of extensions while taking away its capacity to make a change.

My analysis of the formation of children's practices highlights the formation of children's potential and capacities through the mundaneness of their everyday experiences, and how these fit or clash with the requirements of the restructuring society that the children grow up into. The book, for example, showed children's contributions to their family lives, particularly in the area of child care but also through other contributions to domestic work (see Chapter Nine and Eleven); how children shaped public spaces in the neighbourhood by actively engaging with, and reshaping, the tangible environment (see Chapters Five and Seven); and, not least, how they affected, through friendship and peer relationships, the lives and everyday experiences of other children in Kopčany (see Chapter Ten and Eleven). I have presented Kopčany on the one hand as a deprived neighbourhood struggling after two decades of post-socialist transformations in urban and social politics, cultural patterns and economic structures. But I have also shown it as a site of intensive daily dynamics in which several hundred children interact with the world around them as they are becoming new social subjects, uncovering and developing their potential in those circumstances that are present. Children are not just features in broader social and economic patterns; they are also active subjects of care, play, engagements with the public space and emerging social relations. While they are affected by the local circumstances in the Kopčany neighbourhood, their activities also have considerable effect on the local processes, relationships and experiences of other social actors.

These paragraphs should not be read as a call to refrain from intervening in children's lives and letting them live in their own way. Such a thought is clearly absurd and unacceptable. Instead, I wish to question the frontiers between establishing and respecting children's autonomy (Jones, 2013; see also Chapter One) and engaging with them as *both* future *and* present citizens and social subjects. Actually, I also wish to question the frontiers between establishing such autonomy and engaging with it – being able to coexist with children without either subjugating them to adult orderings, which they can hardly affect, or losing the contact with them entirely.

Children's agency, adults' politics

The last section of the book responds to the question about what children's agency implies for adults. I have shown children's agency as ontologically similar to that of adults, and children as agents similar to adults as agents. The difference is in the range and kind of extensions to agency – children do not have all that adults do (as extensions accumulate over time) and they have some that adults might lack (as some extensions recede). This is not a question of morality, however; children in my book demonstrate solidarity, compassion or perseverance, the very same sense of being-in-the-world, as adults do.

Centring on children's practices encourages thinking about childhood not just as a potential for the future (and about children as adults in the making) but rather as an active and transformative *presence* with a potential to take these transformative impacts further. It identifies children in important positions as family carers, as engaging with and consequently reshaping the physical environment in the neighbourhood, or as the source of emotional support or learning, especially for other young people. Rather than exploring how the landscapes of childhood in marginalised areas (such as Kopčany) can fit within the global changes of regions (such as ECE), my proposition is to explore the opportunities that these landscapes offer and the question of how to mobilise children's agency for the benefit of all. This is a political question, a question of action, and my answer is threefold.

First, adults need to acknowledge children's agency ('rematerialise' it) and conceive it as a promise, not a threat. The story of my book is restricted to my stay in Kopčany in 2008–9, but writing it in 2015, when several children from this book are already adults, the neighbourhood has changed significantly, and actions of children *together* with adults (parents, youth workers, others from outside the neighbourhood) were instrumental in this. Elsewhere (Blazek et al,

2015), I offer a story of a new playground, a persistent topic of this book, which materialised largely as an outcome of activities of two young girls, carers in their wider families. The construction of a new sports ground, another key story of this book, is almost finished in Kopčany, and while the Community Centre (not local authorities) were behind its development, the very roots of the initiative come from the narratives and period presented in this book, while the process itself was facilitated by sustained participation of neighbourhood residents – but especially children.

These examples raise a question of how the children's potential corresponds with, or eludes, the visions of other stakeholders – policy makers at the local or national level, adult residents of communities, practitioners, or others – and how they can identify common ground with children, particularly with the wide range of concerns about safeguarding (Philo and Smith, 2013). In Chapter One, I presented the idea of place only as a way of understanding (Cresswell, 2004), but the story of Kopčany suggests it needs to expand beyond this and encompass also ways of acting collectively, where children's capacities *and* needs are respected, supported and sometimes included, sometimes followed. In parallel to the accounts of place as a political opportunity to make the most of the existing juxtapositions of social dynamics (Massey et al, 2009), I suggest that a partial answer to the search for a theory of action is in locating children's agency, rather than incorporating it (for instance through discourses of participation) into adult agendas, and in exploring (and handling) new ways of being-together with children where this is possible (see Blazek and Hricová, 2015).

Second, my work draws primarily on the exploration of local circumstances and the question of upscaling agency would be a likely objection to the proposition discussed. I admit this; while this call addresses key resources in a neighbourhood such as Kopčany, it also creates a risk of segregating children's practices from broader spatial and social contexts. A solution might be to return to Katz's *initial* idea of counter-topography as a comparative method for exploring local experiences as affected by similar processes at various spatial scales. This is a challenge for further research, and tackling the dearth of accounts of children's transformative potential around the globe should go hand in hand with an aggregative analysis of what communities and societies can learn from each other. A 'global' counter-topography has the power to expose the potential of children's agency (together with adults' action) in a 'more associative politics – one that [would be] scale and place crossing with practical entailments that could work across and against received distinctions of "us" and "them"' (Katz,

2011, p.58), whether this stands for for 'adults' and 'children' or any other form of social and spatial dichotomy. This counter-topography can stand for exploring ways in which children can develop their agency away from the neighbourhood, and how their social and spatial mobility can be increased, but also how their potential possibly could be utilised elsewhere, beyond the scope of the neighbourhood, through practical engagement or at least through transfer and exchange or experiences. This is a notion that, against the romanticised idea of local resistance, opens the children's potential as transformative agents to amplification by its connections with knowledge and actions beyond local boundaries, and through a range of social and spatial connections at various scales.

Finally, I want to conclude by articulating a concise theory of action as an account of adult politics, although some elements of this theory have already emerged on the previous pages. In Chapter Three, I theorised how my work in Kopčany was sustained simultaneously by sticking to who I was (as a researcher and a practitioner – but also as an individual with specific histories, motivations and personality) through a focus on my agendas – professional, moral, personal – and by negotiating who I *could be* in the presence of children in 'their' neighbourhood. I see this as fundamental to achieve the propositions formulated in this chapter and the question of how it can be done is central to how children's agency can be rematerialised into a theory of action. There is no universal solution – constantly looking for (re) connections between adults and children in situated contexts, rather than subsuming our understandings of childhood and children into predefined majority models (Chapter One) is the closest to it. This book explored this problem in a site- and time-specific context of Kopčany and this is where its story ends, only for new stories to begin.

References

Aapola, S. (2002) Exploring dimensions of age in young people's lives, *Time & Society*, 11, 295–314.

Adkins, L. (2003) Reflexivity: freedom or habit of gender? *Theory, Culture & Society*, 20, 21–42.

Aitken, S. (1998) *Family fantasies and community space*, New Brunswick, NJ: Rutgers University Press.

Aitken, S. (2000a) Mothers, communities and the scale of difference, *Social and Cultural Geography*, 1, 65–82.

Aitken, S. (2000b) Play, rights and borders: gender bound parents and the social construction of children, in S. Holloway and G. Valentine (eds) *Children's geographies: Playing, living, learning*, London: Routledge.

Aitken, S. (2001a) Fielding diversity and moral integrity, *Ethics, Place and Environment*, 4, 125–9.

Aitken, S. (2001b) *Geographies of young people: The morally contested spaces of identity*, London: Routledgen.

Aitken, S. (2009) *The awkward spaces of fathering*, Aldershot: Ashgate.

Alderson, P. and Morrow, V. (2004) *Ethics, social research and consulting with children and young people*, Ilford: Barnardos.

Aldridge, J. and Becker, S. (1993) *Children who care: Inside the world of young carers*, Loughborough: Young Carers Research Group.

Allan, G. (1989) *Friendship: Developing a sociological perspective*, Boulder, CO: Westview Press.

Allport, G. (1954) *The nature of prejudice*, Reading: Addison-Wesley.

Amin, A. (2006) The good city, *Urban Studies*, 43, 1009–23.

Anderson, B. (2004) Time-stilled space-slowed: how boredom matters, *Geoforum*, 35, 739–754.

Anderson, B. and Harrison, P. (2010) The promise of non-representational theories, in B. Anderson and P. Harrison (eds) *Taking place: Non-representational theories and geography*, Farnham: Ashgate.

Anderson, B. and Tolia-Kelly, D. (2004) Matter(s) in social and cultural geography, *Geoforum*, 35, 669–74.

Andraško, I. (2006) Perception of the quality of life in Bratislava city wards, *Geografická revue*, 2, 227–40.

Andraško, I. (2007) Vnútorná štruktúra mesta z hľadiska kvality života [Inner urban structure from the perspective of quality of life], Institute of Geography, Slovak Academy of Sciences, Bratislava.

Änggård, E. (2015) How matter comes to matter in children's nature play: posthumanist approaches and children's geographies, *Children's Geographies*, forthcoming.

Ansell, N. (2009a) Childhood and the politics of scale: descaling children's geographies? *Progress in Human Geography*, 33, 190–209.

Ansell, N. (2009b) Embodied learning: Responding to AIDS in Lesotho's education sector, *Children's Geographies*, 7, 21–36.

Askins, K. (2007) Codes, committees and other such conundrums! *ACME: An International E-Journal for Critical Geographies*, 6, 350–9.

Åslund, A. (2002) *Building capitalism: The transformation of the former Soviet bloc*, Cambridge: Cambridge University Press.

Aufseeser, D. (2014) The problems of child labor and education in Peru: a critical analysis of 'universal' approaches to youth development, in P. Kelly and A. Kamp (eds) *A critical youth studies for the 21st century*, Leiden: Brill.

Austin, J. L. (1962) *How to do things with words*, Oxford: Clarendon Press.

Banks, G. and Scheyvens, R. (2014) Ethics issues, in R. Scheyvens (ed.) *Development fieldwork: A practical guide,* London: Sage.

Bannister, J., Fyfe, N. and Kearns, A. (2006) Respectable or respectful? (In)civility and the city, *Urban Studies*, 43, 919–37.

Barker, J. (2002) *Alain Badiou: A critical introduction*, London: Pluto Press.

Barker, J. and Smith, F. (2001) Power, positionality and practicality: carrying out fieldwork with children, *Ethics, Place and Environment* 4, 142–7.

Barnes, P. and Kehily, M. J. (2003) Play and the cultures of childhood, in M. J. Kehily and J. Swann (eds) *Children's cultural worlds*, Milton Keynes: Open University Press.

Bauman, Z. (1991) *Modernity and ambivalence*, Cambridge: Polity Press.

Beazley, H. (2000) Home sweet home? Street children's sites of belonging, in S. Holloway and G. Valentine (eds) *Children's geographies: Playing, living, learning*, London: Routledge.

Beazley, H. (2003) Voices from the margins: street children's subcultures in Indonesia, *Children's Geographies*, 1, 181–200.

Beck, U. (2000) Living your own life in a runaway world: individualisation, globalisation and politics, in W. Hutton and G. Anthony (eds) *On the edge: Living with global capitalism*, London: Jonathan Cape.

Bell, N. (2008) Ethics in child research: rights, reason and responsibilities, *Children's Geographies*, 6, 7–20.

Bell, S. and Coleman, S. (1999) *The anthropology of friendship*, Oxford: Berg.

Benjamin, W. (1978) On the mimetic faculty, in P. Demetz (ed.) *Reflections*, New York: Harcourt Brace Jovanovich.

Bezanson, K. and Luxton, M. (2006) Introduction: social reproduction and feminist political economy, in K. Bezanson and M. Luxton (eds) *Social reproduction: Feminist political economy challenges neo-liberalism*, Montreal: McGill-Queen's University Press.

Bissell, D. (2008) Comfortable bodies: sedentary affects, *Environment and Planning A*, 40, 1697–712.

Blaise, M. (2005) A feminist poststructuralist study of children 'doing' gender in an urban kindergarten classroom, *Early Childhood Research Quarterly*, 20, 85–108.

Blazek, M. (2011) Place, children's friendships and the formation of gender identities in a Slovak urban neighbourhood, *Children's Geographies*, 9, 285–302.

Blazek, M. (2013) Emotions as practice: Anna Freud''s child psychoanalysis and thinking – doing children''s emotional geographies., *Emotion, Space and Society*, 9, 24–32.

Blazek, M., and Hraňová, P. (2012): Emerging relationships and diverse motivations and benefits in participatory video with young people., *Children's Geographies*, 10, 151-–168.

Blazek, M. and Hricová, P. (2015) Understanding (how to be with) children's emotions: relationships, spaces and politics of reconnection in reflections from detached youth work., In:in M. Blazek, M., and P. Kraftl, P. (eds) *Children's emotions in policy and practice: mMapping and making spaces of childhood.*, London: Palgrave, London.

Blazek, M. and Lemešová, M. (2011) Integrative, mobile work with children and youth: its contribution to community development in Slovakia, *Children Youth and Environment*, 21, 322–31.

Blazek, M., Smith, F. M., Lemešová, M. and Hricová, P. (2015) Ethics of care across professional and everyday positionalities: (un)expected impacts of participatory video with young female carers in Slovakia, *Geoforum*, 61, 45–55

Bondi, L. (1999a) Stages on journeys: some remarks about human geography and psychotherapeutic practice, *Professional Geographer*, 51, 11–24.

Bondi, L. (1999b) Small steps: a reply to commentaries on 'Stages on journeys', *Professional Geographer*, 51, 465–8.

Bondi, L. (2005a) Making connections and thinking through emotions: between geography and psychotherapy, *Transactions of the Institute of British Geographers*, 30, 433–48.

Bondi, L. (2005b) The place of emotions in research: from partitioning emotion and reason to the emotional dynamics of research relationships, in J. Davidson, L. Bondi and M. Smith (eds) *Emotional geographies*, Aldershot: Ashgate.

Bondi, L. (2005c) Gender and the reality of cities: embodied identities, social relations and performativities. Online papers archived by the Institute of Geography, School of Geosciences, University of Edinburgh. Available at: http://www.era.lib.ed.ac.uk/bitstream/1842/822/1/lbondi002.pdf.

Bondi, L. (2013) Research and therapy: generating meaning and feeling gaps, *Qualitative Inquiry*, 19, 9–19.

Bondi, L. and Fewell, J. (2003) 'Unlocking the cage door': the spatiality of counselling, *Social and Cultural Geography*, 4, 527–47.

Bosco, F. (2007) Hungry children and networks of aid in Argentina: thinking about geographies of responsibility and care, *Children's Geographies*, 5, 55–76.

Bourdieu, P. (1984) *Distinction: A social critique of the judgement of taste*, London: Routledge.

Bourdieu, P. (1986) The forms of capital, in J. Richardson (ed.) *Handbook of theory and research for the sociology of education*, New York: Greenwood.

Bourdieu, P. (1990) *The logic of practice*, Stanford, CA: Stanford University Press.

Bradshaw, M. and Stenning, A. (2004) Introduction: transformation and development, in M. Bradshaw and A. Stenning (eds) *East Central Europe and the former Soviet Union: The post-socialist states*, Harlow: Pearson/DARG Regional Development Series.

Brannen, J. and O'Brien, M. (1995) Childhood and the sociological gaze: paradigms and paradoxes, *Sociology*, 29, 729–37.

Bryant, L. (2008) *Difference and givenness: Deleuze's transcendental empiricism and the ontology of immanence*, Evanston, IL: Northwestern University Press.

Buck-Morss, S. (1989) *The dialectics of seeing: Walter Benjamin and the arcades project*, Cambridge, MA: MIT Press.

Burawoy, M. (1999) Afterword, in K. Verdery and M. Burawoy (eds) *Uncertain transition: Ethnographies of change in the postsocialist world*, London: Rowman & Littlefield.

Burney, E. (2005) *Making people behave: Anti-social behaviour, politics and policy*, Cullompton: Willan Publishing.

Burrell, K. (2011) The enchantment of western things: children's material encounters in late socialist Poland, *Transactions of the Institute of British Geographers*, 36, 143–56.

Butler, J. (1990) *Gender trouble: Feminism and the subversion of identity*, London: Routledge.

Butler, J. (1993) *Bodies that matter*, London: Routledge.

Butler, J. (1997) *Excitable speech: A politics of the performative*, London: Routledge.

Census (2001) *2001 Population and Housing Census*, available at http://sodb.infostat.sk/sodb/eng/2001/oscitani2001.htm

Cerbone, D. (2006) *Understanding phenomenology*, Chesham: Acumen.

Chaney, D. (2002) *Cultural change and everyday life.*, Basingstoke: Palgrave, Basingstoke.

Christensen, P. and O'Brien, M. (eds) (2003) *Children in the city: Home, neighbourhood and community*, London: Routledge.

Christensen, P., James, A. and Jenks, C. (2000) Home and movement: children constructing family time., In:in S. Holloway, S. and G. Valentine, G. (eds) *Children''s geographies: pPlaying, living, learning*, London: Routledge, London.

Christensen, P. and O'Brien, M. (eds) (2003) *Children in the city: home, neighbourhood and community*. Routledge, London.Clandinin, D. J. and Connelly, F. M. (1994) Personal experience methods, in N. K. Denzin and Y. S. Lincoln (eds) *Handbook of qualitative research*, London: Sage.

Colebrook, C. (2002) *Gilles Deleuze*, London: Routledge.

Colls, R. and Hörschelmann, K. (2009a) The geographies of children's and young people's bodies, *Children's Geographies*, 7, 1–6.

Colls, R. and Hörschelmann, K. (2009b) Introduction: contested bodies of childhood and youth, in K. Hörschelmann and R. Colls (eds) *Contested bodies of childhood and youth*, Basingstoke: Palgrave.

Connolly, M. and Ennew, J. (1996) Introduction: Children out of place, *Childhood: A Global Journal of Childhood Research*, 3, 131–45.

Crang, M. (2000) Relics, places and unwritten geographies in the work of Michel de Certeau (1925–1986), in M. Crang and N. Thrift (eds) *Thinking space*, London: Routledge.

Crawford, A. (2006) 'Fixing broken promises?': Neighbourhood wardens and social capital, *Urban Studies*, 43, 957–76.

Creed, G. (1999) Deconstructing socialism in Bulgaria, in M. Burawoy and K. Verdery (eds) *Uncertain transition: Ethnographies of change in the postsocialist world*, Oxford: Rowman & Littlefield.

Cresswell, T. (1996) *In place/out of place: Geography, ideology, and transgression*, Minneapolis, MN: University of Minnesota Press.

Cresswell, T. (2004) *Place: A short introduction*, Oxford: Blackwell.

Crouch, D. (2003) Spacing, performing and becoming: tangles in the mundane, *Environment and Planning A*, 35, 1945–60.

de Certeau, M. (1984) *The practice of everyday life*, Berkeley: University of California Press.

Deleuze, G. (1995) Control and becoming, in *Negotiations 1972–1990*, New York: Columbia University Press.

Deleuze, G. (2001) Immanence: a life, in *Pure immanence: Essays on a life*, Cambridge, MA: MIT Press.

Deleuze, G. (2004) Intellectuals and power, in *Desert island and other texts 1953–1974*, Los Angeles: Semiotext(e).

Deleuze, G. and Guattari, F. (1986) *Kafka: Toward a minor literature*, Minneapolis: University of Minnesota Press.

Deleuze, G. and Guattari, F. (2004) *A thousand plateaus: Capitalism and schizophrenia, vol. 2*, London: Continuum.

Derevenski, J. S. (2000) *Children and material culture*, London: Routledge.

Derrida, J. (1973) *Speech and phenomena and other essays on Husserl's theory of signs*, Evanston, IL: Northwestern University Press.

Derrida, J. (1978) *Writing and difference*, London: Routledge.

Dewsbury, J. D. (2000) Performativity and the event: enacting a philosophy of difference, *Environment and Planning D: Society and Space*, 18, 473–96.

Dewsbury, J. D. and Naylor, S. (2002) Practising geographical knowledge: fields, bodies and dissemination, *Area*, 34, 253–60.

Doucet, A. (2008) 'From her side of the gossamer wall(s)': reflexivity and relational knowing, *Qualitative Sociology*, 31, 73–87.

Dowds, J. (2008) Throwing the baby out with the bathwater, *Children's Geographies*, 6, 103–4.

Dowling, R. (2000) Power, subjectivity and ethics in qualitative research, in I. Hay (ed.) *Qualitative research methods in human geography*, Oxford: Oxford University Press.

Dunn, J. (2004) *Children's friendships: The beginnings of intimacy*, Oxford: Blackwell.

Dyson, J. (2010) Friendship in practice: girls' work in the Indian Himalayas, *American Ethnologist*, 37, 482–98.

Eco, U. (1979) *The role of the reader: Explorations in the semiotics of text*, Bloomington: Indiana University Press.

Ekiert, G. and Hanson, S. E. (2003) Time, space and institutional change in central, in G. Ekiert and S. E. Hanson (eds) *Capitalism and democracy in Central and Eastern Europe: Assessing the legacy of communist rule*, Cambridge: Cambridge University Press.

Elsley, S. (2004) Children's experience of public space, *Children and Society*, 18, 155–64.

Elwood, S. (2007) Negotiating participatory ethics in the midst of institutional ethics, *ACME: An International E-Journal for Critical Geographies*, 6, 329–38.

Erwin, P. (1998) *Friendship in childhood and adolescence*, London: Routledge.

Etherington, K. (2007) Ethical research in reflexive relationships, *Qualitative Inquiry*, 13, 599–616.

Evans, R. (2011a) 'We are managing our own lives ...': life transitions and care in sibling-headed households affected by AIDS in Tanzania and Uganda, *Area*, 43, 384–96.

Evans, R. (2011b) Young caregiving and HIV in the UK: caring relationships and mobilities in African migrant families, *Population, Space and Place*, 17, 338–60.

Evans, R. and Holt, L. (2011) Diverse spaces of childhood and youth: gender and other socio-cultural differences, *Children's Geographies*, 9, 277–84.

Featherstone, M. (1991) *Consumer culture and postmodernism*, London: Sage.

Fine, G. A. (1993) Ten lies of ethnography, *Journal of Contemporary Ethnography*, 22, 267–94.

Finlay, L. (2003) The reflexive journey: mapping multiple routes, in L. Finlay and B. Gough (eds) *Reflexivity: A practical guide for researchers in health and social science*, Oxford: Blackwell.

Fonseca, I. (1996) *Bury me standing: The Gypsies and their journey*, London: Vintage Books.

Foucault, M. (1985) *The history of sexuality, vol. 2: The use of pleasure*, Harmondsworth: Penguin.

Foucault, M. (1988) Technologies of the self, in M. Foucault, H. Gutman, P. H. Hutton and L. H. Martin (eds) *Technologies of the self: A seminar with Michel Foucault*, London: Tavistock.

Fox, M., Martin, M. and Green, G. (2007) *Doing practitioner research*, London: Sage.

Freeman, M. and Mathison, S. (2009) *Researching children's experiences*, New York: Guilford Press.

Fukuyama, F. (1992) *The end of history and the last man*, Harmondsworth: Penguin.

Fuller, R. and Petch, A. (1995) *Practitioner research: The reflexive social worker*, Milton Keynes: Open University Press.

Fyfe, N. (ed) (1998) *Images of the street: planning, identity and control in public space*, London: Routledge.

Fyfe, N., Bannister, J. and Kearns, A. (2006) (In)civility and the city, *Urban Studies*, 43, 853–61.

Fyhri, A. and Hjorthol, R. (2009) Children's independent mobility to school, friends and leisure activities, *Journal of Transport Geography*, 17, 377–84.

Gallagher, M. (2008) 'Power is not an evil': rethinking power in participatory methods, *Children's Geographies*, 6, 137–50.

Gallagher, M. (2011) Sound, space and power in a primary school, *Social and Cultural Geography*, 12, 47–61.

Garfinkel, H. (1967) *Studies in ethnomethodology*, Englewood Cliffs, NJ: Prentice Hall.

Gaskell, C. (2008) 'Isolation and distress?' (Re)thinking the place of emotions in youth research, *Children's Geographies*, 6, 169–81.

Gibson-Graham, J. K. (1996) *The end of capitalism (as we knew it)*, Oxford: Blackwell.

Goodwin, M. (2008) The embodiment of friendship, power and marginalization in girls' interactions, *Girlhood Studies: An Interdisciplinary Journal*, 1, 72–94.

Gough, K. V. and Franch, M. (2005) Spaces of the street: socio-spatial mobility and exclusion of youth in Recife, *Children's Geographies*, 3, 149–66.

Gregory, D. (1978) *Ideology, science and human geography*, London: Hutchinson.

Gregson, N. and Beale, V. (2004) Wardrobe matter: the sorting, displacement and circulation of women's clothing, *Geoforum*, 35, 689–700.

Gregson, N., Crewe, L. and Brooks, K. (2002a) Discourse, displacement and retail practice: some pointers from the charity retail project, *Environment and Planning A*, 34, 1661–83.

Gregson, N., Crewe, L. and Brooks, K. (2002b) Shopping, space and practice, *Environment and Planning D: Society and Space*, 20, 597–617.

Gros, D. and Steinher, A. (2004) *Economic transition in Central and Eastern Europe: Planting the seeds*, Cambridge: Cambridge University Press.

Guillemin, M. and Gillam, L. (2004) Ethics, reflexivity and 'ethically important moments' in research, *Qualitative Inquiry*, 10, 261–80.

Gwanzura-Ottemöller, F. P. and Kesby, M. (2005) 'Let's talk about sex, baby ...': conversing with Zimbabwean children about HIV/AIDS, *Children's Geographies*, 3, 201–18.

Hancock, R. and Gillen, J. (2007) Safe places in domestic spaces: two-year-olds at play in their homes, *Children's Geographies*, 5, 337–51.

Hanson, S. (1997) As the world turns: new horizons in feminist geographic methodologies, in J. P. Jones, H. Nast and S. Roberts (eds) *Thresholds in feminist geography: Difference, methodology and representation*, Oxford: Rowman & Littlefield.

Haraway, D. (1991) *Simians, cyborgs and women: The reinvention of nature*, London: Routledge.

Harker, C. (2005) Playing and affective time-spaces, *Children's Geographies*, 3, 47–62.

Hart, R. (1979) *Children's experiences of place*, New York: Irvington.

Harutyunyan, A., Hörschelmann, K. and Miles, M. (eds) (2009) *Public spheres after socialism,* New York: Intellect Books.

Hemming, P. J. (2007) Renegotiating the primary school: children's emotional geographies of sport, exercise and active play, *Children's Geographies*, 5, 353–71.

Herrera, E., Jones, G. A. and Thomas de Benitez, S. (2009) Bodies on the line: identity markers among Mexican street youth, *Children's Geographies*, 7, 67–81.

Hertz, R. (ed.) (1997) *Reflexivity and voice*, London: Sage.

Hey, V. (1997) *The company she keeps: An ethnography of girls' friendship*, Milton Keynes: Open University Press.

Heywood, C. (2001) *A history of childhood: Children and childhood in the West from medieval to modern times*, Cambridge: Polity Press.

Hirt, S. A. (2012) *Iron curtains: Gates, suburbs and privatization of space in the post-socialist city*, Oxford: John Wiley & Sons.

Hirt, S. A., Sellar, C. and Young, C. (2013) Neoliberal doctrine meets the Eastern bloc: resistance, appropriation and purification in post-socialist spaces, *Europe-Asia Studies*, 65, 1243–54.

Hitchings, R. (2010) Seasonal climate change and the indoor city worker, *Transactions of the Institute of British Geographers*, 35, 282–98.

Holloway, S. (1999) Reproducing motherhood, in N. Laurie, C. Dwyer, S. Holloway and F. M. Smith (eds) *Geographies of new femininities*, Harlow: Longman.

Holloway, S. (2005) Articulating Otherness? White rural residents talk about Gypsy-Travellers, *Transactions of the Institute of British Geographers*, 30, 351–67.

Holloway, S. and Pimlott-Wilson, H. (2012) Neoliberalism, policy localisation and idealised subjects: a case study on educational restructuring in England, *Transactions of the Institute of British Geographers,* 37, 639–54.

Holloway, S. and Valentine, G. (2000) Children's geographies and the new social studies of childhood, in S. Holloway and G. Valentine (eds) *Children's geographies: Playing, living, learning*, London: Routledge.

Holloway, S. and Valentine, G. (2003) *Cyberkids: Children in the information age*, London: Routledge.

Holt, L. (2004) The 'voices' of children: de-centring empowering research relations, *Children's Geographies*, 2, 13–27.

Holt, L. (2010) Young people's embodied social capital and performing disability, *Children's Geographies*, 8, 25–37.

Holt, L. (ed.) (2011) *Geographies of children, youth and families: International perspectives*, London: Routledge.

Holt, L. (2013) Exploring the emergence of the subject in power: infant geographies, *Environment and Planning D*, 31, 645–63.

Hopkins, P. and Pain, R. (2007) Geographies of age: thinking relationally, *Area*, 39, 287–94.

Hörschelmann, K. (1997) Watching the East: constructions of "otherness" in TV representations of East Germany., *Applied Geography*, 17, 385–396.

Hörschelmann, K. (2004) The social consequences of transformation, in M. Bradshaw and A. Stenning (eds) *East Central Europe and the former Soviet Union*, Harlow: Prentice Hall.

Hörschelmann, K. and Burrell, K. (eds) (2013) *Socialist and post-socialist mobilities*, London: Palgrave Macmillan.

Hörschelmann, K. and Schäfer, N. (2005) Performing the global through the local: young people's practices of identity formation in former east Germany, *Children's Geographies*, 3, 219–42.

Hörschelmann, K. and van Blerk, L. (2011) *Children, youth and the city*, London: Routledge.

Hörschelmann, K. and van Hoven, B. (2003) Experiencing displacement: the transformation of women's spaces in (former) East Germany, *Antipode*, 35, 742–60.

Horton, J. (2008) A 'sense of failure'? Everydayness and research ethics, *Children's Geographies* 6, 363–83.

Horton, J. and Kraftl, P. (2006a) Not just growing up, but going on: materials, spacings, bodies, situations, *Children's Geographies*, 4, 259–76.

Horton, J. and Kraftl, P. (2006b) What else? Some more ways of thinking and doing 'children's geographies', *Children's Geographies*, 4, 69–95.

Horton, J. and Pyer, M. (eds) (forthcoming) *Children, young people and care*, London: Routledge.

Husserl, E. (2001) *The shorter logical investigations*, London: Routledge.

Irigaray, L. (1993) *Sexes and genealogies*, New York: Columbia University Press.

Isin, E. and Uestuendag, E. (2008) Wills, deeds, acts: women's civic gift-giving in Ottoman Istanbul, *Gender Place and Culture*, 15, 519–32.

Iversen, R. R. (2009) 'Getting out' in ethnography: a seldom-told story, *Qualitative Social Work*, 8, 9–26.

James, A. (1993) *Childhood identities: Self and social relationships in the experience of the child*, Edinburgh: Edinburgh University Press.

James, A., Jenks, C. and Prout, A. (1998) *Theorising childhood*, Cambridge: Polity Press.

Janssen, D. F. (2009) 'Where' 'boys' 'are': co-constructions of maturities-genders-bodies-spaces, *Children's Geographies*, 7, 83–98.

Jeffrey, C. and Dyson, J. (2008) *Telling young lives: Portraits of global youth*, Philadelphia, PA: Temple University Press.

Jenks, C. (1996) *Childhood*, London: Routledge.

Jirojanakul, P., Skevington, S.M. and Hudson, J. (2003) Predicting young children's quality of life, *Social Science and Medicine*, 57, 1277–88.

Johnson, J. E. and Robinson, J. C. (eds) (2007) *Living gender after communism*, Bloomington: Indiana University Press.

Jones, C., Shillito-Clarke, C., Syme, G., Hill, D., Casemore, R. and Murdin, L. (2000) *Questions of ethics in counselling and therapy*, Milton Keynes: Open University Press.

Jones, O. (2000) Melting geography: purity, disorder, childhood and space, in S. Holloway and G. Valentine (eds) *Children's geographies: Playing, living, learning*, London: Routledge.

Jones, O. (2008) 'True geography [ ] quickly forgotten, giving away to an adult-imagined universe': approaching the otherness of childhood, *Children's Geographies*, 6, 195–212.

Jones, O. (2013) 'I was born but ...': children as other/nonrepresentational subjects in emotional and affective registers as depicted in film, *Emotion, Space and Society*, 9, 4–12.

Kaldor, M. and Vejvoda, I. (2002) *Democratization in Central and Eastern Europe*, London: Continuum.

Kallio, K. P. (2008) The body as a battlefield: approaching children's politics, *Geografiska Annaler: Series B, Human Geography*, 90, 285–97.

Kallio, K. P. and Häkli, J. (2011) Are there politics in childhood? *Space and Polity*, 15, 21–34.

Katz, C. (1993) Growing girls/closing circles: limits on the spaces of knowing in rural Sudan and US cities, in C. Katz and J. Monk (eds) *Full circles: Geographies of women over the life course*, London: Routledge.

Katz, C. (1996) Towards minor theory, *Environment and Planning D: Society and Space*, 14, 487–99.

Katz, C. (2001a) On the grounds of globalization: a topography for feminist political engagement, *Signs*, 26, 1213–34.

Katz, C. (2001b) Vagabond capitalism and the necessity of social reproduction, *Antipode*, 33, 709–28.

Katz, C. (2004a) *Growing up global: Economic restructuring and children's everyday lives*, Minneapolis: University of Minnesota Press.

Katz, C. (2004b) Reconfiguring childhood: boys and girls growing up global, *Revista: Harvard Review of Latin America*, 32, 12–15.

Katz, C. (2006) Los terrores de la hipervigilancia: seguridad y nuevas espacialidades de la niñez., *Documents d''Anàlisi Geogràfica*, 47, 15–29.

Katz, C. (2008) Childhood as spectacle: relays of anxiety and the reconfiguration of the child, *Cultural Geographies*, 15, 5–17.

Katz, C. (2009) Topography, in D. Gregory, R. J. Johnston, G. Pratt, M. Watts and S. Whatmore (eds) *The dictionary of human geography* (5th edn), Oxford: Blackwell.

Katz, C. (2011) Accumulation, excess, childhood: toward a countertopography of risk and waste, *Documents d'Anàlisi Geogràfica*, 57, 47–60.

Kehily, M. J., Mac An Ghaill, M., Epstein, D. and Redman, P. (2002) Private girls and public worlds: producing femininities in the primary school, *Discourse: Studies in the Cultural Politics of Education*, 23, 167–77.

Kesby, M., Gwanzura-Ottemoller, F. and Chizororo, M. (2006) Theorising *other* 'other childhoods': issues emerging from work on HIV in urban and rural Zimbabwe, *Children's Geographies*, 4, 185–202.

Kesby, M., Kindon, S. and Pain, R. (2007) Participation as a form of power: retheorizing empowerment and spatialising participatory action research, in S. Kindon, R. Pain and M. Kesby (eds) *Participatory action research approaches and methods: Connecting people, participation and place*, London: Routledge.

Kitson, M., Martin, R. and Willkinson, F. (2000) Labour markets, social justice and economic efficiency, *Cambridge Journal of Economics*, 24, 631–41.

Kjørholt, A. T. (2003) 'Creating a place to belong': girls' and boys' hut-building as a site for understanding discourses on childhood and generational relations in a Norwegian community, *Children's Geographies*, 1, 261–79.

Kline, S. (1993) *Out of the garden: Toys, TV and children's culture in the age of marketing*, London: Verso.

Kraftl, P. (2006) Building an idea: the material construction of an ideal childhood, *Transactions of the Institute of British Geographers*, 31, 488–504.

Kraftl, P. (2013) *Geographies of alternative education: Diverse learning spaces for children and young people*, Bristol: Policy Press.

Kraftl, P. and Horton, J. (2007) 'The health event': everyday, affective politics of participation, *Geoforum*, 38, 1012–27.

Kraftl, P. and Horton, J. (2008) Spaces of every-night life: for geographies of sleep, sleeping and sleepiness, *Progress in Human Geography*, 32, 509–24.

Latham, A. (1999) Powers of engagement: on being engaged, being indifferent and urban life, *Area*, 31, 161–8.

Latham, A. (2003) Research, performance and doing human geography: some reflections on the diary-photograph, diary-interview method, *Environment and Planning A*, 35, 1993–2017.

Latour, B. (1987) *Science in action: How to follow scientists and engineers through society*, Cambridge, MA: Harvard University Press.

Latour, B. (2005) *Reassembling the social: An introduction to actor-network theory*, Oxford University Press, Oxford.

Latour, B. and Venn, C. (2002) Morality and technology: the end of the means, *Theory, Culture & Society*, 19, 247–60.

Laurie, N., Dwyer, C., Holloway, S. and Smith, F. (1999) *Geographies of new femininities*, Abingdon: Routledge.

Laurier, E. (2001) Why people say where they are during mobile phone calls, *Environment and Planning D: Society and Space*, 19, 485–504.

Laurier, E. and Philo, C. (2004) Ethnoarchaeology and undefined investigations, *Environment and Planning A*, 36, 421–36.

Laurier, E. and Philo, C. (2006) Cold shoulders and napkins handed: gestures of responsibility, *Transactions of the Institute of British Geographers*, 31, 193–207.

Laurier, E., Whyte, A. and Buckner, K. (2002) Neighbouring as an occasioned activity, *Space and Culture*, 5, 346–67.

Law, J. (1999) After ANT: complexity, knowledge and topology, in J. Law and J. Hassard (eds) *Actor Network Theory and After*, Oxford: Blackwell.

Law, J. (2004) *After method: Mess in social science research*, London: Routledge.

Lee, J. (2006) Constructing race and civility in urban America, *Urban Studies*, 43, 903–17.

Lee, N. (2001) *Childhood and society: Growing up in an age of uncertainty*, Milton Keynes: Open University Press.

Lee, N. (2005) *Childhood and human value: Development, separation and separability*, Buckingham: Open University Press.

Lee, N. (2013) *Childhood and biopolitics: Climate change, life processes and human futures,* London: Palgrave.

Lees, L. (1998) Urban renaissance and the street: spaces of control and contestation, in N. Fyfe (ed.) *Images of the street: Representation, experience and control in public space*, London: Routledge.

Leiter, J. (1980) *A primer on ethnomethodology*, New York: Oxford University Press.

Lieten, G. K. (2008) *Children, structure and agency: Realities across the developing world,* London: Routledge.

Longhurst, R. (2001) *Bodies: Exploring fluid boundaries*, London: Routledge.

McCall, L. (2005) The complexity of intersectionality, *Signs*, 30, 1771–800.

MacDonald, R. and Marsh, J. (2005) *Disconnected youth? Growing up in Britain's poor neighbourhoods*, Basingstoke: Palgrave.

McDowell, L. (1997) Introduction: rethinking place, in L. McDowell (ed.) *Undoing place?*, London: Arnold.

McDowell, L. (2001) 'It's that Linda again': ethical, practical and political issues involved in longitudinal research with young men, *Ethics, Place and Environment*, 4, 87–100.

McKendrick, J. H., Bradford, M. G. and Fielder, A. V. (2000) Kid customer? Commercialization of playspace and the commodification of childhood, *Childhood: A Global Journal of Childhood Research*, 7, 295–314.

McLanahan, S. and Percheski, C. (2008) Family structure and the reproduction of inequalities, *Annual Review of Sociology*, 34, 257–76.

McLeod, J. (1999) *Practitioner research in counselling*, London: Sage.

Malbon, B. (1999) *Clubbing: Dancing, ecstasy and vitality*, London: Routledge.

Malone, K. (2002) Street life: youth, culture and competing uses of public space, *Environment and Urbanization*, 14, 157–68.

Marston, S., Jones III, J. P. and Woodward, K. (2005) Human geography without scale, *Transactions of the Institute of British Geographers*, 30, 416–32.

Martin, D. G. (2007) Bureacratizing ethics: institutional review boards and participatory research, *ACME: An International E-Journal for Critical Geographies*, 6, 319–28.

Massey, D. (1984) *Spatial divisions of labor: Social structures and the geography of production*, New York: Macmillan.

Massey, D. (2003) Imagining the field, in: M. Pryke, G. Rose and S. Whatmore (eds) *Using social theory: Thinking through research*, London: Sage.

Massey, D. (2005) *For space*, London: Sage.

Massey, D., Bond, S. and Featherstone, D. (2009) The possibilities of a politics of place beyond place? A conversation with Doreen Massey, *Scottish Geographical Journal*, 125, 401–20.

Mathy, J. P. (1993) *Extrême-Occident: French intellectuals and America*, Chicago: Chicago University Press.

Matthews, H. (1992) *Making sense of place: Children's understanding of large-scale environments*, Hemel Hepstead: Harvester Wheatsheaf.

Matthews, H. and Limb, M. (1999) Defining an agenda for the geography of children: review and prospect, *Progress in Human Geography*, 23, 61–90.

Matthews, H., Limb, M. and Taylor, M. (1999) Reclaiming the street: the discourse of curfew, *Environment and Planning A*, 31, 1713–30.

Matthews, H., Limb, M. and Taylor, M. (2000) The 'street as thirdspace', in S. Holloway and G. Valentine (eds) *Children's geographies: Playing, living, learning*, London: Routledge.

Mauthner, M. (2002) *Sistering: Power and change in female relationships*, Basingstoke: Palgrave.

Mayall, B. (2002) *Towards a sociology for childhood: Thinking from children's lives*, Milton Keynes: Open University Press.

Mayall, B., Bendelow, G., Barker, S., Storey, P. and Veltman, M. (1996) *Children's health in primary schools*, London: Falmer Press.

Menter, I., Elliot, D., Hulme, M., Lewin, J. and Lowden, K. (2011) *A guide to practitioner research in education*, London: Sage.

Merriman, P., Jones, M., Olsson, G., Sheppard, E., Thrift, N., Tuan, Y.-F. (2012) Space and spatiality in theory, *Dialogues in Human Geography*, 2, 3–22.

Mitchell, K. and Elwood, S. (2012) Mapping children's politics: the promise of articulation and the limits of nonrepresentational theory, *Environment and Planning D*, 30, 788–804.

Mol, A. (2002) *The body multiple: ontology in medical practice*, Durham, NC: Duke University Press.

Morris-Roberts, K. (2004) Girls' friendships, 'distinctive individuality' and socio-spatial practices of (dis)identification, *Children's Geographies*, 2, 237–55.

Morrow, V. (2005) Social capital, community involvement and community cohesion in England: a space for children and young people, *Journal of Social Sciences* (special issue), 9, 57–69.

Morrow, V. (2007) 'No ball games': children's experiences of urban space in an English town, in K. Malone (ed.) *Child space: An anthropological exploration of young people's use of space*, New Delhi: Concept Publishing Co.

Morrow, V. (2008) Ethical dilemmas in research with children and young people about their social environments, *Children's Geographies*, 6, 49–61.

Morrow, V. and Richards, M. P. M. (1996) The ethics of social research with children: an overview, *Children and Society*, 10, 90–105.

Moser, S. (2008) Personality: a new positionality? *Area*, 40, 383–92.

Mowl, G., Pain, R. and Talbot, C. (2000) The ageing body and the homespace, *Area*, 32, 189–97.

Musgrove, F. (2012) *The family, education and society*, London: Routledge.

Musil, J. (1993) The transition to democracy, in J. O'Loughlin and H. Van Der Wusten (eds) *The new political geography of Eastern Europe*, London: John Wiley and Sons.

Nagar, R. and Swarr, A. L. (2005) Organizing from the margins: grappling with 'empowerment' in India and South Africa, in L. Nelson and J. Seager (eds) *A companion to feminist geography*, Oxford: Blackwell.

Nast, H. J. (1994) Women in the field – opening remarks, *Professional Geographer*, 46, 54–66.

Nast, H. J. and Pile, S. (eds) (1998) *Places through the body*, London: Routledge.

Nauta, M. M. and Kokaly, M. L. (2001) Assessing role model influences on students' academic and vocational decisions, *Journal of Career Assessment*, 9, 81–99.

Nayak, A. (2003a) 'Through children's eyes': childhood, place and the fear of crime, *Geoforum*, 34, 303–15.

Nayak, A. (2003b) *Race, place and globalization*, Oxford: Berg.

Nelson, L. (2004) Topographies of citizenship: Purhépechan Mexican women claiming political subjectivities, *Gender, Place and Culture: A Journal of Feminist Geography*, 11, 163–87.

Oswell, D. (2013) *The agency of children: From family to global human rights*, Cambridge: Cambridge University Press.

Outhwaite, W. and Ray, L. (2005) *Social theory and postcommunism*, Oxford: Blackwell.

Pain, R. (2006) Paranoid parenting? Rematerializing risk and fear for children., *Social and Cultural Geography*, 7, 221-–243.

Pain, R. (2008) Ethical possibilities: towards participatory ethics, *Children's Geographies*, 6, 104–8.

Pain, R. and Francis, P. (2004) Living with crime: spaces of risk for homeless young people, *Children's Geographies*, 2, 95–110.

Painter, J. (2000) Pierre Bourdieu, in M. Crang and N. Thrift (eds) *Thinking space*, London: Routledge.

Parr, H. (1998) Mental health, ethnography and the body, *Area*, 30, 28–37.

Parr, H. (2008) *Mental health and social space: Towards inclusionary geographies*, Oxford: Blackwell.

Parr, H., Philo, C. and Burns, N. (2004) Social geographies of rural mental health: experiencing inclusions and exclusions, *Transactions of the Institute of British Geographers*, 29, 401–19.

Pattison, V. (2008) Neoliberalization and its discontents: the experience of working poverty in Manchester, in A. Smith, A. Stenning and K. Willis (eds) *Social justice and neoliberalism: Global perspectives*, London: Zed Books.

Peck, J. (2008) Remaking laissez-faire, *Progress in Human Geography*, 32, 3–43.

Percy-Smith, B. and Thomas, N. (eds) (2010) *A handbook of children and young people's participation: Perspectives from theory and practice*, London: Routledge.

Philo, C. (1992) Neglected rural geographies: a review, *Journal of Rural Studies*, 8, 193–207.

Philo, C. (2000) 'The corner-stones of my world': editorial introduction to special issue on spaces of childhood, *Childhood: A Global Journal of Childhood Research*, 7, 243–56.

Philo, C. (2003) 'To go back up the side hill': memories, imaginations and reveries of childhood, *Children's Geographies*, 1, 7–24.

Philo, C. (2004) *A geographical history of institutional provision for the insane from medieval times to the 1860s in England and Wales: The space reserved for insanity*, Lampeter: Edwin Mellen Press.

Philo, C. and Smith, F. M. (2003) Political geographies of children and young people, *Space and Polity*, 7, 99–115.

Philo, C. and Smith, F. M. (2013) The child-body-politic: afterword on 'Children and young people's politics in everyday life', *Political Geography*, 17, 137–44.

Piaget, J. (1995) *Sociological studies*, London: Routledge.

Picchio, A. (1992) *Social reproduction: The political economy of the labour market*, Cambridge: Cambridge University Press.

Piko, B. F. and Keresztes, N. (2006) Physical activity, psychosocial health and life goals among youth, *Journal of Community Health*, 31, 136–45.

Pile, S. and Thrift, N. (1995) Mapping the subject, in S. Pile and N. Thrift (eds) *Mapping the subject: Geographies of cultural transformation*, London: Routledge.

Pilkington, H., Omel'chenko, E. and Garifzianova, A. (2010) *Russia's skinheads: Exploring and rethinking subcultural lives*, London: Routledge.

Prezza, M., Pilloni, S., Morabito, C., Sersante, C., Alparone, F. R. and Giuliani, M. V. (2001) The influence of psychosocial and environmental factors on children's independent mobility and relationship to peer frequentation, *Journal of Community and Applied Social Psychology*, 11, 435–50.

Procter, L. (2015) Children, nature and emotion: exploring how children's emotional experiences of 'green' spaces shape their understandings of the natural world, in M. Blazek and P. Kraftl (eds) *Children's emotions in policy and practice: Mapping and making spaces of childhood*, London: Palgrave.

Prout, A. (2011) *The body, childhood and society*, London: Palgrave.

Prout, A. and James, A. (1997) A new paradigm for the sociology of childhood? Provenance, promise and problems, in A. James and A. Prout (eds) *Constructing and reconstructing childhood: Contemporary issues in the sociological study of childhood*, London: Falmer Press.

Punch, S. (2005) The generationing of power: a comparison of child–parent and sibling relations in Scotland, *Sociological Studies of Children and Youth*, 10, 169–88.

Punch, S. (2007) "I felt they were ganging up on me": interviewing siblings at home., *Children''s Geographies*, 5, 219–234.

Punch, S. (2012) Hidden struggles of fieldwork: exploring the role and use of field diaries, *Emotion, Space and Society*, 5, 86–93.

Pyyry, N. (2015) Geographies of hanging out: connecting everyday experiences with formal education, in M. Blazek and P. Kraftl (eds) *Children's emotions in policy and practice: Mapping and making spaces of childhood*, London: Palgrave.

Qvortrup, J. (1995) Childhood and modern society: a paradoxical relationship? , in J. Brannen and M. O'Brien (eds) *Childhood and parenthood*, London: Falmer Press.

Ramet, S. P. (2014) *Religion and politics in post-socialist Central and Southeastern Europe: Challenges since 1989*, London: Palgrave Macmillan.

Rasmussen, K. (2004) Places for children – children's places, *Childhood: A Global Journal of Childhood Research*, 11, 155–73.

Rasmussen, K. and Smidt, S. (2003) Children in the neighbourhood: the neighbourhood in the children, in P. Christensen and M. O'Brien (eds) *Children in the city: Home, neighbourhood and community*, London: Routledge.

Rautio, P. (2013) Children who carry stones in their pockets: on autotelic material practices in everyday life, *Children's Geographies*, 11, 394–408.

Rawlins, E. (2006) Mother knows best? Intergenerational notions of fashion and identity, *Children's Geographies*, 4, 359–77.

Reinharz, S. (1992) *Feminist methods in social research*. Oxford: Oxford University Press.

Renold, E. (2006) 'They won't let us play unless you're going out with one of them': girls, boys and Butler's 'heterosexual matrix' in the primary years, *British Journal of Sociology of Education*, 27, 489–509.

Riessman, C. (1993) *Narrative analysis*, Newbury Park, CA: Sage.

Ringold, D., Orenstein, M. A. and Wilkens, E. (2005) *Roma in an expanding Europe: Breaking the poverty cycle*, Washington, DC: World Bank.

Robson, E. (2004) Hidden child workers: young carers in Zimbabwe. *Antipode*, 36, 227–48.

Rose, G. (1996) As if the mirrors bled: masculine dwelling, masculine theory and feminist masquerade, in N. Duncan (ed.) *BodySpace: Destabilising geographies of gender and sexuality*, London: Routledge.

Rose, G. (1999) Performing space, in D. Massey, J. Allen and P. Sarre (eds) *Human geography today*, Cambridge: Polity Press.

Rose, G. (2000) Practising photography: an archive, a study, some photographs and a researcher, *Journal of Historical Geography*, 26, 555–71.

Rose, G. (2003) Family photographs and domestic spacings: a case study, *Transactions of the Institute of British Geographers*, 28, 5–18.

Ryder, A., Cemlym, S. and Acton, T. (eds) (2014) *Hearing the voices of Gypsy, Roma and Traveller communities*, Bristol: Policy Press.

Sachs, J. (1994) *Poland's jump to the market economy*, London: MIT Press.

Sakwa, R. (1999) *Postcommunism*, Milton Keynes: Open University Press.

Schatzki, T. (1988) The nature of social reality, *Philosophy and Phenomenological Research*, 49, 239–60.

Schatzki, T. (2001) Introduction: practice theory, in T. Schatzki, K. Knorr Cetina and E. von Savigny (eds) *The practice turn in contemporary theory*, London: Routledge.

Schillmeier, M. (2008) Time-spaces of in/dependence and dis/ability, *Time & Society*, 17, 215–31.

Schneider, B. H. (2000) *Friends and enemies: Peer relations in childhood*, London: Arnold.

Schwanen, T., Banister, D. and Bowling, A. (2012) Independence and mobility in later life, *Geoforum*, 43, 1313–22.

Scott, J. C. (1985) *Weapons of the weak: Everyday forms of peasant resistance*, New Haven, CT: Yale University Press.

Scourfield, J., Dicks, B., Holland, S., Drakeford, M. and Davies, A. (2006) The significance of place in middle childhood: qualitative research from Wales, *British Journal of Sociology*, 57, 577–95.

Setten, G. (2009) Habitus, in N. Thrift and R. Kitchin (eds) *International encyclopedia of human geography*, London: Elsevier.

Shapiro, B. Y. (2001) School-based sex education in Russia: the current reality and prospects, *Sex Education: Sexuality, Society and Learning*, 1, 87–96.

Sharp, J., Routledge, P., Philo, C. and Paddison, R. (2000) Entanglements of power: geographies of domination/resistance, in J. Sharp, P. Routledge, C. Philo and R. Paddison (eds) *Entanglements of power: Geographies of domination/resistance*, London: Routledge.

Shields, S. A. (2008) Gender: an intersectionality perspective, *Sex Roles*, 59, 301–11.

Sibley, D. (1995a) *Geographies of exclusion.*, London: Routledge, London.

Sibley, D. (1995b) Families and domestic routines: constructing the boundaries of childhood, in S. Pile and N. Thrift (eds) *Mapping the subject: Geographies of cultural transformation*, London: Routledge.

Sibley, D. (1998) Social exclusion and the Roma in transition, in J. Pickles and A. Smith (eds) *Theorizing transition: Political economy of post-communist transformations*, London: Routledge.

Sibley, D. and Lowe, G. (1992) Domestic space, modes of control and problem behaviour, *Geografiska Annaler, Series B, Human Geography*, 74, 189–97.

Silk, J. (2004) Caring at a distance: gift theory, aid chains and social movements, *Social and Cultural Geography*, 5, 229–51.

Sills, C. (ed.) (1997) *Contracts in counselling*, London: Sage.

Simmel, G. (1950a) The stranger., In:in K. H. Wolff, K. H. (ed.) *The sociology of Georg Simmel*, New York: The Free Press, New York.

Simmel, G. (1950b) The metropolis and mental life, in K. H. Wolff (ed.) *The sociology of Georg Simmel*, New York: Free Press.

Skeggs, B. (1997) *Formations of class and gender: Becoming respectable*, London: Sage.

Skelton, T. (2000) 'Nothing to do, nowhere to go?' Teenage girls and 'public' space in the Rhondda Valleys, South Wales, in S. Holloway and G. Valentine (eds) *Children's geographies: Playing, living, learning*, London: Routledge.

Skelton, T. and Valentine, G. (2004) Exploring notions of masculinity and fatherhood: when gay sons 'come out' to heterosexual fathers, in K. Hörschelmann and B. van Hoven (eds) *Spaces of masculinities*, London: Routledge.

Smith, A. and Pickles, J. (1998) Introduction: theorizing transition and the political economy of transformation, in J. Pickles and A. Smith (eds) *Theorizing transition: Political economy of post-communist transformations*, London: Routledge.

Smith, A. and Rochovská, A. (2007) Domesticating neo-liberalism: everyday lives and the geographies of post-socialist transformations, *Geoforum*, 38, 1163–78.

Smith, A., Stenning, A., Rochovská, A. and Swiatek, D. (2008) The emergence of a working poor: labour markets, neoliberalization and diverse economies in post-socialist cities, in A. Smith, A. Stenning and K. Willis (eds) *Social justice and neoliberalism*, London: Zed Books.

Smith, F. M. (1997) Contested geographical imaginings of reunification: a case study of urban change in Leipzig, *Applied Geography*, 17, 355–69.

Smith, N. (1984) *Uneven development: Nature, capital and the production of space*, Oxford: Blackwell.

Smyth, C., Blaxland, M. and Cass, B. (2011) 'So that's how I found out I was a young carer and that I actually had been a carer most of my life': identifying and supporting hidden young carers, *Journal of Youth Studies*, 14, 145–60.

Spicer, N. (2008) Places of exclusion and inclusion: asylum-seeker and refugee experiences of neighbourhoods in the UK, *Journal of Ethnic and Migration Studies*, 34, 491–510.

Stenning, A. (2000) Placing (post-)socialism: the making and remaking of Nowa Huta, Poland, *European Urban and Regional Studies*, 7, 99–118.

Stenning, A. and Hörschelmann, K. (2008) History, geography and difference in the post-socialist world: or, do we still need post-socialism? *Antipode*, 40, 312–35.

Stenning, A., Smith, A., Rochovská, A. and Swiatek, D. (2010) *Domesticating neo-liberalism: Spaces of economic practice and social reproduction in post-socialist cities*, Oxford: Blackwell.

Stevenson, S. (2001) Street children in Moscow: using and creating social capital, *Sociological Review*, 49, 530–47.

Strawbridge, S. and Woolfe, R. (2003) Counselling psychology in context, in R. Woolfe, W. Dryden and S. Strawbridge (eds) *Handbook of counselling psychology*, London: Sage.

Stronach, I., Garratt, D., Pearce, C. and Piper, H. (2007) Reflexivity, the picturing of selves, the forging of method, *Qualitative Inquiry*, 13, 179–203.

Sutton, L. (2009) 'They'd only call you a scally if you are poor': the impact of socio-economic status on children's identities, *Children's Geographies*, 7, 277–90.

Swanson, K. (2009) *Begging as a path to progress: indigenous women and children and the struggle for Ecuador's urban spaces*, Athens: University of Georgia Press.

Talbot, D. (2013) Early parenting and the urban experience: risk, community, play and embodiment in an East London neighbourhood, *Children's Geographies*, 11, 230–42.

Taussig, M. (1993) *Mimesis and alterity: A particular history of the senses*, London: Routledge.

Teather, E. K. (1999) Introduction: geographies of personal discovery, in E. K. Teather (ed.) *Embodied geographies: Spaces, bodies and rites of passage*, London: Routledge.

Temelová, J., Novák, J., Ouředníček, M. and Puldová, P. (2011) Housing estates in the Czech Republic after socialism: various trajectories and inner differentiation, *Urban Studies*, 48, 1811–34.

Thomas, M. E. (2009) The identity politics of school life: territoriality and the racial subjectivity of teen girls in LA, *Children's Geographies*, 7, 7–19.

Thomson, F. (2007) Are methodologies *for* children keeping *them* in their place? *Children's Geographies*, 5, 207–18.

Thomson, S. (2005) 'Territorialising' the primary school playground: deconstructing the geography of playtime, *Children's Geographies*, 3, 63–78.

Thorne, B. (1993) *Gender play: Boys and girls in school*, Milton Keynes: Open University Press.

Thrift, N. (1996) 'Strange country': meaning, use and style in non-representational theories, in N. Thrift (ed.) *Spatial formations*, London: Sage.

Thrift, N. (2007) Overcome by space: Reworking Foucault, in: J.W. Crampton and S. Elden (eds) *Space, knowledge and power: Foucault and geography*, Aldershot: Ashgate.

Thrift, N. and Pile, S. (2000) Preface, in S. Pile and N. Thrift (eds) *City A–Z*, London: Routledge.

Tivers, J. (1986) *Women attached*, London: Croom Helm.

Tolia-Kelly, D. P. (2004a) Locating processes of identification: studying the precipitates of re-memory through artefacts in the British Asian home, *Transactions of the Institute of British Geographers*, 29, 314–29.

Tolia-Kelly, D. P. (2004b) Materializing post-colonial geographies: examining the textural landscapes of migration in the South Asian home, *Geoforum*, 35, 675–88.

Tomanović, S. and Petrović, M. (2010) Children's and parents' perspectives on risks and safety in three Belgrade neighbourhoods, *Children's Geographies*, 8, 141–56.

Trell, E. M., van Hoven, B. and Huigen, P. P. P. (2012) 'It is good to live in Järva-Jaani but we can not stay here': youth and belonging in rural Estonia, *Journal of Rural Studies*, 28, 139–48.

Tremblay, M.S., Barnes, J.D., Copeland, J.L. and Esliger, D.W. (2005) Conquering childhood inactivity: Is the answer in the past? *Medicine and Science in Sports and Exercise*, 37, 1187–94.

Tucker, F. (2003) Sameness or difference? Exploring girls' use of recreational spaces, *Children's Geographies*, 1, 111–24.

Valentine, G. (1997) 'Oh yes I can.' 'Oh no you can't': children and parents' understanding of kids' competence to negotiate public space safely, *Antipode*, 29, 65–89.

Valentine, G. (2008) Living with difference: reflections on geographies of encounters, *Progress in Human Geography*, 32, 323–37.

Valentine, G. and McKendrick, J. H. (1997) Children''s outdoor play: exploring contemporary public concerns., *Geoforum*, 28.

Valentine, G., Butler, R. and Skelton, T. (2001) The ethical and methodological complexities of doing research with 'vulnerable' young people, *Ethics, Place and Environment*, 4, 119–25.

van Blerk, L. (2005) Negotiating spatial identities: mobile perspectives on street life in Uganda, *Children's Geographies*, 3, 5–21.

van Nijnatten, C. (2013) *Children's agency, children's welfare: A dialogical approach to child development, policy and practice,* Bristol: Policy Press.

Veitch, J., Salmon, J. and Ball, K. (2007) Children's perceptions of the use of public open spaces for active free-play, *Children's Geographies*, 5, 409–22.

Verdery, K. (1996) *What was socialism and what comes next?* Princeton, NJ: Princeton University Press.

Vermeersch, P. (2003) Ethnic minority identity and movement politics: the case of the Roma in the Czech Republic and Slovakia, *Ethnic and Racial Studies*, 26, 879–901.

Von Eckartsberg, R. (1986) *Life-world experience: Existential-phenomenological approaches in psychology*, London: Center for Advanced Research in Phenomenology and University Press of America.

Vygotsky, L. S. (1978) *Mind in society: The development of higher psychological processes*, Cambridge, MA: Harvard University Press.

Ward, C. (1978) *The child in the city*, New York: Pantheon.

Warren, S. (1996) Popular cultural practices in the 'postmodern city', *Urban Geography*, 17, 545–67.

Whatmore, S. (2002) *Hybrid geographies: Natures cultures spaces*, London: Routledge.

Willis, K., Smith, A. and Stenning, A. (2008) Introduction: social justice and neoliberalism, in A. Smith, A. Stenning and K. Willis (eds) *Social justice and neoliberalism: Global perspectives*, London: Zed Books.

Wilton, R. D. (1998) The constitution of difference: space and psyche in landscapes of exclusion, *Geoforum*, 29, 173–85.

Winchester, H. P. M. and Costello, L. (1995) Homeless youth: a culture of survival, *Environment and Planning D: Society and Space*, 13, 329–48.

Windram-Geddes, M. (2013) Fearing fatness and feeling fat: encountering affective spaces of physical activity, *Emotion, Space and Society*, 9, 42–9.

Woodward, I. (2007) *Understanding material culture*, Sage, London.

Woodyer, T. (2008) The body as research tool: embodied practice and children's geographies, *Children's Geographies*, 6, 349–62.

Woodyer, T. and Cook, I. (2011) The lives of things, in E. Sheppard, E. Barnes and J. Peck (eds) *The new companion to economic geography*, Oxford: Blackwell.

Youdell, D. (2005) Sex-gender-sexuality: how sex, gender and sexuality constellations are constituted in secondary schools, *Gender and Education*, 17, 249–70.

Young, I. M. (1990) *Justice and the politics of difference*, Princeton, NJ: Princeton University Press.

Index

Note: Page numbers for figures appear in *italics*.

Index

G

Gajo 209, 210, 211, 212
Gallagher, M. 45, 46–7
Garfinkel, H. 155
gender 213–17, 218
  affect on friendship 184–5, 186–8, 190, 195
  and child care 169–70
geographical experiences/knowledge 74–6
geographies, circumscribed 154, 156
gifts 129–31, 134
girls
  as carers 169–70
  friendships 184–6, 187–8
Girls Group 35
glasses, wearing 103
globalisation 31
Gregory, D. 57
Gregson et al 150–1
Gregson, N. 127
'growing up' 203–8
Guattari, E. 9, 56, 226
Gypsy 209, 211

H

Harker, C. 8
Harrison, P. 59, 60, 62
health 106, 107
helping process 48, 49
Hemming, P. J. 108
Herrera et al 109
higher education 207
Holloway, S. 6–8, 209
Holt, L. 47, 193, 201, 202
home 76–9, 90
Hörschelmann, K. 23, 24, 89
Horton, J. 70, 123, 213
hostility 190
housing 161, 210
Hricová, P. 42
Husserl, E. 57
hygiene 101–2, 106
hypermarkets 72

I

identity 39, 197–219
illegal economic activities 210
imaginations 61, 62, 99, 100
immanency 62
immateriality 62
incivility 30
inclusion 192
income 73, 74, 161–2
in/completeness 7
independence 72, 73, 127, 199, 229
independent mobility 72–3, 90, 91

individualism, competitive 228
inequalities 31, 45
informed consent 50, 51, 53
institutional ethics 50, 53
interactions 70, 134
interconnectedness 9
intersectionality 198
intersubjectivity 115
intimacy, social 115
invasion 114
Irigaray,L. 33
isolation 29, 31, 203, 229

J

James, A. 177, 180, 182, 198, 202
Janssen, D. F. 218
Jirojanakul et al 106
Jones, O. 8, 89

K

Katz, C. 12–13, 24, 55, 96, 99, 108–9, 202–3, 208
  and 'childhood as waste' 228, 229
  and counter-topography 14, 232–3
  and 'fusion of knowledge and action in children's practices' 225–6
  and minor theory 55, 62
Kehily, M. J. 124
Kesby et al 53
Kitson et al 228
knowledge
  and action 226
  spatial 74–5, 90
Kopčany 11, 12, 14, 21–2, 24–30, 141, 227, 230
  attitude to 75, 76
  families, types of 160–3
  and football 58–9
  importance of experiences from 147
  public spaces 67–94, 115
Kraftl, P. 61, 70, 120, 123

L

lake 72
Latham, A. 139–40, 149
Latour, B. 9, 60
Laurie et al 11–12
Laurier, E. 140, 147
Law, J. 33, 139
Lee, N. 6, 7–8, 10, 61, 147, 226, 230
Lees, N. 88
leisure time activities 73
Leiter, J. 154
lice 103
lines of flight 226
local authorities 29